SALT IN OUR BLOOD

THE MEMOIR OF A FISHERMAN'S WIFE

SALT IN OUR BLOOD

THE MEMOIR OF A FISHERMAN'S WIFE

MICHELE LONGO EDER

SALT IN OUR BLOOD

www.saltinourblood.com

This book is a work of nonfiction although some of the names have been changed to protect the privacy of individuals.

ISBN-13: 978-1-892076-44-1
Library of Congress Control Number: 2008903929
Eder, Michele Longo
Salt In Our Blood: The memoir of a fisherman's wife /
1. Title; 2. Memoir; 3. Fishing; 4. Crab Fishing; 5. Fixed-gear fishing; 6. Oregon Coast fisheries industry.

Manufactured in the United States of America
Book design: Carla Perry
Cover design: Karen Downs Graphic Design
Photo credits:

Front cover photo © Jim Haron
Photos © Michele Longo Eder pages 21, 393, P-1A, P-6
Photos © Bob Eder pages 16, 47, P-1B, P-2A, P-3A
Photo © Ben Eder page P-4A
Photo © Jim Hanselman page P-3B
Photo © Leah Brooks page P-7B
Photo © Register-Guard page P-8
Photo © Carla Perry page 395
Photo © Phoebe Morris page 431
Back cover author photo © Colin Park

Permissions to reprint:
Articles from the Newport *News-Times* granted by the News-Times
Poem, "Four men drowned today," granted by Taylor Bortz
Articles and letters from the Portland *Oregonian* granted by the *Oregonian*
Article from the San Francisco *Chronicle* granted by the *Chronicle*

DANCING MOON PRESS
P.O. Box 832, Newport, OR 97365
541-574-7708
www.dancingmoonpress.com
carla@dancingmoonpress.com

FIRST EDITION

"I really don't know why it is that all of us are so committed to the sea… All of us have, in our veins, the exact same percentage of salt in our blood that exists in the ocean, and, therefore, we have salt in our blood, in our sweat, in our tears. We are tied to the ocean. And when we go back to the sea, whether it is to sail or to watch it, we are going back from whence we came."

President John F. Kennedy
Newport, Rhode Island
September 14, 1962

Acknowledgements

Thank you, most deeply, to Yvonna Weiland to whom I entrusted my earliest memories of the events that follow, and who, with her compassion and good humor, supported my dream of writing this book. And to Tami McAvoy, who spend months editing and revising the manuscript. Yvonna's and Tami's insightful comments, unending patience, and kindness made possible the recounting of this journey.

I would also like to thank Kim Lehmann and Lynn Jeffress whose suggestions allowed me to make the cuts required to get the book to a publishable length. I am also grateful to Kim, and the late Mary Ridings, for every moment they stood beside me, then and now. Thanks also to Don Riddell, who provided the quote that became the title of this book.

My husband, Bob, read and critiqued my work. He helped me describe more accurately the fishing activities, and when he complained I didn't talk enough about fishing, it gave me the opportunity to tell him to write his own damn book.

It is Carla Perry's pen, however, that made my writing crisper, sharper, and stronger. She gave me confidence to persevere. Without her belief in this book, and her ability to bring it all together, I'd have never made it to publication. Thank you, Carla.

There are crewmen, families, friends, community members, and total strangers who came together to support us in our time of grief. We remember you all. A special thank you to the Newport Fishermen's Wives, and to my friend, Ginny Goblirsch.

Finally, thank you to Bob and Dylan, who encouraged me to write this book, and allowed me to share their private emotions in order to tell my story the very best way I could.

For Bob, Ben, and Dylan

Seattle
Washington
Astoria
Warrenton
Portland
Newport
Toledo
Coos Bay
Oregon
Port Orford
Crescent City
Bodega Bay
San Francisco
Nevada
Santa Cruz
California
Los Angeles
San Diego

INTRODUCTION

"Go, go, go!" the deep voice shouted, right near my ear. Bob's calloused hand, which had just been caressing my thigh, grabbed the source of the sound: a black, hand-held VHF radio, located on the rickety nightstand next to the bed in the hotel room where we lay. The digital clock, lit with red numbers, showed 2 a.m.

"I'm coming," Bob said, having flipped the radio into transmission mode. He jumped out of bed and grabbed his blue jeans, pulling them on.

"What are you doing?" I asked. "I just got here!"

"Time for me to go, honey. That was Spelbrink on the radio. He's been watching the wave heights. The bar is safe to cross." Bob leaned down, kissed me, and left me sitting upright in bed. Taking a long, last look, he said, "Have a safe drive home," and closed the door tight behind him.

That was December 1987. I was at the Best Western Motel in Crescent City, California. Bob was a commercial fisherman, owner and skipper of the 40-foot aluminum Fishing Vessel *(F/V) Nesika*, and it was the start of the fishing season for Dungeness crab. Although Bob was home-based in Newport, a town of 8,000 people on the central Oregon Coast, he, and his running buddy Bob Spelbrink, thought that the season's crab would be found in Northern California. They moved their vessels, crew and gear southward 250 miles.

Bob had called me earlier that day at my law office in Lincoln City, Oregon, about 25 miles north of Newport. "Drive on down and see me," he cajoled. The weather's bad here. We're stuck in port and not going to get out across the bar for a while."

"How far a drive is it?" I asked.

"Four hours, maybe five," Bob said. "On the way down, stop and grab something to eat at the Blue Heron Café in Coos Bay. You'll like that place—it's good."

"You'll be in port for a few days?" I asked.

"Oh, well, I don't know about that, but we're in town right now and probably tonight, too. Come on, honey. I could really use your company," he said.

I'll bet, I thought. But my trial for the next day had settled out of court, and so I had some unexpected time on my hands. Oh, what the hell, I thought. I'll go. Dating this man, a fisherman, sure was different. "I've got to wrap up a few things, then I'll be down," I told him. I could hear him smile over the phone. Hanging up, I told my secretary what I was about to do.

"He must really be something," she said, and shook her head, grinning.

As I went out, I looked back at her and said, "This fishing life is crazy. No matter what I do or say, don't ever let me marry this guy."

Six months later, we were husband and wife.

I am a fisherman's wife. As a feminist, it is hard for me to believe that I define myself as an appendage to another person, particularly a man. But he isn't just any man. He is a commercial fisherman, and he is my husband.

Bob Eder, the middle son of three boys, was raised in Los Angeles. A body-surfing beach habitué, no one thought he'd grow up to be a fisherman. Hebrew-schooled and bar-mitzvahed, Bob had been accepted and was on his way back East to Phillips Exeter Academy when his father, Benjamin Eder, a warm, optimistic and energetic man, was diagnosed with brain cancer. Bob was 14 years old.

It took five years for Benjamin Eder to die. Edie, Benjamin's wife, emerged from their suburban Jewish enclave, "the neighborhood," and went to work to support her three sons. Bob never made it to prep school. While enrolled at Venice High School, he helped care for his dying father and smoked a lot of dope. He read, wrote poems, played guitar, surfed, and then went to the University of California at Santa Cruz, where he read, wrote some more poems, played guitar, surfed and smoked a lot more dope. He graduated from college in 1973 with a major in "Aesthetic Studies" and a minor in Art History, and then wound his way up the coast to the town of Port Orford, a Wild West fishing port on the southern Oregon coast. He was a prolific and talented poet, but needing to feed himself, he found a job as a crewman on the back deck of a salmon troller.

Despite never having seen a diesel engine or wielded a wrench, Bob learned basic mechanics and taught himself to fish. He saved every dime he made. After working as a deck hand on a boat for a year and driving a school bus, he bought his first boat, the *If and I,* in 1975. Looking now at yellowed photos, it appeared to be a wooden disaster waiting to happen, but he patched the boat and rigged it to fish for Dungeness crab and salmon, and bought the necessary gear. For crew, he found teenagers who, as students, had ridden the school bus he drove, or he pressed old friends like Steve Ganz, and his younger brother, Alan Eder, into service. In the early days, it's been said that Bob wasn't a lot of fun to work with on the boat. But every dime Bob had was tied up in the venture. He had no safety net. Bob's diet consisted of eating fish he caught and a lot of beans and potatoes.

Within a year, Bob sold that boat and bought another, the *F/V Spirit.* By 1979, he'd earned enough money to commission the building of an aluminum vessel he named the *Nesika*, a word that means "ours" in the language of the Siletz Indians. The boat, a Nils Lucander design, was 40 feet in length, the maximum size the port hoist could handle. The Port of Orford was an unprotected cove; boats were literally hoisted 50 feet into the air, water streaming from the gunnels, and then set down on trailers on the land each time they returned from the sea. Like a king salmon, the *Nesika* was shiny: silver, fast, and responsive.

Bob launched the *Nesika* in 1979, christening it with the words "May the life of this boat be bountiful and safe." With him was his wife Anita, pregnant with their son-to-be Benjamin Alan Eder, born the following spring.

Bob and Anita separated in 1982 when Ben was two and

Anita was pregnant with Dylan. When they finally divorced, Bob, found by the judge to be the far more sound parent, received custody of 3½-year-old Ben and their 9-month old son, Dylan. With the help of his mother, his brothers Harvey and Alan, assorted nannies and friends, Bob raised the boys.

Broke again after his divorce, but rich in the assets that mattered, his children, Bob relentlessly re-established himself financially. With his family relatively stable, he was ready to look further afield. Bob decided to move his fishing operation and family from Port Orford to Newport, a small town on the central Oregon coast, the county seat in which I practiced law. It was here, in the spring of 1987, that I met him.

Upstate New York is where I am from, born in the capital, Albany. The city is abloom in tulips in the spring, awash with humidity in the summer, rich with color in the fall, and blanketed with snow in the winter.

I grew up in the suburbs of the city, born of second-generation Italian, French-Canadian, Polish and English parents. My parents were the first in their families to complete high school, and my dad, by the grace of the GI bill, graduated from Syracuse University. He was a war hero but didn't call himself one; as a bombardier he'd flown over 70 missions in Europe in World War II and held the Distinguished Flying Cross. My mother neither worked outside the home nor drove a car, but the home she commanded was well run and rich with tradition. Coming home from school on any given afternoon, I never knew whether I'd be greeted with the smell of cabbage rolls from the Polish side of the family or ziti from the Italians.

After graduating from high school, I went to The Johns Hopkins University in Baltimore, Maryland, earning a bachelor's degree and good enough grades to get into law school. Most of my free time in Baltimore was spent with friends, watching lacrosse, eating raw oysters and bushels of Maryland blue crabs steamed in beer and layered with rock salt and Old Bay seasoning.

At the beginning of my senior year in college, I read *Sometimes a Great Notion*, and became convinced Oregon was my Mecca. I opened a law school catalog, looked at the Northwestern School of Law of the Lewis and Clark College in Portland, Oregon, and said out loud, "Hey—I can get in there!"

My parents, who had traveled around the world, loved the Northwest, both for its people and its natural beauty. They were reluctant to have me leave the Northeast, recognizing then, as I did not, that it was probably a permanent move. But ethnic families have a very tight hold on their children and I knew if I didn't get further away, I'd be sucked back into attending law school in Albany, a fate, which at 21, seemed worse than death. I moved to Portland, Oregon in the summer of 1976, and settled in Lake Oswego, a small community just a few minutes away from the school.

In the summer after my second year in law school, I rented a house in Newport, Oregon, a small fishing and tourist town on the coast and clerked in the District Attorney's office, prosecuting misdemeanor crimes. Then, before graduating and passing the bar exam in the summer of 1979, I was offered a job as an associate in a small law firm in Lincoln City, a town 25 miles north of Newport.

Moving to Lincoln County after graduation, I did criminal defense trial work and loved it. I made a living and saved enough to open my own practice in Lincoln City, and in 1987, bought a piece of property for myself with two buildings on it, one that I used as a home; the other as an office.

When I first met Bob, early in 1987, in addition to meeting his beautiful sons, then 7 and 5 years old, he insisted I had to see this boat of his, the *Nesika*. I put him off about the children, for I doubted I could resist them, having met their soft spoken, thoughtful, literate and handsome father. I did not wish to involve myself in the boys' lives if I wasn't going to be a permanent fixture. But I did agree to check out his boat. An ignorant landlubber, it was a struggle for me to be dutifully impressed, though I thought its silver aluminum hull was prettier than many of the old steel boats that lined the commercial docks, badly in need of paint. I remember how Bob quietly told me that in the previous year he'd landed more crab from his 40-foot boat than any other boat owner in the local fleet. A newcomer to Newport, he'd already made his mark as a producer.

Only later did I understand how out of character it was for Bob to talk about how much fish and crab he had caught, and by implication, how much money he earned. But he was romancing me, and he thought he had to tell me how good he was at what he did, or I would lose interest. He also knew I was dating a Porsche-driving, sailboat-racing lawyer in Portland, that I owned my own law practice and property, and tried cases for a living. What he didn't know was that I was broke, lonely, miserable, and dying to have a family.

Ben and Dylan, Spring 1988

And then I met the boys. Ben, 7, had warm brown skin, dark blonde hair and deep rich dark eyes that were old beyond his years. Ben was protective of little Dylan, who was only 5. Dylan had an open face, a nose splattered with freckles, white-blonde hair, an unmanageable cowlick, and was utterly fearless. He had the sunniest disposition and was the happiest child I had ever met. Ben, the first day we met, asked, "Can I call you 'Mom'?" I replied, "Let's wait until your Dad and I get married, honey." And on May 7, 1988, with Ben and Dylan as our ring bearers, we became a family.

Wedding Day, May 7, 1988. Bob, Michele, Ben and Dylan

For the next 13 years, I interwove my life as a fisherman's wife and mother of two boys, with being a practicing attorney. In 1992, I joined a law firm in Newport, in a position known as "of counsel." It meant I was neither partner nor employee with the firm, but, instead, was able to pick and choose my cases and manage the flow and demands of my legal work.

Bob's fishing business continued to flourish. He participated in sustainable, healthy commercial fisheries: Dungeness crab, and sablefish, a deepwater groundfish caught with baited traps. This method of fishing was "species specific," meaning no unwanted fish were caught or wasted at sea. These were Bob's ethical choices.

Working together as a family, in 1989 we bought another boat, the *F/V Argos*, and with continued success, in 1996, lengthened and widened the *Argos* into the 66-foot *F/V Michele Ann*. Bob's renaming of the vessel after me was an enormous honor, a gift I will always cherish.

Beginning with the opening of the Dungeness crab season in Oregon in December 2000, I began to keep a journal of our lives as a commercial fishing family. As my husband, our sons, and our crew worked throughout the year in a variety of fisheries on our two boats, I wrote about the challenges they faced and the roles I played as a working partner: wife, mother, bookkeeper, gofer, cook, and legal advisor.

In November 2001, I began to edit my manuscript, planning to query agents and publishers. As December 2001 approached, and the start of another year's crab season, Bob and his crew prepared the *F/V Michele Ann* and its gear for opening day. Our other vessel, the *F/V Nesika*, was now owned by our sons, managed by my husband, and skippered by long-time local fisherman Rob Thompson.

Bob and his crew left port early the morning of December 11, 2001 on the *F/V Michele Ann*, heading south of Newport. The *F/V Nesika* left the dock a couple of hours later, at about 8 a.m., and headed north. Our oldest son, Ben, then 21, was home from college and joined the crew of the *F/V Nesika* as an "extra man" to help set gear.

Sometime between 9:20 a.m. and 10:45 a.m., while Bob was setting crab gear and I was at work at my law office, the *F/V Nesika* capsized. The accident occurred just off shore, within sight, and in front of, our oceanfront home. The vessel was discovered upside down in the water by the skipper of another boat. Despite an intensive Coast Guard search by lifeboats and helicopter, and local crab boats that rushed to help, all four men, including our son, Ben, died at sea.

Rather than abandon the journal I had begun, I decided to continue to write. By obtaining Coast Guard reports, and assembling other's recollections of the tragedy through taped interviews, I have reconstructed the events of that day. This book chronicles not only our unusual lives before the accident, but the aftermath of December 11, 2001; the challenge of grieving and honoring our son and our men, at the same time dealing with insurance company investigators and lawyers, and financial claims from surviving heirs.

I have also written of how we confronted ourselves, questioning the fundamental nature of our lives, our sea-going culture, and whether we can, or even wish to, remain a part of the commercial fishing community.

DECEMBER 2000

F/V Michele Ann in Yaquina Bay

Monday
December 11, 2000

Four-thirty a.m. I'm awake. The *F/V Michele Ann* is being loaded with the last of its crab pots, ready to leave Newport and head north to Astoria, a port on the Columbia River. Tomorrow at 8 a.m., hundreds of boats will go to sea loaded with crab gear stacked on their decks and then dump those pots into the ocean. Each pot will be dropped to the ocean floor, and marked with a colorful buoy, specific to the owner of the pot. The pots are baited one by one, with the individual crabber's secret recipe stuffed into plastic jars that have holes drilled into them, so the scent of the bait attracts the crabs. "Hanging bait," or fresh fish carcasses, are also attached to the pot.

After the gear is laid, the boats will then start retrieving their pots, hopefully full of crab. The pots are hydraulically hauled on board the vessels and emptied. Only male crabs of a certain size are kept for sale, and all females are returned to the sea to protect future stock. The pots are then rebaited and reset, pushed off the side of the vessel, line and buoys trailing, so they can be found and retrieved again.

However, we have been getting calls from fishermen at the Columbia River, and further north that the crabs aren't "ready," meaning they might not yet be full and heavy with crab meat. Worse yet, an agreement with the buyers about the price has not yet been settled. Cynically, Bob and I wonder if that means they are trying to discourage the Newport boats from coming north to fish.

We both roll out of bed, Bob to the shower and then to the computer to check the NOAA (National Oceanic and Atmospheric Administration) website for weather conditions; me to dress then load cardboard boxes into the back of his pickup truck. The boxes contain frozen dinners I made: chicken enchiladas, pork loin with sour cream noodles, pot stickers, scalloped potatoes and ham, chili, goulash, turkey with dressing and gravy. I double-check the list I assembled for him yesterday: reading glasses, fishing permits, cash, checkbook, prescriptions. I put empty duffle bags in front of the stacks of his work clothes I'd washed, folded and laid out on the loveseat in our bedroom. Bob left first for the boat, and I followed in the Explorer, pulling into the loading dock at the fish plant. His crew untied the boat from the port dock and drove to the fish plant to load pots, bait and the food I brought.

When I left the house at 6 a.m., the boys were still asleep. I am nervous about their day. Dylan, a high school senior, is skipping school. He and Ben, home from college, are taking Bob's white and blue Ford pickup and driving to Astoria. They're hauling a trailer loaded with the "shelter deck," a 10-foot by 10-foot two-sided aluminum shelter that will be bolted onto the deck of the boat for the guys to work under during bad weather. It had been taken off the *Michele Ann* to maximize room to stack crab pots on the deck, but would be re-attached to the vessel once the gear was laid and fishing underway.

I thought it wouldn't be cold enough for the roads to be icy, but Highway 101 north to Astoria traverses mountains in the Coast Range and goes through a tunnel. It isn't easy driving that route in a car at the best of times, let alone a truck hauling a trailer loaded with thousands of pounds of equipment on slick pavement.

Dear God, please let them be safe. I often lurch from prayer to prayer, from husband to sons to crew. *Dear God, just please let them all be safe.*

People often ask if I worry. I blithely assure them I don't. For if you really thought about the dangers involved in commercial fishing, you'd be paralyzed. Frozen with worry.

Tuesday
December 12, 2000

Bob, somewhere on the ocean heading north to Astoria, called me yesterday from the boat. "We may not lay our gear," he said. "The crabs aren't ready. Processors will pay only $1.25." That amount was far less than what the crabs are worth. Would there be a strike?

Later in the afternoon, Bob called again. "The gear isn't going in the water, honey," he said.

Oh, brother, I thought. Meanwhile, Bob said that Ben and Dylan had arrived in Astoria in fine shape, with the truck and trailer of equipment intact. The boys were going to the crabbers' meeting near Astoria, to keep Bob in touch with what was going on with the local fishermen. It was a matter of timing. Bob did not want to cross the Columbia River bar to "lay up" with the guys on strike, and then suddenly see crab boats loaded with gear headed down the river toward him. If the strike was going to settle soon, he'd stay on the ocean waiting, and not set any gear until the strike broke. Bob sent Ben and Dylan to the crab meeting so they could relay the latest information to him to help decide what to do.

"What the hell?" I said. "For Christ's sake, Bob, tell those boys to come home. Jesus, the roads are freezing; there's black ice all over. Some of the roads are closed, Dylan's got school…."

"Okay, okay," Bob said. "I'll get them out of here. Take it easy, they're fine."

The phone rang at dinner time. The boys? I thought. Are they okay? Bob? Is he okay? I live with this litany running through my head every fishing season. But it was Russell Smotherman on the phone, a crabber at the Columbia River. "What's up, Russell?" I asked.

"No gear's going in the water. We aren't fishing," said Russell.

Russell was shouting against loud background noise. I

suspected this conversation was not just for my benefit, but for the Astoria crabbers sitting in the bar that served as the meeting room.

"What's the news?" I asked.

"Nobody's gear goes in the water, everyone's holding," Russell said.

"I'll tell Bob, Russell. You can call him on his cell phone, but I will tell him, too. That's no problem," I reassured. "Bob's with you." These crabbers at Astoria were panicking that Bob and the other fishermen from Newport would lay their crab pots and start fishing before they did.

I called Bob and gave him the information from Russell, which, as it turned out, Bob already knew.

"Ben called me," Bob said. "I told Ben it was important for me to know what was going on, but for him to just listen."

I thought, Oh, for God's sake. There are my two kids, in a bar somewhere, with a bunch of uptight fishermen. The Astoria crabbers all knew Bob was coming north, along with Todd Whaley, on the *Miss Sarah*, the largest crab vessel on the coast, and Justin Yager, another very talented fisherman.

"I told Ben that if the subject came up, to tell the men we were on our way to the river, and that we will do whatever the fishermen at the river do," Bob said.

It is hard to describe the energy of these fishermen just before a season starts; they're like thoroughbred racehorses in the starting gate. The men are extremely keyed up and ready to bolt. Many at the meeting were there only to make sure no one else left the dock early to go fishing. They were distrustful of one another, and did not want anyone to get the jump on them. One of the fishermen in the Astoria meeting announced that Bob was on his way north. As instructed by Bob, Ben stayed silent. But then Al Gann, a very productive fisherman himself, said "I wouldn't trust Bob Eder any further than I could throw him." It was then that Ben stood up.

"I know what Bob Eder's going to do," Ben said.

Al Gann jumped up, physically confronted Ben and said, "Who the fuck are you?"

Ben looked at Al Gann straight on and said, "My name is Ben Eder and Bob Eder is my dad. And he told me to tell you he'll do whatever you guys decide—set gear or sit and wait for a better price."

Ben is so brave. I've been in rooms full of angry, uptight fishermen and it isn't an easy place to be—not even for me—a grown woman lawyer. I couldn't imagine what it was like for Ben to hear someone talk about his father in a disrespectful manner. I am enormously proud that he stood up in that group of men and defended his father. Not one of those men did Ben know, except for crazy Dennis Sturgell, a talented crabber of ill repute. Sturgell later told Bob that he needed a wheelbarrow to carry Ben's balls out of the room that day.

"After the meeting, Sturgell laid $2,000 bucks on the bar and bought drinks for everybody," Ben told me that evening, wide-eyed.

"Yeah, and I had to stay outside the whole time," Dylan complained.

"I knew you'd kill me, Mom, if I'd taken Dylan into the bar," Ben said with a grin.

So last night, after Bob tied up the boat at the dock in Astoria, the devastated crew took the bait off the boat, put it in the freezer at the fish plant, found a slip in a very crowded harbor, and returned to Newport. Ben, home for the holidays from Reed College, had planned to finance the next six months traveling in South America with crab money, but he hadn't earned a dime yet. And here was Bob, suddenly back home, who yesterday I kissed goodbye, thinking he wouldn't be sleeping in our bed for the next couple of months.

Saturday
December 16, 2000

I slept in until 9:30 this morning. Evidently, I am exhausted. For the last two weeks I have focused on working out at the YMCA five days a week, doing step aerobics, and lifting weights twice a week. I am five pounds lighter, but still have 24 to go. It is going to take a while to get the weight off, especially since I am constantly confronted with holiday food.

In fact, on Thursday, our regular December Fishermen's Wives Board meeting was instead a Christmas lunch at the home of Chris Carley, the wife of a crab and shrimp fisherman. Chris works part-time as a school bus driver. The boys had ridden her bus to school when they were young. I'd get a call from Chris if the boys were up to no good, which, truth be told, happened only once. One great thing about living in a small town is that there are hordes of other moms who love your children and we keep an eye on them all.

Chris is an excellent cook. For lunch she made an elegant crab, shrimp and scallop fettuccine with a cream sauce—there went my diet. Her home was beautifully decorated for Christmas and her dining table sparkled with crystal, silver and china. Ginny Goblirsch, President of Fishermen's Wives and a Marine Sea Grant agent, had thoughtfully bought crab and fish ornaments for each of us as a Christmas gift.

Bob is back in Astoria, having left again on Friday morning. He let the crew stay home an extra day with their families, but wanted them back on the boat Sunday morning. The crabs are now in good shape, hard-shelled and full of meat. But they still can't get a decent price out of Pacific Seafood, the largest processor on the West Coast.

Despite the impasse on the crab price, I am feeling rather glorious today. For years we have been trying to get an individual quota system in place for West Coast fixed-gear sablefish, our other major fishery. Instead of fishermen being forced to catch all their fish in one very short season, an individual quota program would allot a certain number of pounds to each fisherman, based on their catch history, allowing them to take fish over a longer season when weather, price, and availability were most favorable. Because IQ programs are politically controversial, Congress is now poised to extend a previous four-year moratorium for another two years, despite the recommendations of the Ocean Studies Board of the National Academy of Science to implement IQs as a management tool in the nation's fisheries.

Bob Alverson, of the Fishing Vessel Owners Association in Seattle, has been instrumental in getting language included in a bill in Congress to provide an exception to the IQ moratorium for our fixed-gear sablefish fishery. No one thought it could happen. The West Coast Seafood Processors Association, represented by Rod Moore, vehemently opposes the bill. Alverson works tirelessly with Congressional staff, explaining the problem and why we need this exception for our fishery. For my part, I wrote an editorial for the local Newport newspaper and for *The Oregonian* this past September, explaining the changes we need in the management of our sablefish fishery:

***The Oregonian,* September 11, 2000**

For shame, seafood processors! Rather than supporting Congressional legislation that would amend the Magnuson-Stevens Act to allow an individual quota system for fixed-gear sablefish in waters off Washington, Oregon and California, the West Coast Seafood Processors Association, led by their lobbyist, Rod Moore, is actively working against it.

Sablefish are found in deep waters, from the Aleutian chain to the Mexican border, in approximately 100 to 700 fathoms. Also known as "black cod," their pearl white flesh is especially valued by the Japanese.

Two categories of gear are used to catch sablefish: bottom trawl and fixed-gear. Fixed-gear comes in two types—hook longlines and fishpots. A longline is an anchored ground line with baited hooks attached at intervals. Fishpots are baited steel frame traps covered with nylon mesh.

This fishery is regulated by the Pacific Fishery Management Council, responsible for managing salmon and 83 groundfish species off the West Coast. Each year the Council sets limits as to how much fish may be landed by the commercial fleet.

In order to curtail the effort in the groundfisheries, the Council has implemented a limited entry program restricting participants to those with historical landings, has enacted a sablefish endorsement criteria, again restricting those who could fish, and assigned poundage limits to each permitted vessel. At present, there are 164 permits in the limited-entry sablefish-endorsed fixed-gear fleet on the entire West Coast. Still, the directed season for fixed-gear sablefish has been dramatically reduced. From a ten-month season in 1987, the season this summer was only nine days long.

For the last ten years, fixed-gear fishermen from all three states have advocated the use of individual quotas as a method of managing this fishery. An individual quota system would allow fishermen to take their poundage limits over a several month period of time, thus allowing them to choose when to fish based on safety, weather, fish quality and availability, and price. IQs have been utilized in Alaska for sablefish and halibut with resounding success. The consumer gets fresh product over a longer season and the loss of boats and lives has been reduced.

Despite the Pacific Council's efforts to implement an IQ program for this fishery, in 1996 Congress enacted a nationwide moratorium on any new IQ plan until further studies could be completed. The Ocean Studies

Board of the National Academy of Science was charged with the task of evaluating individual quotas as a management tool. In their final report, in addition to endorsing the use of IQ programs, this nationwide study specifically mentioned that IQs would be particularly useful in the management of Pacific fixed-gear sablefish.

Members of the environmental community also support the use of individual quotas. In 1996, Dr. Rod Fujita of the Environmental Defense Fund stated, "Our study indicates that IQs can reduce the pressure to over exploit the resource if properly designed and used in conjunction with a risk adverse harvest guideline and appropriate conventional management measures."

Finally, the Pacific Fishery Management Council, in its Draft Strategic Plan of June 2000 specifically recommended that in the event that the Congressional moratorium on IQs expires, the Council should move forward expeditiously to immediately develop a transition plan to an IQ fishery for fixed-gear sablefish.

Why, then, would the West Coast Seafood Processors Association seek an extension of the moratorium and oppose a limited exception for fixed-gear sablefish? To give you a glimpse of their reasoning, here's an excerpt from a very recent letter to West Coast Congressional representatives from Rod Moore, the processors' lobbyist. He stated that until the Pacific Council develops an IQ program for all fisheries and gear types and establishes a permit program for processors, they will not support an exception to the moratorium for fixed-gear sablefish.

Is that fair? No. In general, processors oppose IQs because their implementation gives the individual fisherman more control over where, when and for what price they fish.

Who are we? Nobody. No lobbyist. No organization. I saw Senator Wyden at a local gathering in Newport last week and spoke with him briefly. He said he was "sympathetic." Well, thank you, Senator, but will you help us?

I haven't seen the movie *The Perfect Storm*, and I don't intend to. As a fisherman's wife and mother of two sons who participate in this fishery, that's a little too much reality for me. Commercial fishing, even in the best of circumstances, is a dangerous business and I've learned to accept that. But what I can't accept is the political activity of the monopolistic seafood processors that control not only our economic well-being, but who are intent on opposing legislation that would dramatically improve conditions for the resource, the consumer, and coastal fishing families. That's right, Mr. Moore. It's not fish you're buying—it's men's lives.

Michele Longo Eder
Newport, Oregon

Monday
December 18, 2000

Fishing continues to be an upside down world. We are lurching again back to a schedule where Bob will be fishing over the holidays. Ben is back in town after visiting friends at Reed College in Portland, and his girlfriend, Phoebe Morris, is home from Antioch College in Ohio. Dylan's lovely friend Leah Brooks is also home from college in Eugene, and so they all came to dinner Saturday night. I laid the table with silver and the Christmas china, made dinner, and we then decorated the Christmas tree. The girls added a civilized touch to the whole tradition instead of the boys goofing around and me nagging them to "Come on, do it right." The four of them had fun putting ornaments on the tree. The boys took pride in explaining to the girls some of our Christmas traditions. It was sweet. They ate dessert and sat around the kitchen table with me until 9 p.m., then scattered. I was happy to get off to bed and read, as I was tired.

Yesterday morning I went to the office to download weather charts and fax them to the boat in Astoria for Bob. First, I retrieved weather forecasts from the NOAA weather site and the "buoy report," which is information from buoys moored in the ocean at various points. Some of the buoys are close to shore and some are several hundred miles offshore. The buoys report wind speed and wave heights. I also checked the Navy's reports, which show oncoming weather patterns, wind direction and wave heights for the next five days at 24 hour intervals. The maps are in color, corresponding to wave height, and it's not unlike reading topographical maps. Because my fax machine doesn't print color, I download and print out the maps from my computer, handwrite the wave heights on the chart for Bob, and fax those to him, too.

That task accomplished, I went off to Fred Meyer, a local variety store, to try and solve the mystery of why I blew several sets of outside Christmas lights. It turns out I had too many sets strung together, of course. Then I further aggravated the problem, and myself, by buying the wrong size fuses. Pete and Leah Fones's and their children stopped by the house on Sunday afternoon and Pete fixed the problem.

Pete and Leah are two of my dearest and oldest friends. Pete, 50 years old and a retired Oregon State Police Sergeant, is now getting his bachelor's degree, and wants to study to become an Episcopal priest. Leah is a nurse in charge of infection control at the hospital in Lincoln City. They have four grown children and our families have gathered together for various holidays over the years. After downing some Martinelli's sparkling apple cider and coffee, Pete and Leah left and I got down to the business of the day: making rugelach.

Rugelach, a cookie made with a cream cheese and butter dough, is a traditional Hanukkah treat. I rolled the dough out in a circle, brushed it with melted butter, sprinkled it with sugar and cocoa and finely chopped nuts, cut the circle of dough into triangles, and individually rolled the cookies into small crescents. I was dusted head to toe in flour when Ben came in the back door. I thought he had left port early this morning to go fishing with our skipper, Richard Wood, on our other boat, the *Nesika.* But he said that although the wind had laid down, the Yaquina Bay bar still looked sloppy, and Richard had decided to wait until tomorrow morning to leave.

Ben spent the day chopping frozen mink carcasses at the fish plant, while the other crew members stuffed bait bags with the mink to put inside the pots. Having thrown his clothes in the wash with a heavy dose of disinfectant, Ben and Brent Barton sat at our kitchen table, wolfing down a meal I cooked for them. Brent, a high school friend of Ben's home from Stanford University, is the son of another local lawyer. I listened to them and laughed; their energy spilling all over the table, long legs and arms waving as they spoke. They made plans to go out that evening. Ben assured me he would be home early and would get enough rest before going out fishing at 4:30 tomorrow morning. I was doubtful. I didn't hear him come or go, which was not unusual. Most probably he found someplace to lay his head with girlfriend Phoebe, and left for fishing from wherever he woke.

The phone rang at 5:30 this morning. It was Bob, calling from Astoria. He is full of nervous energy. The price has settled, finally, and the crab gear would be set at 8 a.m. tomorrow. There is a possibility they will have a delivery of crab before Christmas, but as far as he knew, every crew member except one said he wanted to stay on the boat to go fishing, instead of getting off the boat for Christmas. Bob told me to tell Dylan to stand by, ready to go, as Dylan might need to be the replacement on the *Michele Ann*, since Ben was out fishing with Richard on the *Nesika*. Uh-oh. Ben would be mad if Dylan went out on the first *Michele Ann* crab trip instead of him. The *Michele Ann* would likely catch twice the crab that the *Nesika* could hold. Ben was still counting on fishing money to support his travels and education, and with the delays in the start of the crab season, the money hadn't materialized.

Saturday
December 23, 2000

I'm all ready for Christmas, or so I think. I stayed up late last night wrapping gifts. I hope the boys like everything.

I had chest pain all day yesterday, until I went to aerobics class at 5:30 p.m. I have lost only six pounds, but I have now made it through three weeks straight of aerobics, five days each week. I'm impressed with myself. But chest pain. That worries me.

It started with a call from Bob in Astoria. The weather was horrible, but he was going to try and make it out on the morning tide. He was disgusted. His crew had gone out to dinner the evening before, but a couple of them hadn't returned until 3 in the morning. Bob was incensed. Although Bob thinks they won't get out fishing until this evening, for his crew to go and get fucked up the night before the first day of crab season is so unprofessional. They are about to embark on the most physically rigorous portion of their season. Bob let the guys sleep in that morning, as long as he could, but when Bob opened the door to the foc'sle where the crew slept, he found that two of the four men were missing.

The *Michele Ann* would miss the tide on the first day of crab season! Oh. My. God. Boats were leaving the harbor to go out fishing ahead of the *Michele Ann.*

Bob said he needed Ben to come to Astoria, in case he couldn't find his crew, so that the *Michele Ann* could get out on the next tide. I hustled to gather stuff Ben would need and gassed up the Subaru. What a drag. It means thousands of dollars of lost income to not be on the fishing grounds at the first opportunity, but worse, it was the immaturity of it all. These are crab jobs that can earn our crewmen forty to fifty thousand dollars a year. These men are people with families to support. It is just self-destructive behavior.

My chest pounded all day, sharp pain, and I knew it was

anxiety. I talked with Bob several times yesterday and during every phone call, I cried. He was upset and would speak abruptly to me. I was oversensitive, took everything to heart, and couldn't help but absorb his stress. But it ended up that Ben didn't have to go to the river to fish. During my last conversation with Bob, he said his missing crew had returned, the boat was underway, and he was approaching the Columbia River bar.

A calmer man, Bob was now focused, and looking forward to the job at hand.

Monday
December 26, 2000

I cried Christmas morning. I rose early, as always, and tiptoed downstairs into the living room, excited for the day to begin. As I was re-arranging presents piled under the Christmas tree, the tree fell over. Crash! Ornaments broke. Damn it.

For years we've had a tradition of giving ornaments to the children for Christmas, and my mother has given me one for the last 25 years as well. Luckily, only one of the precious ornaments broke, but unfortunately, it was Ben's 1998 shiny sparkling ball, the one with his name emblazoned on it. Shit, shit, shit. I could barely lift the tree. I yelled for help, but the boys were still asleep on the south side of the house. To scream any louder would only waken my neighbors. I managed to shove the eight-foot Noble fir upright, my arms scratched and pricking from the branches. While holding the tree in place with one hand, I used the other to unplug one of the numerous extension cords that kept 500 lights from shorting out and going dark. I then wrapped the extension cord around the tree, and taped the end of the cord to the window with duct tape. Then I cried some more.

But not for long. I miss Bob, but my misery over his being away and fishing on Christmas is pointless. This is just another holiday he isn't home, and we are all accustomed to that. I reminded myself of all the people who work on holidays, then considered what real misery was, and stopped whining. Instead, I got to work making cinnamon rolls and quiche, anxious for Mary's arrival.

Mary is an "aunt" to my children and a dear friend to me. We've known each other for 20 years and she welcomed the boys into her life as if she was my biological sister. Vibrant, sparkling eyes and smile, always stunningly dressed (at a fraction of retail), Mary is living proof that a person can light up a room. She is an aunt of the very best kind. Mary draws the boys into interesting conversations, and buys them the simplest and most perfect gifts that they put to immediate use.

We had a nice Christmas day. Bob and the boys gave me a great gift—a rock tumbler! For the 12 years we've lived here, I've come back from the beach walking lopsided, my pockets full of agates and jasper and other stones that caught my eye. And now I have my very own rock tumbler to smooth and polish my collection.

I had spoken with Bob two evenings before, on Christmas Eve. The fishing was dismal, he said, despite predictions to the contrary. Crabbing was no better at the Columbia River than it was off Newport; in fact, it was worse. Bob said that when he set the gear it didn't feel "crabby" to him and that attitudes on the boat were deteriorating quickly.

It is difficult for the crew. Accustomed to big first trips, and the possibility of making four thousand dollars each trip for the first few weeks of the season, the prospect of a mediocre crab season was depressing. It is one thing to be away for the holidays if you were making a ton of money. It is another thing to be away from family when your earnings on the first trip will barely cover the draws you've been extended in the weeks before the season's start. The crew has been counting on big pulses of income and it isn't going to happen.

Friday
December 30, 2000

I spent today at my law office, answering correspondence, arranging a tennis game for tomorrow morning, and paying the end-of-year business bills to maximize deductions. I called all our major suppliers for our December invoices and paid them, rather than wait to receive the bills in January. I prepaid as many bills as I thought would withstand IRS scrutiny, including our insurance bill for the two boats, which is a whopping $33,000 per year. That one just floors me. I am just grateful that we have the funds to pay it. I prepaid our state income taxes, which are $25,000. I have to pay our estimated Federal tax on January 15, which will be $55,000.

After visiting Bob yesterday, I came home to Newport. Rain, rain. I loved the drive, and with the music cranked up, it went by in a flash. I saw Dylan momentarily, then dashed off to a 5:30 step aerobics class, came home and collapsed in bed. I'd only slept a few hours the night before and I was exhausted. I could not understand how my husband did it.

At 9 p.m. the phone rang—it was Bob. He was so bummed. They'd gotten back out on the ocean, and their first set of gear looked great. It was a string they'd set just the night before. First pot, 15 crabs; next pot, 22 crabs; next pot 20 crabs! Jesus Christ, they were "in them." The crew was elated! Then a two-crab pot, and a pot whose lid was fastened incorrectly. Then two crab, and another pot that had been tampered with. And so on. The crew hoisted the gear on a string of 50 pots only to discover they'd been robbed. While Bob and the boat were at the dock unloading his catch, some captain and his crew were stealing from our men's hard work. Thieves!

It is the worse kind of poison when this happens. You can't defend against it. The asshole, whoever it was, obviously waited for Bob to leave the crab grounds to go into port. The crew was demoralized. On the phone I was shrieking, "Call the cops, call the cops," but Bob refused. "They can't do anything, Michele," he said.

We decided to call the guy who ran the crab protective association in Newport. Every crabber throws in a couple hundred bucks per boat for a reward fund. If someone is stolen from, a reward is offered—a substantial one—for information leading to the arrest and conviction of the thief. For $5,000, often a guilty crew member will come forward, and, if credible, he gets paid. It is a Wild West kind of system. I had discovered that reward money paid out by the protective association could be recouped as restitution in the criminal process. A person convicted of stealing crab and/or crab pots could be required to pay not only fines and restitution, but also could be required to reimburse the crabber's protective association for the $5,000 reward, which keeps the coffers full.

At 10:30 p.m. the phone rang again. It was Richard Wood, our skipper on the *Nesika*. He said one of his crew was injured with a severely bruised thumb. Ouch. I said I would call the injured guy the next day.

We have a $2,500 deductible which means we will pay the emergency room bill, the doctor, follow-up care and the crewman's wages for whatever is earned by the boat while he is off work, up to $2,500. After that, the insurance will kick in. Plus we will pay the crew member that took the injured man's place, which, I hoped, would be Dylan. If I had to pay double, let it be to a family member.

Richard was going to rustle up Ron, his brother-in-law who occasionally crews for us, and he wanted Dylan as well. I told him to call Dylan on the boys' phone line and see what he was up to; I was going to sleep. It was Dylan's choice to go out fishing, or not. I didn't feel like going downstairs and nagging him. I feel guilty about the amount of pressure I put on the kids to drop whatever they are doing to get out and work at a moment's notice.

Up Saturday morning, and out the door to go to my office to work, to write and to make calls. I have no idea if Richard is going fishing or if Dylan is going with him. I need to call our injured crewman. Richard will call me with landing information and grocery receipts so I can pay him and his crew. And I need to do payroll for the *Michele Ann.*

January 2001

Tuesday
January 2, 2001

New Year's Eve. I spent a quiet one at home on the sofa, watching old *Godfather* movies. Bob, Ben and Dylan are out fishing. Richard, the *Nesika's* captain, needed a substitute crewman, so Dylan went. I can't get over how mature Dylan looks. Before he left the house to go fishing, he came into the living room to say goodbye. Dylan's long, long legs were capped with brown Extra Tuff boots, and he wore an old red Stormy Seas jacket and black fleece pants. It is unnerving when they are all gone to sea, and worse, when one of the boys is fishing on a boat without Bob. I can't decide which is scarier, having all my men on one boat, or split up between the *Michele Ann* and the *Nesika*. The background buzz in my thinking, the worrying about them when they are out fishing, doesn't quiet down until they are all safely home.

Outside, now sheltered in our carport, I have chunks of albacore tuna smoking in a Big Chief smoker. The smoker was a gift from our friends and neighbors, Jim Hanselman and Joann Ronzio.

When I smoke up a batch of tuna using my Big Chief Smoker, I pay close attention to the brine. The right proportion of salt and sugar is very important, much more so than the ingredients in a marinade. With the smoker set up in my carport, the smoke from the mesquite chips wafts throughout the neighborhood. I'm surprised the smoker hasn't been tipped over by local hoodlum cats.

Last August, Bob had called from the ocean and said a friend of ours, Denny Berg, had a couple of tuna for us as a treat, and would I please go down to Denny's boat at Dock 7 and get them.

Denny Berg is a sweetheart of a guy. He graciously carried two albacore wrapped in green plastic sacks up the dock, loaded them into the back of my car in and waved a genial goodbye.

Denny thought I'd be taking the fish home to my men to clean them, but I knew the last thing Bob wanted to do when he got home from a fishing trip was to clean fish.

So, what to do? The Oregon State University Marine Extension office was ably "manned" by Evelyn Brookhyser, the queen of all food preparation, who dispenses all manner of advice. I wandered into her office, a 20-pound albacore tuna under each arm, and explained my predicament to the laughing office staff. Evelyn hustled me into the on-site kitchen. "Aprons on," she said, and loined the first one for me, showing where to cut into the fish, to draw the line around the gills, to pull the skin back, and then to dig my fingers in along the backbone to "roll" the loin out. We repeated the process in each quarter of the fish to get four loins. I loved digging my fingers into the flesh, along the red line of blood and separating the loin. It was very tactile, and no skill with a knife was necessary. As thanks, I gave Evelyn a couple of the loins and made my way home, problem solved.

Bob and the boys and crew also caught tuna while fishing for sable last summer. We generally don't fish for tuna commercially. It's a recreational fishery for the guys, one they do in late summer while on the ocean and sablefish season is underway. Between the *Nesika* and the *Michele Ann*, the crew landed almost 500 pounds of tuna. Bob asked the fish plant to loin the tuna and then he brought it all home in the back of his pickup. I telephoned our crew to come and get some for their families. Bob and Dylan, assembly-line style, had wrapped the fish for freezing. Nothing fancy; into Ziplock bags it went. Ben told me we needed to buy a vacuum sealer, and he was right. I stashed the tuna in freezers in our garage, but Bob said to stack the fish so there was circulating air between each loin. I quickly ran out of wire racks to separate the layers of fish, so resorted to kindling laid crosswise, to make sure the fish would freeze evenly. "Honey, that's pretty ingenious of you!" Bob said.

Ben loves to take a tuna from the freezer and have a barbecue with his urban college friends. He's become quite particular about his marinades and cooking process. I'm proud of him. My style is to take a loin or two, throw it in a half gallon Ball jar, pour soy sauce, water, leftover oil and vinegar dressings, whatever leavings I can find from bottles of A-1 and Worcestershire sauce, and give the jar a good shake to mix the ingredients. I let the tuna marinate in the jar for 24 hours in the fridge, then grill the loin on the barbecue.

Dylan and Ben with a tuna caught for fun during sablefish season aboard the *Michele Ann*, 2000

Thursday
January 4, 2001

Dylan was funny last night. While we sat around the dinner table, he described to his friend, Leah Brooks, his most recent fishing trip with Richard on the *Nesika.* Richard said that Dylan and Ron, Richard's brother-in-law, got through the gear in half the time it had taken two of his other crewmen. That was high praise from Richard. I asked Dylan how he liked the trip. Dylan snorted. "Well," he said, "Ron ordered me around most of the time and Richard didn't talk, but other than that it was okay." I laughed. Dylan, only 18, is always at the bottom of the totem pole, despite his skill and work ethic. He is at least as good, or better, than many of the crewmen aboard the *Nesika* or the *Michele Ann.*

In great detail, he told Leah about his duties on deck while fishing. "One of my jobs is to chop bait," he said. "The bait is stuffed into bait jars, which go inside the crab pots. The jars have tiny holes in them, and the crabs can smell the bait. The bait better be fresh and sweet smelling, or the crabs won't come near the pots. I really love the squid. It's frozen and you cut it up fast, like a chef," Dylan said, making fast chopping motions with his hands on the kitchen table. "But I get yelled at for that. Because squid goes bad first, it's supposed to be "made up" last, but I don't care. Richard and Ron come out and yell at me. My least favorite bait to chop is the mink," Dylan grinned.

"Mink?" Leah asked, astounded.

"Yeah, mink, like in mink coats," Dylan said. "See, they raise mink for their fur and they skin 'em, and there's nothing to do with the carcasses, until we discovered they're great crab bait. Now there's a market for them, and the ranchers get money for 'em... But they're disgusting! Long, lean, muscley, chop them up, ya get all bloody and gosh, do they ever smell."

Leah pushed her plate away "Yuk," she said. "I've had enough."

Dylan wasn't kidding. There's no worse smell on this planet than chopped mink. The carcasses reek. Imagine you've got your nose stuck in the pants of an old drunk who's peed himself so many times he's stuck to the pavement. It's worse than that. Whenever the boys come home from chopping bait, I put their clothes into the washing machine in a separate load with a strong disinfectant. Whew.

Leah's eyes were big. I realized Dylan didn't talk much about the realities of his fishing work to even his closest friends. I was surprised this was the first Leah heard about Dylan chopping bait. It's a part of the crew's job on deck at sea. But like any profession; the people you work with know the nitty gritty of the day-to-day work, and everyone else has just a general idea of what you do for a living.

Bob just called. They're going to be in port tomorrow or Saturday morning. I'll go up to Astoria to see him. Bob mentioned they caught about 16,000 pounds, which means they found a few more crab than they had on the boat just a day and a half ago. Bob said it looked like he would sell his crab to fish buyer Brian Catton again, given that Catton would pay $2.25 per pound, a quarter more than Pacific Seafood. Twenty-five cents times 16,000 pounds of crab is $4,000 more for the boat, which is quite a chunk of change. Four thousand more than Pacific Seafood would pay for the exact same crab, delivered in the exact same port. Crazy.

Friday
January 12, 2001

It's been a tumultuous week.

Bob is still fishing out of Astoria. This season is dismal. It's the worse crab season of our marriage. I'm still waiting for a check from the fish buyer, Brian Catton in California, for Bob's first big trip. I need it to pay our estimated taxes for last year. Bob spoke with Brian Catton as to the whereabouts of the money. Catton said he'd mailed the check on Monday. If it doesn't get here by Saturday, I have to float the checks to the Feds for our estimated taxes, trusting that the Catton money will get here, or else dip into a line of credit. I'm also advising a client regarding seizing his vessel back from a buyer in default with "self help," and, testifying in front of a U.S. Senate Commerce Subcommittee hearing being held here in Newport and chaired by Oregon Senator Ron Wyden. Yikes! Too much on my plate.

Last weekend I went to see Bob in Astoria when the boat came in. It's a three-hour drive north on Highway 101 to the Astoria dock. Jeez, how the wind blew. It was clear and cold and the wind whistled through the fish plant. Phoebe was already there to visit Ben. I was cordial to her, warm even, but it felt so weird. It was good to see Ben's joy. It was clear he felt loved by Phoebe and I was glad for that. But I am still in the process of letting go of my adult son. It's creepy. Here I am in Astoria, remembering the places I took the boys when they were young, when we made road trips in our old Volvo station wagon to see their dad. I drove past the hotels, the shops, the maritime museum, the parks, the baseball card stores, the laundromats, the grocery stores, the repair shops and the fish plants—and now here was Ben with his "own woman."

Bob was exhausted. He was glad to see me, but overtired and short-tempered with everyone. For Bob, that is unusual. Even when exhausted, my husband usually exhibits extraordinary good manners. Damn, did he ever need some sleep. The unloaders from the plant weren't handling the crab well as they removed them from the boat. Bob yelled at them to stop unloading, then proceeded to give the men detailed instructions on what to do. "Crabs can't be offloaded upside down!" he shouted from the dock down to the boat.

I wandered off. Bob is rarely loud or agitated, but this time he was both. I hope Bob returns to his usual good-natured self after he gets some sleep.

Bob and I left the boat to do the grocery shopping. I had nagged him to let me go alone so he could rest at the motel room, but when I suggested it a second time, Bob barked at me, "Don't bug me about this," so I left him alone. I am starting to regret having come up to Astoria. All this anticipation, 30 seconds of pure joy of seeing Bob, then the rest of the time I have to deal with his exhaustion and the pressure he feels. I am not good at isolating myself from Bob's tension. I absorb all of it, and it makes me ill.

But off we went to Costco, with a grocery list a crew member prepared. I supplemented the list by looking through the cupboards and the fridge on the boat. And Bob added items as we drove. Between the three of us, we had a complete list.

At Costco, Bob and I sat down at a small table in the area where hot dogs are sold. He sipped on a latte we'd bought at a drive-through on the way to the store. I pulled some papers out of my purse to share with Bob. It was an essay Dylan wrote for one of his college applications.

My Father
by Dylan Eder

Did you ever notice that some people have everything imaginable yet they are still not happy; while at the same time, others have nothing and somehow they are always smiling? This is because happiness is not something you can buy. It comes from having a good attitude about life. It comes from seeing the goodness and beauty in everything and everybody. This outlook can come from many places, but usually you will find that the best way to get it, is to surround yourself with people who have it. In my case I didn't have to look very hard to find someone with the right attitude. My dad has a better outlook on life than anybody else I know.

He was born in Los Angeles and was raised as a Jew. While taking part in all of the Jewish tradition, he thought freely and maintained his own ideas about spirituality and religion. Though he rejected some of the more orthodox Jewish beliefs, my dad did embrace one of most important ideals in the Jewish faith, that of focusing on living and not on dying. Of making the best out of life, and not dreaming of a better life in death. His dad, Benjamin, got sick when he was still a young teen, and he had a hard time dealing with his loss. Ben was a very influential man in my dad's life, and even on his death bed, my grandpa kept teaching my dad valuable lessons. My father has told me time and time again about what my grandpa told him while he was breathing his last breaths. He said, "It's just great to be alive." My dad told me that he said this over and over again, even when in great pain.

Whether it was the words of his father, or the ideals of his faith, something in my dad's childhood had a deep and lasting impact on his outlook on life. After my grandfather died of brain cancer, my dad was heartbroken. His life continued but he was obviously very affected. He did, however, continue his success in school, and after high school he attended the University of California at Santa Cruz. There he spent most of his time studying the art of expression. He wanted to be either a poet or an English professor. He was a very good writer and a book of poems, "*Burning the Slash,*" was published while still in school. He told me that he wanted to be a poet because he sees so much beauty in the world and he wanted to express it.

After graduation my dad continued his writing while he traveled around gathering material. One of these trips took him out on a fishing boat to see the ocean. While out there he helped out a little bit and found that he loved the environment and the work. From this point on he was a fisherman by trade and a poet at heart. He now owns a corporation consisting of two fishing vessels, at least seven full time employees, hundreds of fishing traps, and multiple fishing permits for California, Oregon, and Washington. He doesn't fish because it is the easiest way to make a lot of money; it's not at all. He fishes because he loves it. My dad sees so much beauty in fishing, he doesn't even have to be doing well to be happy. He thinks that the ocean is one of the most beautiful places in the world, and he appreciates and honors its size and raw power. He finds the animals which he catches to be incredible, and he sees beauty and grace in their movement and their physique. My father even finds his place in the world to be a very natural thing. He feels like an important part of the food chain; delivering healthy, natural food to people for their consumption and enjoyment.

My dad is not only happy when he is fishing or out at sea. He savors every moment he has to spend with his family at home. He almost always portrays a good attitude and continually looks on the bright side of things. He never stops appreciating life and he never forgets how lucky he is to have a nice home and a loving family. Even during the most hectic periods, I can see him look around and smile in appreciation. Every morning, when my dad gets out of the shower, he goes into his room and sits on the edge of the bed. He just sits, in silent contemplation, staring out the window at the ocean. I have sat there with him before and I got the feeling that he sees just as much beauty in that view now as he did when we first moved in.

Although my dad spends a lot of time fishing out of town, he still has a superb influence on my life and my attitude. He taught me the value of a good outlook on life

> as well as the value of education. My dad has not passed on a lot of what he learned about Judaism, but he has passed on what he feels are the important aspects. When asked about death, my dad admitted that he doesn't know what will happen. He says the only thing he knows is that we are here now, so we should focus on life and living each day to its full potential.
>
> It is obvious to me that the things my dad told and showed me through example have had a major impact on who I am. Not only do I find myself staring out at the ocean, thinking about how beautiful this earth is, I also try hard to put things into perspective. I try to be grateful for what I have, and anytime I feel down, I just think of those that are less fortunate, and it helps me appreciate my life. I try to find beauty in all things. People who seem unpleasant have good sides too, and things that seem commonplace or simple are actually amazing if you consider where they come from. I just hope that I can go through life with the same good attitude that my dad has and that I can have the same inner peace that he has found.

Bob was crying even before he finished reading Dylan's essay. "I can't believe this," he said, wiping his eyes with the back of his hand. "Dylan loves you so much, honey," I said. Bob stood, shaking his head in wonderment at the beauty of what Dylan wrote.

When we finished loading the groceries, Bob went back to the boat, while I went to Fred Meyer to buy items not available at Costco. Back to the boat I went and unloaded the rest of the groceries. Bob drove the boat from the fish plant over to the fuel dock. I paid the fuel bill—$3,300—and then sat in my car on the dock. The boat would still need to be driven from the fuel dock up the river to the boat basin in Warrenton, and parked, before the men could call it an evening and get some rest.

The boat got underway, and I drove by land to the dock in Warrenton to wait for its arrival. Phoebe sat with me for a while and we talked. Making sure the boat was securely tied and hooked up to shore power, Bob and the crew finally left the boat. At the hotel, Bob slept for 12 hours straight. While he was conked out, I woke up at 3 a.m., unable to sleep. I was worried about Dylan at sea with Richard on the *Nesika*, fishing out of Newport. I don't like either of the boys fishing on the ocean without Bob aboard. The next morning Bob and I went to the Columbia Cafe for breakfast, our favorite restaurant in Astoria, where we ate delicious omelets, with homemade toast and jam.

I drove the three hours home to Newport, and Dylan was there to greet me. He'd had a good, if short trip on the *Nesika.* Dylan said he had "run the block" this trip. My eyes widened, eyebrows lifted, and Dylan smiled. Being the "block man" meant you caught the crab buoy with a buoy stick as it bobbed on the seas, grabbed the line attached to the crab pot sitting on the bottom of the ocean, and put the line in the crab block, which looks like two shallow and wide steel bowls glued back to back. The line caught, the hydraulics were engaged and the line flew on board, bringing the crab pot up from the ocean floor to the rail of the boat. It was the most skilled job on the deck and also the most dangerous. Block men were often missing fingers, and ran the danger of getting hit in the head with the steel sheaves. Still, I was proud of him, and Dylan, I could tell, was proud of himself.

By then it was Sunday evening, January 7, and I collapsed on the sofa to watch the family favorite, *The Simpsons.*

Bob called. They'd gotten underway after we ate breakfast that morning, and he expected he'd be back in port on Tuesday. "Ben's got to get off the boat," he said. Ben was leaving to travel in South America for six months, and as far as I knew, he plans to leave Newport next week. Ben said he wanted to spend a couple of days in Portland first, with his friends from Reed. I called Phoebe and offered her my car so she could go pick up Ben in Astoria, and she happily accepted.

Friday
January 19, 2001

Ben came home from fishing on Tuesday and was a whirlwind getting ready to go on his trip. He sorted through his belongings; huge piles of items scattered around his room. I watched as Ben made a tightly-packed first-aid kit. He bought an insulated sleep sack and a new backpack. But the backpack couldn't look too new, Ben told me, or he'd be a target for theft. Ben was a far more experienced traveler than I. In addition to having been to Israel and Venezuela while in high school, he'd been on the beach in Rio de Janeiro for the millennium in 2000, had crisscrossed the U.S. and Mexico in a marathon road trip, and traveled to Santo Domingo last spring. This trip was to take him through much of South America.

Watching him pack, I felt useless. He was so grown up. I couldn't tuck cookies in his knapsack anymore, knowing he'd safely return home to me from school at the end of the day. Instead, I looked for books I thought would interest him, to read on the plane.

Meanwhile, I was in a flurry of my own. Oregon Senator Ron Wyden's Commerce Subcommittee hearing regarding the groundfish industry is being held in Newport. I've been asked to testify about issues of concern. I invited some of his staff and that of the Commerce subcommittee to dinner. I'd picked up a dozen crabs from the fish plant, bought sourdough bread, tossed a green salad and bought some spicy Szechwan pasta from Canyon Way restaurant. After I returned home from shopping, Ben announced he was leaving for Portland that very evening, to spend time with his college friends, before departing for South America. I was surprised, but couldn't very well cancel the dinner guests at the last minute to spend the evening alone with Ben, as I would have preferred.

That evening, while we were gathered around the kitchen

table eating crab, Ben appeared, his fully loaded pack on his back.

"Well, what do you think?" he asked with a smile, turning around to show us his old-looking new pack. "I'm leaving," Ben announced. "Peter's here. He's taking me to Portland."

I got up from the table, as composed as I could manage, to hug and kiss him goodbye. Although I'd mothered Ben while he'd been home the past week, his leave-taking was so sudden. I knew Ben planned it that way. It was another step in asserting his independence. One of my guests, a young man of 30, was clearly envious.

"Boy, that's the life," he said. "I just wish I had the chance to do that. I'd be gone in a flash."

I went outside with Ben and waved at him, as he and his best friend, Peter, pulled out of the driveway. I kept waving until they were out of sight. Tears ran down my cheeks, but I wiped them away and went back in the house to rejoin my guests.

FEBRUARY 2001

Sunday
February 25, 2001

Home alone. Well, not quite. Dylan is out and about with friends. Ben is somewhere in Brazil. And Bob is still in Astoria crabbing. I'm happy for Bob tonight, though. This weekend was the Fourth Annual Fisher Poets gathering at the Wet Dog Café in Astoria. Started in 1998, Bob has been invited to attend and read his poetry each year, but since it's always held during crab season, he hasn't been able to go. This year, Bob came in from fishing, unloaded his crab and, after being up all night, made his way to the café to read.

Bob called me today, excited about the event, and was so pleased he'd been asked to participate. "It was amazing, Michele," he said. "A packed house, and I was pretty nervous." This was the poem he read.

END OF SEASON GUTTING SONG

As we rip
the bloodharp gills
the useless jewels
the shrimp and smelt from their bellies,

as we feed
the gulls we want
one function: muscle that moved them.

A fish heart
like a forget-me-not
jerks and blooms
across the deck.

Birds fight
for torn, milt-filled
sacs. They trail
intestines
like ladders to heaven.
From females
we save the small
and bulging eggs
the dreams of fins
dreams of eyes
their first sight
the current.

Tomorrow
only the river
will catch salmon
only the eggs
will catch bending
constant and uncertain
our lord of light.

—Bob Eder

March 2001

From: **Ben in Argentina**
Date: **Tuesday, March 13, 2001**

Mother, brother and father,

I have now been for almost an hour in Argentina, and quite relieved the border here is so slack that nobody seemed to mind I overstayed my visa in Brazil. Yesterday, I visited the world's largest hydroelectric dam, a joint venture between Paraguay and Brazil, providing all of Paraguay's power and 25% of Brazil's. This dam will still produce more power per year than the Three Gorges Dam in China.

I did not go to the nearby Ciudad de Este in Paraguay, which is an international free trade zone, shopping bonanza, and the stolen goods and smuggling capital of South America. It has a huge Lebanese population and significant funding base for the Hamas and PLO. Today I visited the truly bitchin' Iguacu Falls from the Brazilian side, and will see them from the Argentina side in the morning, before I leave on a twenty-four hour bus ride to the capital. I have exciting news to report that if all goes according to recently made plans, Phoebe will be flying into Buenos Aires on the 16th and staying for her spring break. I still don't quite believe it myself, but better go soon if I'm to meet her on time. I'm very excited to be working on Spanish again, though I keep spewing out Portuguese words and phrases I didn't know I knew until I left Brazil. I was wondering what the most current thoughts are for travel down to the southern core. I miss you all and would be deeply honored and excited to receive you as my guests in Latin America. Take care, and learn, learn, learn.

—Ben

Thursday
March 15, 2001

I'm laughing today remembering the dinner at our home last night. Scott Price was a guest. Scott is one of our former crew members. I arrived home from working out at the YMCA, soaked in sweat. There was no room for me to park my car at the house. At first I didn't recognize the extra truck out front and I wondered who the guest was and if we had enough for an extra plate for dinner.

We did—I'd marinated tuna loins in an amalgamation of balsamic vinegar salad dressing and soy sauce. Mmm, I ticked off in my head: plenty of salad fixings and two bunches of asparagus—that will work. I opened the back door, saw Scott, and said hello. I threw the tuna in the oven and ran upstairs to get a quick shower, leaving the guys in the living room to talk.

With the tuna, I served the fresh, slender, steamed asparagus and a red leaf and spinach salad, with fresh hand-grated Romano cheese and an olive oil and lemon juice dressing. Dylan, Bob and I sat around the kitchen table and listened to Scott's stories.

Scott asked to join our crab crew late this season, as he needed the money. I was glad to rehire Scott. He genuinely believed in Bob, and was a supportive team worker. A talented and knowledgeable mechanic, Scott had a great attitude.

I got to know Scott during crab season in December of 1996. Bob, his crew and the *Michele Ann* were leaving Newport to go to the Columbia River to fish out of Astoria. They were late getting away from the dock in order to make the tide and a window of good weather. The bait was loaded and the boat was at the fish plant dock, ready to pull away. They'd been working so hard up until the very last minute, that the guys hadn't made plans to have their trucks picked up from the bayfront and returned to their homes, or any long-term parking arrangements. I'd barely had time to pack for Bob and throw duffle bags of clothes for him on the boat. Scott jumped off the boat to move his truck from its short-term parking space, and retrieve the stuff he would need while fishing. I followed Scott in my car, waited for him to park legally, and then I was to drive him back to the boat with his gear.

Scott got out of his antique 1955 pickup truck with a duffle bag in one hand and a 45 caliber six-shooter, long barreled Vaquero Ruger in the other.

"What are you doing with the gun?" I shouted.

"Well, I can't leave it sitting in the truck, Michele. The truck doesn't lock," Scott said reasonably.

"Well, you can't take it on the boat, for Christ's sake!" I yelled at him.

"Okay. Here. You keep it for me." Scott handed the gun to me and laughed.

"Oh, shit, Scott, is it loaded?" I asked.

"Well, of course it's loaded, Michele. "What good would it be if it wasn't loaded?" Scott smiled and his eyes twinkled, amused by my discomfort as he climbed into my car.

Scott did have a point. I pulled up in front of the fish plant, stuck the gun in my purse, and ran with Scott out to the dock, where they were beginning to untie the boat. Scott jumped on board. The wind was blowing so hard, there were whitecaps in the bay and the bar was really snotty.

"I'll never forget that day, Scott," I said, recalling the incident and laughing at dinner last night. "I do a lot of things to help out crew members, but that was the first gun I'd stashed in my handbag."

Saturday
March 17, 2001

"I'd better hurry up and call Jack before he gets drunk and turns his phone off," Bob said, in a droll manner. Bob was getting ready to round up his crew, to let them know they would be leaving to go fishing tomorrow.

Whether it is Jack or someone else, we continually struggle with drug and alcohol addiction among our crew. For the last five years we have done pre-employment drug screens and random drug testing for everyone, including, to their umbrage, our own children. Neither Ben nor Dylan appreciate being required to take a drug test, that is for sure. And Ben, in particular, lets me know it.

"You say you wanted to be treated like crew; well, you will be. Get down there and get drug tested," I said to my sons. Ben, in return, insisted that Bob and I get tested. Ben railed at me that drug testing was an extreme indignity and a violation of his civil rights. Ben is right; it is. But Ben sure did like the money he earned, and I sure did like having a clean crew.

Before we began drug testing in 1997, I just knew that some of the crew were using methamphetamine. Bob would confront them and they would deny it. It had to stop. It was insane. People were risking their lives to make a living on the ocean. We were risking their lives and our business. And it wasn't just a safety issue on the boat either. The last straw for me was when a crew member, who had been fired for meth use, angrily came to our home while Bob was at sea. He pounded on every door, screaming at me in a meth rage, and when I wouldn't answer the door, threatened to beat it down. I called 911, only to have the operator ask if I had previously forbidden the man to come to our home.

"Oh, right," I said. "Is this what emergency personnel said to Nicole Simpson? Do I have to get the shit beat out of me first, before help will arrive?" I asked. I hung up angrily, and eventually, the meth freak left. It was after that incident that I began to practice target shooting and kept a loaded firearm nearby. Then I took a class so I could get a concealed weapons permit.

Everyone denies the extent of the drug problem in the fishing industry. Crew members deny it. Boat owners insist that if they drug-test potential crew members, they'd never get crew. As a recovering alcoholic myself, turning a blind eye to addiction in my own business, made me crazy. We were offering good jobs to good men but they had to stay clean. We promised we'd re-employ crew members upon successful completion of treatment. That didn't work. So instead, we began to drug test. We finally got both our boats "cleaned up," but we can only keep them that way with pre-employment and random drug testing. Nowadays, the word is out, and few people who can't pass a screen apply for a job with us.

There is one issue that persists. Marijuana. Like the National Basketball Association, marijuana use is rampant, but unlike the NBA, pot use disqualifies you for a job on our team. Richard, our skipper on the *Nesika*, and Bob are both irritated that pot disqualifies crew for employment. It isn't that Richard or Bob endorse the use of pot, but it's difficult to find strong young men, suitable as crab fishermen, who don't also smoke weed. And Bob says that as long as they smoke only in the off season, he'd rather employ a pot smoker any day than a drinker.

Monday
March 19, 2001

Ben will be 21 on Thursday. It doesn't seem possible. Some days I still see Ben as the seven-year-old boy I met 13 years ago.

He was so excited back then. Ben knew his family was different; a mother had been missing for a long time and he just wanted his family to be whole.

We waded through his grade school years with his friends Daimeon and Derick and Peter. Ben initially struggled with reading and speech, but excelled in math and science. He led the Chess Club and competed in chess tournaments, tying for second Place in the Oregon State Championship when he was in the fifth grade. There were glorious teacher conferences twice a year, where his many talents were praised; cool fall days, standing along the sidelines watching Ben and hordes of others run up and down the soccer field; and lazy days in spring, sitting in bleachers, watching Ben play baseball, me talking with the other moms. Ben entered middle school, where the social groups evanesced and Ben was relegated to being a brain, which meant not cool. This changed radically in his junior year when he emerged into a stud of a man, with a beard and a fishing job, academically strong and confident. He was crowned King at the Prom, named salutatorian of his graduating class, and in 1998, rode a wave of success into the academically challenging world of Reed College in Portland, Oregon.

There, Ben met his match. At Reed, he entered a pool of highly talented people and, at times, was frustrated by his slow reading ability. Ben wanted to take part in all Reed had to offer both academically and socially, with the same gusto he approached all of life.

We worry about Ben. Last year I thought he would explode from self-imposed pressure. Always a traveler, Ben took off for a road trip last spring to Baja, Mexico. When he finished his sophomore year at Reed in the spring of 2000, Ben announced he was taking a leave of absence for a year, to travel, and then maybe attend the University of Oregon in order to take classes he would need as a biochemistry major at Reed. Ben said it would take him at least five years to get through college, and if that were the case, doing a year at the University of Oregon would make it more economical.

I was not happy. In fact, Ben's announcement sparked the worst argument Ben and I ever had. I thought Ben needed to go straight through school or he wouldn't finish. Ben complained that there were so many subjects he was interested in that it was too hard to decide on a major. My retort was that there were thousands of college kids out there who had decided on a major, and he could, too.

After finishing his spring semester 2000 at Reed, Ben came back to Newport for the summer. He and Phoebe rented a house from a friend of ours, located just down the street from us. They set up housekeeping, inviting us for dinner and to visit. It was strange to have Ben living down the street, but it was better than Ben living at home. Ben fished all last summer, drove Phoebe back to college in Ohio, then enrolled at the University of Oregon for the fall quarter of 2000 and lived at a co-op in Eugene. Taking courses from Neurobiology to Russian history, he earned straight A's. He returned home in December, fished a little more, and then left for South America in mid-January, where he's been traveling ever since. We communicate by email.

Phoebe has just written to me. She joined Ben in Buenos Aires for spring break and will be with him to celebrate his birthday. They went on a ferry to Uruguay to enjoy the beaches. Meanwhile, Ben wants Bob to come to South America and join up with him, maybe in Santiago, Chile.

I was invited, too, but I don't want to go. Traveling on the cheap without a clear itinerary is not my cup of tea.

All Bob needs to do is to pick a date and get a plane ticket to and from Santiago. Ben said he would meet Bob there. But Bob is hesitant. I suggested that Bob ask Dylan to go with him. Bob liked that idea, which made me realize he didn't want to travel alone. Dylan thinks it is a great idea, too.

Dylan is having a happy spring. He's been accepted at the University of Oregon and offered a partial tuition scholarship for four years. He's also been accepted at UC Santa Cruz, Bob's alma mater. I dug out an old UC Santa Cruz t-shirt of Bob's, gave it to Dylan and said, "Here, wear this to school tomorrow," and Dylan did, with obvious pride. Then Lewis & Clark College wrote and Dylan was accepted there, too, and they offered him a $6,000 scholarship for four years, for $24,000. Whew—that is a lot of money.

It's now March 19. Notifications are expected by April 1. I wonder if the offers with money are sent out first, then the general acceptances, then the rejections. Dylan is still waiting to hear from Whitman College in Walla Walla, Washington. Walla Walla is my not-so-secret first choice for him. Dylan is undecided between UC Santa Cruz and Whitman College, assuming he is accepted there.

In any event, Dylan is enjoying his life. He volunteers at the soup kitchen, plays racquetball, stays up until all hours watching movies, makes beautiful ceramic pieces, and plays guitar. Dylan is "finding himself" in every sense of the expression and his life is coming up roses.

Wednesday
March 21, 2001

Newport News Times
Annual Blessing of the Fleet set for Yaquina Bay

Newport's Blessing of the Fleet will take place at 1 p.m. March 24 in Yaquina Bay.

Newport's Fishermen's Wives will coordinate with the local fishing fleet, ministerial association, U.S. Coast Guard Motor Lifeboat Station Yaquina Bay, and Coast Guard Air Station North Bend to present the day-long event.

Survival-suit races begin at 9:30 a.m. at the Tradewinds dock below Mo's Annex. A service in memory of fishermen lost at sea will take place at 3:30 p.m. at the Fishermen's Memorial Sanctuary at Yaquina Bay State Park.

The custom of blessing the fleet originated centuries ago in the Mediterranean. Through centuries of change, this custom remains a standard in fishing communities on every United States coast and worldwide. The religious denomination, time and place of ceremonies vary by community, but the purpose remains the same: asking for protection at sea, good catches, and peace of mind for families who wait at home.

Vessels will line up near the Port of Newport International Terminal at noon. Boats should begin to move up at 12:45 p.m. so that the first boat can be blessed at 1 p.m. The Coast Guard will lead the procession.

Special recognition will be awarded to the best decorated vessel. The choice will be made by the Newport Loyalty Days and Sea Fair festival court.

After the blessing, a special glass float will be taken out to sea and launched in memory of all fishermen lost at sea.

Survival suit races have become a modern tradition. Teams of three don survival suits and swim to a life raft anchored 50 feet out in Yaquina Bay, and then pull themselves into it. Emphasis is on speed, being prepared, and knowing the equipment before it is needed. Teams can be made up of fishermen, family members, Coast Guard, and community members. Prizes that include "Newport Fishermen" sweatshirts and glass floats, will be awarded for first, second and third teams and individuals.

The day's events close with a memorial service at the Fishermen's Memorial Sanctuary in Yaquina Bay State Park for all the fishermen lost at sea who called Newport home.

Monday
March 26, 2001

Whew. I'm tired. The Blessing of the Fleet was on Saturday, just two days ago. I'm still recovering from the festivities.

At 7 that morning I flew out of bed. I had 50 people coming to ride on the back deck of the *Michele Ann*, and I'd promised them lunch! Other than order assorted Subway sandwiches, I'd done nothing else. Yikes! I hit the grocery stores, assembling quantities of soda, hot chocolate and coffee, and the nicest looking desserts that could be eaten by hand. The complicating factor was the weather. Could I set up outside on the deck of the boat, or would everybody have to stoop through a narrow passageway to get inside the cabin to eat and drink? Aaaargh! Plan on rain. Had to. I made a last-minute stop at the stationery store to grab large paper doilies for the plastic trays of desserts. I laughed—my mother would be so proud of me!

I raced from the stores to Dock 5 where the *Michele Ann* was parked and met Bob there, dropped off a load of stuff, then ran down the bayfront to a charter boat dock where the Survival Suit Races were taking place. Prizes were awarded for the best team and individual times, but as Connie Kennedy, organizer of the event said, it was "bragging rights" that counted when the whistle blew.

The *Michele Ann* had a team: Tony Kennedy, Rockey Green and Dylan. Friday night, Dylan practiced in our living room, with Bob timing him. Dylan had never donned a survival suit before, but, as Bob pointed out, Dylan was an old hand at putting on gear like this, given Dylan's extensive experience surfing in a wet suit. I even managed to get into a survival suit that evening. After watching Dylan's technique, I saw that I could do it, too.

At the dock this morning, I was breathless. There were teams from a couple of other boats, the Coast Guard and the Loyalty Days Court. The young ladies of the Court were all friends of

Dylan's and he wanted to show off. The girls went first, did very well, and the race was on! Dylan came in second in the overall individual competition, beating out the Coast Guardsmen. I was so pleased for him. Unfortunately, Rockey didn't pull the zipper on his suit all the way up before he jumped into the bay, and water got in, which slowed him down. Our crew placed third overall in the competition—barely in front of the ladies.

Noon approached. On board, Dylan was decorating the hull of our vessel with hundreds of feet of red, white and blue plastic bunting left over from the previous Fourth of July. The *Michele Ann* had a navy hull with a white cabin and mast; it looked particularly patriotic with the bunting. Tony Kennedy set up the hydraulics and the fire hose, aided by a special nozzle provided by the retired Coast Guard Chief, Tom McAdams. It is a tradition for the boats to have water fights while milling about the bay, waiting to line up for the parade. With the flip of a switch, and the help of the nozzle, the hose shot water in an arc 100 feet high. I ran around making pot after pot of coffee and hot chocolate, and setting up various serving stations on the boat for sandwiches and desserts.

Guests began to arrive: friends, lawyers, staff from my office with their families, our crew members' families and friends, and the Lincoln County Commissioners. The three Commissioners are personal friends, but it is good that the politicians responded to the official invitation from Newport Fishermen's Wives to join us on our vessel. The Wives are an effective voice in this community, and the economic base that the fishing industry contributes to the local economy is important. One Commissioner was quite surprised when I explained that the crew payroll, just for our boat in the preceding year, had been $400,000.

Although it seemed I spent most of my time in the galley, I did get out on deck to mingle with our guests. "You certainly do know how to have a good time," one guest exclaimed, taking another brownie from the platter. That made me smile.

Bob drove the boat up the bay, and Tony took aim with the fire hose, showering other boats and their guests with spray. At 1 p.m. the vessels lined up and proceeded under the Yaquina Bay Bridge in groupings of salmon trollers, longliners, crabbers, shrimpers, and trawlers. Then, the boats turned around and passed by the Coast Guard lifeboat *Victory*, which bobbed in the bay and carried the ministers that would bless us. Also on board the Coast Guard vessel were the Loyalty Days Princesses who, dried out after their jump in the bay, judged the best-decorated vessel. Many of the boats were decked in multicolor flags. The parade of boats was broadcast on the local AM radio station, with fisherman Gene Law doing commentary. I listened as we passed by the *Victory*, and as a former Catholic, I crossed myself superstitiously as we were blessed. The boat returned happily to the dock.

Our guests were sated, the sun had come out—it had been a glorious Blessing. Later, I heard that we'd won the award for the best-decked vessel! Bob and I laughed. We felt a little sheepish—the girls were all seniors in high school with Dylan—perhaps it was a bit much to expect 18-year-olds to be impartial. But the *Michele Ann* was the prettiest boat overall certainly, and we did, after all, have the fire hose!

Back at the dock, our guests lingered, then gradually departed. It had been a good party. Sharon, my new secretary, gestured me aside as she and her husband were leaving. Looking at Bob, she nodded. "Do you know," she asked, "how much he loves you?" I was taken aback by her question. It was an intensely personal thing to say. Sharon and I barely know each other, but I recognized immediately that it was a message I was meant to hear, regardless of where it came from. "Yes, yes I think I do," I said slowly. "But thank you for reminding me. Sometimes we take it for granted, don't we?" I replied.

With a quick cleanup from all the "Kennedy girls" and Dylan, Bob and I left the boat. We went to the Fishermen's Memorial for the annual remembrance of our fisherman lost at sea.

Tuesday
March 27, 2001

From: Ben in Buenos Aires

Mi madre, muchos gracias para el dinero. Yo tuve un cumpleanos muy bien y divertido. I had a nice evening with Phoebe in Colonia, Uruguay to celebrate my 21st.

You would be proud of my reading activity as of late, seeing that with the exception of my recent visitor, I have not been able to communicate at any level of complexity with those in my environment. Having been on many long bus rides and customary waits that plague all travel, when available in English, I have turned to books. Here in Buenos Aires, I'm one of those bearded guys you see in the café with books, journals and periodicals stacked about his table, pen in hand, black cap on the head and an involved, concerned look on the face. I must thank you for your strong early influences in this realm. You will find it funny, given that you've corrected so many of my papers and heard me speak, but I discovered yesterday here in Buenos Aires, that I can easily find well paying employment teaching English, with absolutely no experience or documentation. The demand far outstrips the supply of teachers and English being one's first language is qualification enough.

Glad to hear you're doing a lot of writing. Are you working to complete any particular project? I have been doing a fair amount of writing myself, but just in my journal or notes for my reading.

I was in a discussion concerning law school the other day and realized some of my opinions are quite weakly explored and wished to ask you a question: Do you think that law school fundamentally changed the way you think and analyze situations in life, or did it just add skills and

knowledge to an existing and accepting framework? And would you separate from your own experience how you think this question would be answered by the majority in the field? Well, I must be off. Thank you once again for the money. Talk about a gift with utility. Take care, *pura vida,* and learn, learn, learn.
—Ben

April 2001

Sunday
April 1, 2001

In the early days of our marriage, in the winter of 1988 when we still owned only the *Nesika*, Bob came home from fishing and announced that Steve Leake's wife, Becky, had made Bob's favorite cookies and sent them to the boat with Steve, who was then fishing with Bob. Another time, Bob told me that that Tasha, Shawn Bertini's wife, had sent a cake that was really good. Shawn was also a crew member, and later, the skipper of the *Nesika.* Tasha often cared for Ben and Dylan when the boys were small, along with her own two children, Shyla and Shelvin.

Humph, I thought. I already have more than a full-time job representing clients in my law practice. I was co-counsel in the defense of a woman charged with murder, working with famed trial lawyer Gerry Spence. The case would eventually be the subject of a book, *The Smoking Gun.* The trial took me away from home for weeks at a time. Most importantly, I had the shared responsibility of raising our two young boys, albeit with the help of a live-in nanny. And now Bob wanted food? Cooking for my family was one thing, but cooking for the crew on the boat?

Humph, again. But I loved to cook, and the challenge of the logistics interested me. The crew needed good food, securely packaged and easily reheated. Virtually every inch of space on the *Nesika* was dedicated to fishing. The living quarters aboard the boat were miniscule: a tiny refrigerator, a mini microwave, a sink the size of one you'd find in an airplane toilet. Hot meals are a treat for the crew, given that most food eaten on board by the men are sandwiches, hastily slapped together.

So I started production. First, I bought a dozen 20-ounce Rubbermaid rectangular containers on sale for $1.79. I own hundreds of them now, the lids and containers stashed in cupboards and nooks throughout the house. Each year, particularly before crab and sablefish season, I gear up to begin cooking boat food.

What did I make? Over the years, I learned that crew favorites are chicken enchiladas; sausage, biscuits and gravy; and Chicken Malibu. Depending on my schedule, I buy whole chickens and simmer them, saving the broth, cooling it and skimming the fat. I pick the chicken carcasses clean of meat, hand-grate the sharp cheddar cheese, and even make the enchilada sauce from scratch using freshly roasted green chilies. Other times, when I am in a hurry, I'll grab already-baked chickens from the market, shredded cheese in bags, canned enchilada sauce and chopped chilies, for quicker assembly. The enchiladas taste the same either way. To me.

For sausage, biscuits and gravy, the biscuits could be made from scratch or canned. I'd been busted once by a crewman familiar with the brand of refrigerated biscuits I'd used, and who pronounced, indignantly, "Hey, these biscuits aren't homemade!" For the sausage gravy, I brown packages of Italian sausage in two cast iron pans, then drain off some of the grease. I scrape the bits of meat from the bottom of the pan, add flour to thicken, and then broth and milk to smooth out the gravy. Chicken Malibu is a dish that originated from eating at a Sizzler restaurant when the boys were small. It was Ben's favorite, and I duplicated it at home to his delight. Chicken breasts are pounded thin, dredged in flour, soaked in beaten egg and milk, rolled in bread crumbs, then sautéed in a hot cast iron pan, sizzling in cooking spray. Once nicely browned on both sides, I place the chicken on a cookie sheet, layer it with a thin slices of deli ham and Swiss cheese, then broiled it. Chicken Malibu freezes well. I boiled huge pots of egg noodles, buttered and seasoned them with dill weed, and label the packages a side dish to the Malibu.

I also make beef pot pies, quiche Lorraine, ravioli with pesto or red sauce, pot stickers, meatloaf and crusty fried potatoes, pork loin with orzo, meaty chili, and turkey, dressing and gravy. And then there are the desserts. My apple pie was Bob's favorite, followed by German chocolate cake, triple layer orange cake, carrot cake and cinnamon rolls. They love it all!

What Bob likes best about "boat food" is that first, I cook it and secondly, it makes him feel closer to home. If he wasn't compelled to fish, there is no place he'd rather be than with the children and me.

As opposed to the tight quarters on the *Nesika*, the galley on the *Michele Ann* is equipped as nicely as any kitchen in a home. There is a full-sized, side-by-side refrigerator-freezer, a JennAire gas range and oven, and four microwaves. A blender, toaster, three coffeemakers and an espresso machine complete the equipment.

Saturday
April 7, 2001

From: **Ben in Chile**

My thoughts are with you all this evening. Please give everyone my love and know that I will be having my Passover seder in Hebrew with a bunch of Israelis, in Puncon, Chile. By chance it seems I have ended up where they all meet in this part of the world. Yesterday I climbed a 10,000 foot active volcano, saw lava spewing into the air, and slid a good part of the way down, with an ice axe for a brake. Today I can hardly walk and will focus on reading, laundry and fighting off illness. Next year in Jerusalem.

Love,
Ben.

Tuesday
April 17, 2001

I am enjoying the freedom that only a mother and wife can truly savor—an empty house. Bob and Dylan left the Portland airport on Sunday to join Ben in Santiago, Chile. At 4 a.m. this morning the phone rang. It was Ben calling from the Santiago airport. It appears that Bob and Dylan's flight into Chile has been canceled.

"You know where they are, Mom?" Ben asked.

"Nope. Haven't heard from them. Let me know when they arrive, Ben. I love you, sweetie." I hung up the phone. I didn't fall back to sleep, but neither did I worry. How refreshing. I felt, in a word, free.

A few hours later I received an email from Ben saying that Bob and Dylan had arrived, but without their luggage. Bob was crashed at the hotel, sleeping, according to Ben, but he and Dylan were already exploring the city. Good. Hopefully, their bags will turn up.

Last week was a whirlwind of getting ready for their trip. I got cash for them at the bank, did loads of laundry, made copies of their passports, picked up items at the store. To some extent I was sorry I wasn't going. But this sojourn was what I call a guy trip. My preferred mode of traveling does not include backpacks, sleeping bags, or tents.

Meanwhile, I've been looking for another sablefish permit to buy. Last week, Monty Gonsalves, a crabber and sablefish pot fisherman from Crescent City, called and said he wanted to sell us his sablefish pot permit. He called in response to a mailing we'd sent out, asking if any of the current permit holders wanted to sell.

I love doing business with fishermen. Here's how the deal went. I told Monty how much we would pay for the permit—$150,000. Monty said "OK." He knew the market for the permits, and so did we.

Monty said, "My only concern is that you not turn around and sell this permit for a profit. I don't want to look stupid."

I laughed and reassured him. "We want to fish it, Monty."

"Well, then, okay," Monty said. "You do up the papers, I'll send them in."

I sent him an earnest money agreement, with a down-payment.

Monty called me. "Got the paperwork. Signed it all. Filled it out. Looks good to me. I'll transfer the permit to you," he said.

"And I'll pay you," I said.

"Great," he said.

"Great," I said.

"See ya," he said.

"See ya," I said.

He mailed the transfer documents. I mailed him the check. And the deal was done. Done!

I wish everything in my life was that easy.

Tuesday
April 24, 2001

It's been a tough week. I've had a lot of challenging work to do for clients and I am exhausted. I don't write in this journal about my legal work; it's confidential. Suffice to say that with the exception of a few weeks out of the year when I am immersed in helping Bob, I'm also working full-time at my law office.

I arrived home last Friday night and collapsed. Later that evening, on the computer I checked our bank accounts online, intending to download and categorize transactions on Quicken. A Returned Item for $14,000 was debited to our fishing business banking account. Holy shit!

Fucking Catton's check for payment for our last two crab deliveries bounced. I stomped around the room, then ran back to the computer screen. I could not believe my eyes. What was worse, not only had he stiffed us for this money, he still owed us money for trips 12 and 13, another $26,000. Catton was now in the hole to us for $40,000. Jesus, Mary and Joseph!

What to do, what to do? I first tried to reach Catton at all the phone numbers I had for him. No answer. It was 10 p.m. on Friday night, but I left messages all over the place for him to call me. I called Bill Lang, who ran the unloading dock for Catton. I woke him up, but Bill wasn't upset with me. Bill understood the problem, and he promised he'd try to get a hold of Catton.

Well, I didn't get much sleep Friday night. I had fantasies of taking a gun to Catton's head and saying "Your money or your life." That fantasy segued into taking one of his refrigerator trucks and holding it hostage, until we got paid in full in cash for every dime owed. I figured no jury in Newport would convict a fisherman's wife who had been stiffed by a processor. My last resort would be a human chain across the entry road to Catton's dock, our crew's families, particularly those four Kennedy girls, holding banners saying "Pay us what you owe us."

Instead, the next morning, Saturday, I drove across the Yaquina Bay bridge to South Beach and sat in the dock shack with Bill Lang. "Shack" is a perfect description—10 feet by 10 feet, just studs and plywood, a structure that felt like it would blow over any minute. Bill sat behind the desk and genially offered me a cup of coffee.

Catton just happened to call Bill Lang while I was there. Bill grinned and handed the phone to me. I was as angry as I've ever been, but I thought it pointless to shout. I just wanted to know when I was going to get paid in full.

My resolution not to shout lasted about 30 seconds, just long enough for Catton to tell me how busy he was, because he was leaving on a trip to Brussels the next morning at 6 a.m. Big fucking deal, I thought.

"Hey, Mr. Important," I said to Catton. "I hope you have a fucking good time in Brussels, since you are going there on our money!" I yelled. "Is your house payment paid? Do your kids have shoes? Is your wife's car payment made?"

Catton stuttered a response. I told him I had seven families who depended on us and I wasn't going to be his float or his credit line. I told Catton the only business he needed to be concerned about today was how he was going to pay us. Brussels? Bullshit!

I asked Catton when would he have our money. I demanded that he pay in full. He told me he'd have $80,000 on Thursday.

I asked, "From where?"

He said, "The Economic Development Commission in Crescent City."

"Oh, for God's sake," I said. "Do you think I'm stupid? Look Brian, that money is never for operating expenses, and besides, will you really have the money that day?" I asked.

"Well, no," he admitted. He was hoping for approval from a government agency. Then Catton told me about his receivables, and what he expected in payments to him this week.

"Give me their names, Brian," I said. "I'm going to call them and see if they really do owe you money." But I was getting tired of my tirade. There was no point in further shaming the man. All that mattered was whether we got paid. Catton's word with me was ruined, and it was clear that it didn't matter to him anymore, if it ever did in the first place.

That is what is amazing in this fishing business. It is all built on trust. Your word is all you have. The product is perishable. Once sold, you can't track it or seize it, and the fisherman are often the last to know of the money problems of a buyer. Your word has to be good. When I first married Bob, I was shocked at how many hundreds of thousands of dollars were exchanged by virtue of someone's word. Paper really meant nothing. It was simply whether a person did what they said they were going to do. I yelled some more at Catton.

"We went to bat for you, Brian. We used our personal capital, to vouch for you with the Port of Newport, to make sure you got dock space, so you could buy fish here. You've burned us financially, but worse yet, you've burned the very people who went to bat to help you as well."

Of course, it was in our best interest for Brian Catton to be buying fish in Newport, and to be successful. We needed competition among buyers. Otherwise, we were stuck selling to one or two processors: Pacific Seafoods or Bornstein's, which didn't negotiate a price—they just told us what the price was going to be. Bob knew this, and it was why he was willing to sell to Catton.

Now, what to do? I'd already paid the crew for their share of trips 12 and 13. If Catton's check didn't clear on redeposit, not only were we out the $14,000 he owed us, but we were also in the hole for the crew payments I had made, another 30 percent or $4,300. The crew also needed to get paid for trips 14, 15 and 16. Under their crew agreements, crew weren't entitled to get paid until we actually got paid for the product. But these were men with families, responsibilities, bills; they couldn't wait. I always tried to pay our crew every two weeks, even if the buyers were slow with payment. I assured Tony Kennedy and the other men that we were good for their crew share. They would get paid on schedule as usual, regardless of the fact that Catton's checks had bounced. I couldn't do it any other way. The crew had no voice in where or to whom the fish were sold, so I felt we assumed the risk.

So, where did I stand? My husband was in Chile. The *F/V Michele Ann* was at sea, skippered by Tony Kennedy, with live crab on board, due to deliver that evening, and I had no fucking buyer! This time of year, I didn't have a lot of time to find a buyer. These weren't the hard shell crabs found in December; it was April, and it was important to get the live crabs off the boat, fast, and not have them sitting around the dock. The crabs could die. I called and talked to Tony on the *Michele Ann*, and told him not to deliver to Catton. We'd be making other arrangements.

I left the shack at Catton's and headed over to Bornstein's dock. Hopefully, they were still buying crab. I parked my car on the bayfront, and walked out onto the dock to find the foreman, Rick. I explained the situation to Rick and asked if they were buying crab.

"Sorry, no," said Rick. "I don't have a price for you, and we're not set up to take crab off the boat and hold them. Why do you want to sell crab to us, anyway?" Rick asked, teasing me. "Catton not buying?" he asked.

"Well, he might be buying, but we're not selling," and I grinned. "You figure it out." I said.

Rick smiled. What else was I to say? We had been burned by Catton. It was bad that I was there, standing on the dock looking for a market. The word would be all over the port that we hadn't been paid for our crab and it would scare everyone off selling to Catton. That was exactly what I didn't want to happen. What I needed was for product to keep coming across Catton's dock, so that he'd get some money, and we'd get paid.

I left Bornstein's. Now what? It was now 1 p.m. and Tony Kennedy said they were coming in tonight. He estimated he had

1700 pounds of crab on board. I called a company that served the Asian markets, Nor Cal in Oakland. I spoke with a guy named Kevin. Kevin said they wanted our crabs and would pay $4 a pound, but they couldn't send a truck until Monday. Okay. So I called Rick at Bornstein's, and Rick said they'd unload for me.

"Great," I said. "Boat's in tonight, you unload on Sunday and hold them, and Nor Cal will pick them up on Monday."

"Okay," said Rick. Great.

I called Kevin again in Oakland. "Deal's done," I told Kevin. "You can pick the crab up from Bornstein's on Monday."

Driving around town doing errands that afternoon, I was so relieved. I'd done every other aspect of the business before, but hadn't actually sold fish.

But before I could draw too fresh a breath, I got a call from Jeff Princehouse, the manager at the Bornstein plant. The dock manager, Rick, had called Princehouse, his boss, at home. Quite blunt, Princehouse said they would not off-load our crab and would not accept the risk of dead crab if Nor Cal wasn't picking them up until Monday. "No deal," Princehouse said, overriding his dock man.

That meant we'd have to keep the crabs alive on the boat and pump on them. Oh, shit. I remembered what Bob said to me in an earlier email when he heard Tony had crab on the boat: "Tell Tony to sell them. The risk of loss is too big to keep them on the boat."

Now, after talking to Jeff Princehouse, I had to find a solution. Fast.

I called Princehouse back. "By the way," Princehouse said, "if you want to get those crab off your boat, we'll buy those crab from you tomorrow morning, and at your price, too. I can sell them."

Well, what do you know? I've made a deal to sell our crab to Nor Cal. But Princehouse will offload us only if he gets the crab. I really don't have a choice but to sell them to Princehouse if he won't hold the live crab until Monday. He wins. This time.

I called Kevin at Nor Cal. I am embarrassed and apologetic (after all, your word is all you have), but Kevin just laughed when he heard that Jeff Princehouse wouldn't take the crab off the boat and hold them until Monday.

Kevin said, "Oh, hey, I'll just call Jeff Princehouse and buy them from him."

Which confirms for me that I probably could have gotten more money from Kevin for the crab. Instead of our boat getting a higher price, Bornstein's will get the middleman cut, for a profit that should have been ours, and Nor Cal will pay more for the end product. But, this is my first time selling crab, and I am learning.

Sunday
April 29, 2001

Bob and Dylan will arrive home on Thursday. I only wish Ben were coming, too. Maybe he'll surprise me. I would love to see all of them together.

I am still amazed at how much I have enjoyed being alone while my guys have been in Chile. Truly. I know, now, that I could live alone again, as I have in the past. Yes, there would be loneliness, and an ache for a partner, a child, if indeed all were gone, or if I'd never had them. But I have them, and no matter what, will always have them to sustain me. I am now less worried about the angst I will feel when Dylan's gone to college this fall. In fact, I'm almost looking forward to it! This fall will be a honeymoon for Bob and me. We've never lived together without children.

I haven't, however, heard from the guys for a couple days and I do get nervous. Last I knew they were in Punta Arenas and, according to Ben's last email, they could see the bottom of the Earth. Wow!

The fishing business has gone more smoothly this week. Per instructions, I re-deposited Catton's check and it cleared. Whew. But the money Catton said he'd have for me on Thursday for trips 14, 15 and 16 hasn't arrived, and I haven't received any reassuring phone calls that it's on its way.

May 2001

Monday
May 7, 2001

Today is our 13th wedding anniversary. Yippee! Bob says it's really our 26th: 13 years for him and 13 years for me. Not all fishing marriages make it. Sometimes I describe our marriage as a corporation whose shareholders make love. As you can imagine, my shy husband turns bright red when I say that. We are lucky. The flames for each other still burn brightly.

Bob and Dylan arrived home from South America last Thursday, as projected. It's good to have them home, but I am already missing my time alone. Dylan has grown another few inches. The stories of the dynamics of Bob, Ben and Dylan traveling together in Chile entertained me even more than the photos of the sights they saw. Each of them can speak some Spanish, but it took the talents of all three to negotiate transactions. Bob said that when they had to make an arrangement, Dylan, with the most recent education, would formulate the questions in Spanish in advance. Ben would do the actual speaking in his Spanglish, and Bob would listen for the answers and translate into English. I laughed so hard.

Rolling into work today, the first thing I saw was a message that the fish buyer, Brian Catton, had called. This can't be good news, I thought. Catton wasn't calling to tell me I'd just won the lottery.

I called him back. Sure enough, his second check, the one for $24,000 bounced, too. He was calling to get my account number to wire the money to our bank to cover the bad check. "Fine," I said, matter-of-factly. No screaming at him this time, not on my part. All business.

"Here is the account number Brian," I said. There was nothing more to say. Catton will not get our fish again, not without cash payment upon delivery, and not without some sort of an apology. I know it's in our long-term best interest that he survive and continue to buy fish and provide competition to the other buyers, but at what cost? I don't trust him. Still, Bob pointed out to me that because Catton paid a higher price per pound, we made $70,000 more this winter selling our crab to Catton, rather than selling to Pacific Seafood. Which is a lot of money.

From: **Ben in Bolivia**
To: **Mom**
Date: **Wednesday, May 9, 2001**
Subject: ***Hola, mi familia***

I hope you are all well. I don't know if the American media is covering the situation here in Bolivia, but I wanted to assure you I'm ok, have a reasonable working understanding of the situation, and will be gone before the next wave of possible strikes.

I have gone back to my old ways after you guys left (hope the trip home went well). I took a 23 hour bus ride to Calama, then went the next morning to San Pedro de Atacama. Soon after my arrival in the beautiful little oasis in the middle of the driest desert on earth, I rented a bike and made it out to the giant sand dune overlooking the surreal valley of the moon to watch the sunset.

The next morning at dawn I was in the Jeep that was to take me to Uynie, Bolivia. After three days' journey I was in country I could not have imagined existed and cannot possibly describe in any worthy manner. We spent the first night at over 4500 meters on the shore of a multicolored mineral-rich lake, full of flamingos and chunks of salt that look like giant icebergs, fed by the world's hottest hot springs and surrounded by high snowcapped mountains and brown slopes inhabited by wild llama and vicuna.

Anyway, I got into Uynie last night and jumped in the first bus to La Paz, which was a 16-hour experience very near hell, except it was freezing, the whole trip. Thank you for the use of that sleeping bag (it was -20 Celsius the first night). I am now here in La Paz to get a night's sleep and clean up before I go up to Lake Titicaca, probably *manana.* Thank you, Dad and Dylan, for coming and visiting (and spoiling) me, and the best of luck to you all with your various endeavors. Take care and learn, learn, learn.
Love, Ben.

From: **Ben in Peru**
To: **Mom**
Date: **Sunday, May 13, 2001**
Subject: ***Buenos Dias***

Mom, Happy Mother's Day. My plan was to call you, but I wasn't the only one with the idea. My current understanding is that it is not possible today. I am in Cuzco, Peru, arrived early this morning after a couple days in the Isla del Sol in Lake Titicaca, where I camped and helped locals build a house, proving quite an asset when the walls got high, and using some bait stacking skills with the mud bricks that are sure to revolutionize the process. *Manana*, I plan to climb the Inca trail to Macchu Picchu. If all goes well, it will take 3 or 4 days. I hope all is well with you and look forward to coming home. Happy Mother's Day, take care, and learn, learn, learn.

Love
Ben.

From: **Ben in Peru**
To: **Mom**
Date: **Thursday, May 17, 2001**
Subject: **Re: *Hola, mi familia***

Alive and very well; shaved a day off the official time for the Inca trail to Macchu Picchu without a guide or porters. Enjoyed the beautiful scenes, was awed by the ruins, and am now very, very sore and shiver at the sight of stairs.

In the last three days we hiked over 52k, with so little of it flat, it is not worth mentioning. It was great and I'm very glad to have done it. One of the three major passes we crossed was 4200 meters and snowing, something my sea level lungs didn't like so much. I hope all is well at home and give my love to Dad and Dyl. Please let Dad know that the reason his compass was worthless in Chile is because there are 5 magnetic zones on earth, each requiring a different compass, with the exception of some special global compasses not sold by Orvis. Take care, good luck with everything, please make sure we have plenty of nonfat milk and cold cereal at home, and learn, learn, learn.

Love
Ben.

Friday
May 18, 2001

"One price, good crab," Bob said.

Sitting at our kitchen table, red-faced and angry, Bob was shouting at Sam, the owner of a seafood market in Portland. I can count on one hand how many times Bob has raised his voice in the 13 years of our marriage. But his voice is raised now, and loud.

"I have pride in what I sell," Bob continued. Slow to anger, Bob was on a roll. "I have sold hundreds of thousands of crabs in a single season, all good. You ask any buyer up and down this coast, you just ask them about my reputation," he sputtered.

In order to get the best price for the crab, Bob made arrangements for Sam to send a truck and two men down from Portland, to unload our crab at the public port hoist instead of at a fish plant. They were "dry packing" the crab back up to Portland. Packed live in 50-gallon plastic garbage cans, covered with ice, they'd be fine for the trip. There would be some loss of crab, yes, but minimal, which is to be expected with their mode of transport and the time of year.

But Sam was telling Bob that some of Bob's crab arrived dead, and the loss was more than expected. We had already been paid by Sam for the crab, having insisted on payment in full at the time of delivery. If the buyer was unsatisfied, he could still put a stop payment on the check. But it was the same old story—the buyer would have our crab and we'd have little recourse.

Bob didn't believe that the percentage of crab loss was as high as Sam stated. And as the conversation continued, and Bob challenged Sam about just how much crab had died, Sam's story started to change.

Bob said, "Let's get to the point. Are you saying you don't want to buy anymore crab from me? Is that what you are telling me?" No, in fact that wasn't it. Sam wanted to know when Bob was going fishing next, so he could buy more of Bob's "bad" crab.

After he hung up the phone, Bob was upset. Clearing the table and doing dishes together, he asked me: "Do you really think there was that much crab loss?"

"No, honey," I told him, "I think he was trying to shake you down somehow; maybe get a concession on the price for the next trip, and after a while, when you didn't budge, he just gave up."

Bob thought about that for a minute. He was still shook up. "Sam said my crabs were bad." Bob was genuinely injured. A fisherman prides himself on the quality of what he delivers. If Sam was trying to bargain down a price, he picked the wrong guy to squeeze. And to top it all off, Sam called back that evening. He still wanted to buy more crab from Bob. We couldn't help laughing. Here the man had insulted Bob to the depths of his professional pride, and he was now calling back, wanting more crab! Sam offered the best price ever: $4.50 per pound.

Wednesday
May 23, 2001

Yesterday, I went to Salem to attend a meeting of the "Emerging Democrats." I was invited to go by a guy from the House Democrats Political Action Committee, also known as FUTUREPAC. It was a session for people from around the state interested in running for a House seat. The Democrats are motivated to get back a majority of seats in the State Legislature, and especially in our legislative district. This district is a bit of an embarrassment to the Democrats, as the seat last session was won by Alan Brown, a Republican, even though the majority of registered voters are Democrats.

It was an interesting day in Salem. I've long thought about running for office, but delayed the idea. My hands are full with an absent husband, our children, and a career. But the time might be right, now, what with Dylan leaving for college and my interest in the practice of law seriously waning.

I asked Dylan what he thought of Alan Brown. Dylan had spent a day at the state legislature this spring.

"Mom, you can't run against Mr. Brown. He's a really nice guy." Dylan seemed almost outraged that I would consider it.

"When I was there, the other kids got stuck standing around in the back," Dylan said. "Mr. Brown called me down to his desk on the House floor and I spent the day with him. He explained everything that was going on. "Don't do it, Mom. I don't think you will win."

Wednesday
May 30, 2001

So much has happened. Ben came home. It was glorious to see him. He was filled with travel stories of South America, of sights he'd seen, people he'd met, books he'd read. The simple act of setting the table for four people once again, with placemats and napkins and silver, made me happy. We ate big meals together, with lots of seafood. Ben's friends from high school and college wandered in and out. It was good to see Ben, good to see these young people. Ben commented that I, too, seemed happier. He was right. I am happier than I have been in a long time. My sons are healthy and happy and equipped with everything we can give them to help them get started in a productive life.

With Grandma Betty and Grandma Edie in attendance and Ben and Dylan's friends, Dylan graduated from high school very near the top of his class. With the exception of a B in typing, he was been a straight A student. Dylan was definitely ready to go to Whitman College in the fall.

The day of Dylan's graduation ceremony left me somewhat exasperated. It was important to arrive early as at all small town graduations the "good seats" are always taken first. Dylan had to get there early for the lineup, but as the time approached for us to leave the house as a family, Ben had yet to arrive. I was, in a word, pissed. Finally, Bob and I, and the grandmas left for the high school, leaving tickets for the ceremony behind for Ben and friends.

But, as usual, despite my constant worrying, all turned out well. Ben and friends arrived at the high school gym on time to find seats right behind us. They had changed from the raggedy, sloppy clothing they had previously worn while working at our shop, into sport jackets, ties, shirts and slacks. At first I beamed at them, but on closer inspection it appeared there'd been a wholesale ransacking of all the men's closets in our home. The outfits they created were quite resourceful. I burst out laughing. It was impossible to stay mad with Ben.

The ceremony began. Dylan, our freckle-faced, sparkling-eyed boy had grown into a smart, warm, loving son, which gave me shivers of joy. The little boy of five I met, just starting school, was now this confident and kind man. He had faced so many challenges, and conquered them. I couldn't hold back the tears, and I wept.

The valedictorian speech was given by Nathan Ball, Dylan's friend since childhood. Nathan's older sister Leah, a sweet girl, was a good friend of Ben's, and our families had been close. As Nathan spoke, instead of tuning out the usual drone of a valedictory speech, his words caught my ear, and I grabbed Bob's arm. Nathan spoke of his mentor, one person who most inspired him upon entering high school. It was Ben Eder who taught him to reach beyond his grasp, and to forever "Learn, learn, learn!" Our family smiled with joy. Although it was Dylan's graduation ceremony, I knew that he was proud that his older brother Ben still inspired others to achieve.

My mother and Edie were a hoot together during their visit. One afternoon they went off on a shopping trip to the local factory outlet mall. Bob and I and the boys were scattered elsewhere. We arrived home to find the grandmas sitting happily at the kitchen table, surrounded by their shopping bags. Having eschewed the dinner I had carefully prepared to meet their dietary needs, they were literally "eating dessert first": an apple pie I had made.

My husband and I love each other, talk about our goals, and are making plans. Life feels good.

June 2001

Friday
June 22, 2001

This is the first day of summer. It doesn't feel like summer. The temperature is cool and damp, which is what I love and hate about living on the Oregon Coast. The weather is never uncomfortably hot, but then, I never really get warm, either. Some dry heat would feel good right now.

Looking back over the last two weeks, it has been a maelstrom of activity. The boys left on a road trip through the southwest and I expect them home the beginning of July. I went to a Pacific Fishery Management Council meeting in San Francisco. The Council is one of eight regional councils throughout the United States that manages fisheries from three to 200 miles out to sea. Going to San Francisco on business sounds like fun, but the reality is pretty grim. The meeting was held at a cheap hotel, in South San Francisco, with tiny rooms. The showers had no water pressure, and the pool and workout facilities were closed due to remodeling.

The only fun event was joining a group of fishermen and their wives to see the San Francisco Giants play the Anaheim Angels. That was great. From the hotel, we walked to the train station and took Cal Tran directly to Pac Bell Stadium. The new stadium is beautiful. Along the first base line and right field, the stadium opened onto a sea wall and San Francisco Bay. It was a warm June evening, with little wind where we were sitting in the nosebleed section, tickets courtesy of Squeak Morrison, a trawl fisherman friend from Astoria who organized the outing. We had the most beautiful view of the water, yachts, tankers, and the sea wall, where ferries pulled alongside to pick up and deposit passengers. I wolfed down an Italian sausage sandwich on crusty bread, dripping in peppers and onions, then ate a huge order of garlic fries covered in oil, chopped garlic and parsley. And Barry Bonds hit a home run out of the park and into the Bay, Number

12 on the Splash Meter. With the All Star break just around the corner, he was on track to bust open Mark McGuire's record.

But back to work. As well as attending the public sessions of the Pacific Council's meeting, I went to the Groundfish Advisory Panel meeting. The panel was made up of fixed-gear and trawl fishing representatives, a conservation representative, and charter boat and sport fishermen from all three states. I'd known most of these people for years. The GAP discussed matters pertaining to all aspects of groundfish management, from in-season trip limits to strategic long-range plans. Its role was to advise and make recommendations to the Council.

In the meantime, I needed to transfer two of our sablefish permits to Ben and to Dylan, because by owing five permits, we exceeded the regulations. Worry, worry, worry. Most of our cash was tied up in these sablefish permits; $320,000 had been invested in the past couple years. We needed to make our money back, and then some, and as soon as possible.

Last week, I met with two staff members from the Oregon House PAC, the political action committee for the Democratic caucus. I am their first choice to run for a seat in the State Legislature for our district. This is in part because I am a good prospect as a candidate, but also because no one of any significance has stepped forward. It was a long meeting, discussing the ins and outs of what to do next—meet with people throughout the district, compile donor lists, etc. Actually, what I have to do is make the decision of whether or not to run. And to do that, I need Bob's input.

I feel like I've made so many decisions on behalf of others during this entire marriage—for Bob, for the children, and for what has been in the family's best interests. Now, I want to make some decisions that are in my best interests. And if anyone is going to put my interests first, it is going to have to be me. I just wish, every once in a while, that there was someone out there cheering for me in the way I have been cheering everyone else on. But I live with men, and a particularly self-focused breed of them.

I think if I want to change my life, I will have to make those changes for myself, and see if the others who love me want to come along.

At lunch today, I went down to the boat. Bob was stressed; Tony might quit. Tony said he could earn at least $50,000 during the upcoming squid season, according to the owner of the boat offering Tony the new job.

"Hoo boy. I'd take that job, too, if I could make $50,000 in a couple of months," I said. The likelihood of that actually happening was probably not high, but if Tony believed the owner could guarantee him that kind of money, then I wished him well. Tony wasn't going to crab for us in December anyway, so his leaving for another job solved one problem: having too many crew for sablefish this summer. What it didn't solve was some relief for Bob. With Tony leaving, we would have no alternate skipper. Bob was so bummed because his feelings were hurt. I pointed out that Tony's quitting wasn't personal. In the last 10 years of Tony's fishing career, Tony had moved on frequently, changing jobs to meet his family's needs.

From: **Ben in Santa Fe**
To: **Mom**
Date: **Tuesday, June 26, 2001**

Mother, we are fine, healthy and having a very good time. We are expecting to get key parts for our van this afternoon and begin putting the thing back together. We hope to get all working, and be right on schedule, but I thought it fair to warn you of complications on the transportation front. Sorry to hear about Tony leaving. He really is a hell of a fisherman. I am missing seafood and looking forward to some salmon for your birthday. Take care, give Dad my love, and stay the hell away from my cherished periodical.

Love
Ben.

I laughed reading Ben's e-mail. The boys were on a road trip, returning from the Southwest. The cherished periodical he was referring to was his subscription to *The Economist* magazine that now arrived at the house. I had written Ben that Bob and I were reading it in his absence.

Wednesday
June 27, 2001

Yesterday, Phoebe dropped in at my law office. She has just come home to Newport from Chiapas, Mexico, where she was an observer for a human rights organization, watching what was going on with the Zapatistas. Very interesting. We talked about the people she saw, the food, the politics, the language, her art, and her college, Antioch. It was a lovely visit and she promised to come over for dinner soon. I sent Ben an email, "Hurry home. Phoebe's here."

It's Halibut Day today. Halibut are fascinating flatfish that live near the ocean floor and can grow to over 100 pounds. Both their eyes are on the same side of their head. They're delicious. According to a publication of the International Pacific Halibut Commission, which manages the fishery, "The North American Pacific halibut fishery was started many centuries ago by the various indigenous peoples inhabiting the northwestern coastline of North America. The fishery has since become a thriving industry shared by the descendants of those early fishers, sport fishers, directed commercial fishers (those who target halibut), and incidental commercial fishers (those who take halibut as bycatch in other commercial fisheries.)"

Unlike the halibut fishery that takes place in Alaska, we have a very small commercial fishery off the West Coast. This year, the commercial fleet can access only 195,000 pounds. Worse yet, the amount you catch is not based on your ability, but is restricted by the length of your boat. For example, the *Nesika* can catch 1745 pounds of "dressed" fish this year, and the *Michele Ann* can catch 3500 pounds. "Dressed" fish means the heads are still on, but they've been gutted and bled while still on board the vessel.

So both Bob on the *Michele Ann*, and Richard on the *Nesika*, are out on the ocean today. The "season" lasts one day, from 8 a.m. until 6 p.m., regardless of the weather. The weather forecast was for the crummiest day in months—35 knot winds. Bob went out to sea last night to secure the location on the grounds that he wanted, but he was still nervous about not getting the fish. He hadn't been out prospecting, meaning looking for signs of halibut, and wasn't sure what he'd find. If he was "on the fish," then great; if not, we are screwed. At $2 per pound, it could mean a good day of earnings, or a bust. Last night, Bob said a lot of the small boats weren't out on the ocean yet. They were waiting at home to see if the weather would lay down. As I sat in my office, it wasn't blowing shoreside, but that didn't mean it wasn't blowing hard on the ocean.

I talked with Rick today. He's one of the partners at the law firm. "Should I run for state representative?"

He was astounded I'd consider it. Rick quoted comedian Bill Murray, "Next time you want to be rich and famous, try just being rich and see if that won't do it." Rick might be right. He said, "Run for judge, for God's sake. At least then you'd get paid."

Financially, for me to run for the House would be a real money loser. What they pay for my time as a State Representative might cover my travel expenses, but what my absence would cost our fishing business would be huge. And there would be no income from my law practice, although that amount is not significant compared to Bob's fishing income.

Bob just called from the ocean. He's on his way in. They caught their limit of halibut, but the weather is holy hell out there. Richard on the *Nesika* gave up on fishing and is coming in. Geez. It must be really bad. Bob said the ocean came up big about 1:30 in the morning and they'd been getting beat up ever since. Another boat, similar in size to the *Nesika*, had been jogging on the ocean for two days, holding its spot, waiting to fish, but when the weather came up so bad, it went back in to port without even setting its gear. Another boat lost a window; whether it was blown out by wind or struck by a wave, I don't know. I asked Bob to call and leave a message when he got across the bar. He's following Richard in, and because of the bad weather, they're only making about three knots. The usual boat speed is seven to ten knots. Bob says they'll be in late tonight or very early in the morning. They're cleaning fish on the way in, and the crew is just now getting fed and hydrated. What a hard life they lead.

F/V Nesika **crabbing, summer 2001**

Thursday
June 28, 2001

Bob got home from halibut fishing a little after 1:30 a.m. He undressed and climbed into bed next to me. Listening to him, I drew a vivid picture of what happened on the boat. They caught their limit of halibut on the *Michele Ann*, but they were the only ones in that area to do so.

Our crew spent the day before sharpening hooks and making bait. "Every bullet has to count," said Bob, referencing the fact they weren't fishing much gear.

Sharpening hooks. I remember doing that with the boys the first spring I was married to Bob. Ben and Dylan, then 8 and 5 years old, and I sat in the living room of the first house we lived in together, in the Nye Beach neighborhood of Newport, and the boys and I sharpened hooks and made gangions. These are made of twine, with hooks attached at one end and snaps on the other, attached to a groundline for halibut fishing. It was the first sign to me that our marriage was going to be a little different.

It felt surreal that Bob caught his limit of the halibut, where everyone else had gotten skunked. Uncanny. Other fishermen had laid their gear as close as a quarter mile, both inside and outside of Bob's. Even Bob mused aloud at his luck; that he would succeed when other talented fishermen hadn't. It is hard on Bob sometimes. The expectations of him are so high. His crew relied on him to do so well every time. None of them on the boat know any kind of failure with Bob, which leads to unrealistic expectations and unwarranted pressure on Bob. He is, after all, human.

The fish were all big and beautiful. "Lions of the jungle," Bob called them, "and they ate everything in sight."

"How did you know to lay the gear where you did?" I asked.

"Well, the day before I saw large numbers of fish schooling up—a good feeding place for the halibut."

Bob described the sets of gear as they were hauled back on board. On the first two sets, there were just a few fish, which was discouraging to the guys. Then the next set, 30 fish, and so on. Big fish, too. Bob said Tony called for help bringing one fish aboard. Just as Tony yelled for a hand, a big wave hit, came over the rail, surfed the fish onto the boat and knocked Tony on his ass. Everyone laughed. The fish weighed in at 110 pounds.

Bob, half asleep, was still awake enough to complain about the price. And rightfully so. At the fish plant he'd get between $1.60 to $2.00 per pound, with the higher price being paid for fish that weighed over 40 pounds. In the past, we've gotten as much as $3.30 per pound for the same fish—twice the price. Once again, prices are depressed, and so are we.

July 2001

Wednesday
July 11, 2001

It's "Halibut Day" again. Because of the horrible weather, not many were caught in June, so there's still a substantial quota of fish left, making it worthwhile for both our boats to again participate.

And the boys are home! Ben is out fishing on the *Nesika* today with Richard; Dylan is on the *Michele Ann* with Bob, Ron and Javier.

I turned 47 on July 4. I'm healthy, happy and lucky. Saw my cardiologist just two days ago and my blood pressure is great: 100/70. My HDL/LDL ratio is incredible and my "bad" cholesterol is low! Yippee! But I've long known I don't have heart disease. It's the damn mechanical workings of my heart that I need to concern myself with—that the valve doesn't fail. In 1998, two days after Ben graduated from high school, I had open heart surgery to repair a damaged valve. I asked Dr. John, my beloved cardiologist who had been monitoring me for the last 10 years, just how long I could expect my repaired valve to last. "About 10 years," he said, "if all goes well." Shit. That is not very long. But so far, post surgery, with the exception of one hospitalization to have my heart shocked back into rhythm, I've been doing great.

The Fourth of July is a very ritualized holiday at our house and not just because it's my birthday. This year my 16-year-old niece, Marcel, visited us from her home in upstate New York where my brother, sister-in-law and parents still live. Marcel is a sweetheart, and I am so glad she is here.

The day always starts with a funky parade in Neskowin and a party at Aunt Mary's house. Mary invites an eclectic gathering of relatives and friends: artists, professors, stockbrokers, babies, children, and old people. We all bring food and the spread is always delicious. This year I roasted marinated pork loins, sliced them very thin, and laid the slices on a bed of purple kale, dotted with red cherry tomatoes, served with horseradish sauce and onion rolls on the side. Very colorful! Bob had promised me a salmon, but instead he came in the day before the party with a limit of crabs. When the boat delivered, Marcel and I loaded 50 pounds of live crabs in the back of the old Volvo station wagon, and we sped home to clean and cook them.

Arriving home, Ben took me out on our back deck and gave me careful instructions. I usually just throw the live crab whole in a pot of boiling water with a ton of salt, bring the pot of water back to a boil, and cook the crab for 20 minutes. I then cool the crabs to the point I can handle them, remove the shells and clean them. But today Ben told me it was time to learn a new skill.

"OK, Mom," Ben said, as we stood overlooking the ocean. He picked up a live crab. "Watch this. Grab the legs and claws with each hand, close in to the body, so the crab can't pinch you. Then slam the edge of the body on the edge of the deck rail. That will pop the back of the shell off. Then just peel down the apron, scrape out the guts and lungs, and rinse with the hose." Ben's eyes twinkled, hoping I'd rise to the challenge.

All right, I thought. I can do this. But damn, it hurt! My hands weren't tough, and I should have been using rubber gloves. The pointy bumps on the crabs' legs dug into my palms as I slammed the edge of the back of the crab on the rail of the deck. But the backs popped off easily and the crabs cleaned up nicely.

"Way to go, Mom," Ben laughed.

I dropped the cleaned crabs into a pot of boiling salted water and when they were done, no further cleaning was necessary.

So the guests at Mary's party had crab for the holiday, and everyone raved. I piled the red crab in wide, white bowls lined with beds of curly, green leaf lettuce. So pretty. Colorful fruit and pasta salads and fabulous deviled eggs. Ben went through the buffet and took a plateful of eggs. I elbowed him to put some back. They were so delicious, though, I understood his appetite. I know I ate more than my share, too.

Dylan's friends, Allison and Leah, joined us for the party at

Mary's. They are such nice girls and spent time hanging out with Marcel, making her feel welcome and comfortable.

After the parade and the feast at Mary's, we sat and talked, then left for home. Pete and Leah Fones and their children, Isaac and Aliza, who had also been at Mary's, were to join us for dinner. I made Ben's favorite spinach salad: spinach, with feta cheese, mandarin oranges, crisp crumbled bacon, and a balsamic vinaigrette dressing. We had good bread, fruit salad, and grilled halibut. I had basted the fillets with olive oil and dill, and Bob and Pete grilled them. Perfect. I can still smell them and taste them as I write.

After dinner we went down to the *F/V Michele Ann*, as is our tradition, to watch fireworks over the bay. I hauled a birthday cake down to the dock and climbed over the rail onto the deck. I've been making the same cake every year since the boys were little: a huge sheet cake decorated as an American flag, with blueberries for stars and raspberries and heavy whipped cream for the stripes. It is corny as could be, but I love it.

Hundreds of people lined the hillsides, the docks, and the back decks of boats to watch the display. Fireworks, legal and not, exploded over the bay as we awaited darkness and the big show. Dylan and Ben, pyromaniacs both, set off noisemakers galore along the dock. Dylan's friend, Leah, joined us, and Phoebe, and Isaac and Aliza, and Marcel were there, too. The young ones climbed on top of the mast on the wheelhouse of the boat for the best vantage point.

For my birthday, Dylan gave me a cookbook about New York deli food, and Ben and Phoebe gave me two novels. I lit the candles on the cake and everyone gathered in the cabin of the boat and sang *Happy Birthday*. I made my wish, the same wish I've made every year of our marriage, and blew out the candles. It was the best Fourth of July and the best birthday ever. I looked around at everyone's faces and thought, It doesn't get better than this. Surrounded by family and friends I love, I am so grateful.

Saturday
July 14, 2001

It's a gorgeous Saturday morning. I went to the beach with Sally, our 11-year-old black Labrador Retriever, for a walk. Then I was off to Saturday Market. I bought dense, sturdy rounds of rye and sourdough bread, and a half flat of raspberries.

Bob and Ben are out crabbing on the *Michele Ann*, along with Richard and Javier. It's time to bring in the last of the crab gear, and all hands are needed on deck. Although the season is legally open for another month, the quality and the quantity of the crab are such that it's time to stop. Richard is doing most of the boat driving, which means Bob is working on deck. Bob is strong, but I worry about his back. Still, he likes being in the midst of the deck work, and he enjoys the physical labor. It's good for Bob's crew to see that there isn't anything on the boat he can't do, and skillfully, too.

As much as I have enjoyed the last couple of weeks, I am troubled. My family is upset with me. Ben found a place to live with Phoebe and so I have insisted that he clear his stuff out of his room. He had come home from South America in May, dumped his belongings all over the house, then left for a road trip, came home and dumped more stuff. He and Phoebe then slept at various places around town. I don't want them living with us. To top it off, Ben and Dylan had driven back from their road trip in a pickup truck that isn't operable without two people to start it.

One night this week I was awakened at 2 a.m. by loud noises. I wrapped myself in a robe and went downstairs. The garage door was wide open, music was playing full blast, and Ben was banging away on the engine of their truck, oblivious to the fact that he'd woken me and half the neighborhood. That was it. It was time for Ben to get his own place.

As we sat at the kitchen table last night, Bob gave me the

information for payroll so I could write the checks for crew shares today. Bob said Ben was upset with me. I told Bob I felt that 21-year-old men who slept with women were old enough not to leave messes at their parents' house, and if he was living with his girlfriend, it was time for them to find a place of their own.

Why does everyone think I am a jerk? Of course, when I came home yesterday and saw all of Ben's stuff was gone, I was stricken with sadness. But I know it's the right decision, for Ben and for us. He and Phoebe rented a studio apartment in town. Friends live above them, and I think they'll settle in just fine.

Thursday
July 19, 2001

Ben invited me over to dinner at his studio apartment last night. He broiled halibut, and made a cream sauce with a subtle orange flavor. I watched him sauté garlic and finely chopped onions, add orange juice, reduce it, add heavy cream, reduce it. The sauce was excellent! I am very proud of him. He loves good food, cooking and enjoys entertaining. He is definitely my son.

But I worry that Ben is living beyond his means regarding his approach to travel and food. Eating dinner out at sushi restaurants, traveling extensively in foreign countries; can he afford to do that? I know he does it cheaply, but nevertheless, he still has an education to pay for. It is a topic that leads to conflict between us. Ben feels he should do what he wants with the money he earns, relative to travel, etc. I think as long as his father and I are contributing to the cost of his education, the money he earns should also go toward paying for his education. I feel stupid sometimes, working hard to save money, when Ben is eating $40 sushi dinners with his girlfriend and planning trips to foreign countries. Worse yet, I am concerned he won't get a degree.

"Mom," Ben said, over the sauced halibut and a spinach salad. "You've got to trust me, believe in me. I'll get a degree."

I sighed. "All I know, Ben, is that your father and I have contributed $40,000 after taxes to your education so far. We're committed to giving you another $20,000. I'm going to be upset if you don't have a Bachelor's degree in two years. You're 21 now, and it's time to move ahead."

Ben poured himself a glass of white wine. "Well, what if I want to travel some more?" Ben asked. "I wish you could just be glad for me, and see how good it was," he said.

"Well, Ben, I like to hear of your adventures, they're entertaining!" I told him. We sat on the floor of his apartment, at a low table. I drew a crust of bread through the orange sauce on my plate and popped it in my mouth. "And I'm glad you had a good time. But do I consider the trip a luxury? Yes, I do," I said.

Ben was perplexed. He wanted to extol the virtues of travel; he thought I didn't understand him.

"And, in answer to your question, Ben, what if you want to travel more? That's up to you. We'll continue to pay for your education, but we're not going to pay for your lifestyle."

"Well, OK, Mom," he said. "But I'm sorry you feel that way." We hugged, and shortly thereafter, I left.

I told Bob this morning as I was getting ready for work that the most beautiful words in the English language that Ben could say to me are, "I told you so, Mom," when he graduates from college. I'll sing on that day.

Last night, I sat down at our big, maple kitchen table with Bob. He was so tired. His eyes were red. Bob is spending too much of his time doing physical labor. At 50, I think he needs to take it a little easier on his body. That's why we have a crew, and in particular, a young crew, like our two sons. But Bob has a hard time not showing he is both willing and able to do everything that anyone is ever asked to do on our boats—and do it better. For the last couple of years, though, it had been taking its toll on him.

Eating a bowl of multicolored pasta, Bob told me about his day. I couldn't remember a time when our boats were still out crabbing this late in the year, but now it's time to bring in all the gear. The crew unloaded a deck full of crab pots, about 400, six at a time, using the crane at Bornstein's dock. Once unloaded from the boat, the pots were power-washed, then stacked on wood pallets. The bait jars, rope and buoys were removed and cleaned. Then all the gear was loaded and trailered to our shop, located at Steve and Becky Leake's property, four miles up the Bay Road. Once there, the gear was unloaded, stacked, and covered with tarps.

Bob chatted away, amusing me with stories of his day. He had met up with fellow boat owners Ted Gibson, Gary Ripka and Jerry Bates on the docks. Jerry, a former seafood processor, just bought a boat and was getting it ready to go tuna fishing. He was a tall, loquacious good old boy, and you can't help but like him.

"Those cocksuckers will steal you blind," Jerry said, referring to one of the local processors.

"But Jerry," Bob said in his quiet way, "until a little while ago, you were one of those cocksuckers." There was a pause, then everyone, including Jerry, cracked up laughing.

I had a busy day, as well. I'd had lunch with one of the four main lobbyists that financially support Democrats in the legislature. It is clear to me that in order to get significant financial support in the House race, I will have to bow down to the Oregon Education Association, the Oregon Trial Lawyers, the Oregon Nurses Association, and the labor unions. If you didn't vote the party line on their issues, you won't get the financial contributions necessary to win a race. Conservatively, the race would cost $175,000. It isn't just the Democrats; the Republicans are just the same, except if you run as a Republican, it is the Association of Oregon Industries, the Oregon Restaurant Association, insurance defense lawyers, and a few other groups who "own" you. My political, social and economic beliefs are somewhere in between the extreme of these various lobbying groups. You might get their support for a session if you say the right words, but if you deviate significantly from their agenda in your legislative votes, you will never see another dime in contributions. And I don't want to spend $175,000 of our own money to pay for a campaign and the privilege of serving in the Oregon Legislature.

In my heart, I know our business will need me more, not less, in the next few years. We will have to develop new markets, sell our own fish, explore new fisheries, and be far more aggressive than we have been recently to create new ways to earn money. I am good at that. Bob and I are an enormously good partnership already. It could only get better.

That was what I should do. On the other hand, I felt I have a different future, more to contribute, than selling fish.

"Look, Michele," Bob said after he listened to me. "Commercial fishing isn't what I set out to do, either. Who would have thought it? Me, a poetry major! I thought I was destined to produce a collection of work that changed the way people thought about life. Instead, I catch fish for a living." He shrugged, self-deprecatingly. "But it's what we have. It's good. We can make it better."

Who knows what lay ahead? Is it crazy to run for a public office that pays virtually nothing, and committed me to months away from home and the rubber chicken circuit? Probably. Right now, even though the demands of the fishing business and my law practice are intense, I still have total control over my life and schedule, to work, to write, and to play as I choose. It would be foolish to change that.

August 2001

Wednesday
August 1, 2001

Dealing with federal regulators in the fishing business is a nightmare. To the core, bureaucrats are dedicated to making the lives of small business owners miserable.

The latest rant of mine is due to the ownership issue of our sablefish permits. The federal agency that regulates this fishery restricts the number of sablefish permits a person or business may own to prevent "excess accumulation." Argos, Inc., the corporation in which Bob and I are shareholders, owns the *F/V Michele Ann* and the *F/V Nesika.* Argos, Inc. also owns three sablefish permits. Each permit is allowed to catch a certain poundage of fish. As individuals, Ben owns one sablefish permit and Dylan owns one sablefish permit. The plan was for Ben and Dylan to work with Richard to fish on the *Nesika,* and place their two permits on board that vessel.

But some bureaucrats at the National Marine Fisheries Service decided that because Argos, Inc. owns three permits and, also owns the *Nesika* and the *Michele Ann,* that to allow Ben and Dylan to assign their two sablefish permits to the *Nesika* would, in essence, give Argos, Inc. control over five permits. Legally, Argos, Inc. owns only the legal limit of three permits. Allowing Ben and Dylan's permits to be fished on the *Nesika* would be illegal, they said. "Violates the spirit of the law," said the bureaucrats. With much back and forth, in phone calls and faxes, the Feds agreed that if we transferred ownership of the *F/V Nesika* to our two sons, then Ben and Dylan could fish their two permits on the *Nesika.*

But Jesus, Mary and Joseph! I didn't think we were quite ready to do that! And what if the boys didn't want to own the *Nesika?* I called a family meeting for last night, and Ben and Dylan settled in at the kitchen table. They were tired. Both boys had been fishing and hadn't caught up on their rest. After dinner, I served cheesecake and explained, as simply as I could, what the problem was and that we needed to transfer to them the ownership of the *Nesika*.

"If something bad happened, can we get sued?" Dylan asked.

"Yes," I explained, "but you'd be on the insurance policy—you'd be covered, like we would."

"Are there tax consequences?" Ben asked me. "I don't want to pay more in taxes than what I would otherwise," he said.

"Yep," I said. "We don't know exactly how we are going to structure it. We're meeting with attorneys and the accountant tomorrow, but whatever income the *Nesika* earns fishing, it'll get expensed out. It will all flow back to us in management fees, so there will be no increase in your taxes, but if there is, we will pay it."

Bob explained to Ben and Dylan that we were being forced to do this by the Feds, or lose our ability to fish two of the sablefish permits on the *Nesika*. Both the boys said they'd do whatever needed to be done to keep the business going and sign whatever needed to be signed so we could fish all the permits. Whew.

Dylan, in particular, looks exhausted. But before everyone left the table, I had to talk about one more matter, and it was difficult. I told both the boys that they'd need to execute wills, conveying ownership of the *Nesika* and the two fishing permits back to us in the event of their death. What they wanted to do with the rest of their property was up to them. Both Ben and Dylan have assets in the thousands of dollars, savings they have diligently accumulated from years of hard work.

Tears started to run down Dylan's cheeks. He wiped them away with the back of his hand. "I can't believe you'd say that, Mom," Dylan said. "If someone I loved was to die, the last thing I'd be thinking about would be getting their property. That's disgusting." Dylan jumped up from the table, left the room, and ran down the hall to his bedroom. His door slammed and I heard the lock turn. Ben, Bob and I looked at each other, then walked down the hall. We knocked on Dylan's door and tried to get him to talk to us. Dylan wouldn't come out, not even when Ben asked him to come back to the kitchen. Christ, I thought. What have I done now?

Sitting back down at the kitchen table, Bob, Ben and I all pushed around our empty dessert plates. I felt terrible.

Ben said, "Well, Mom, it's kind of like the discussion you had with Dylan and me about needing prenuptial agreements before we get married. It's pretty awful, the assumption that people might get divorced, before you even walk down the aisle. But I understand the financial necessity for it. Remember, these are things you are used to talking about at your work every day. Same thing with the wills. I understand that we need to do it, but it's just hard on Dylan," he said.

Ben got up to leave and together we walked out to his truck. "Look, Mom, anything I own—I want it all to go to Dylan. And I'll explain this all to him. Don't worry, Mom."

Ben patted me on the shoulder, then hugged me, and got in his truck to go back to his studio apartment.

God. Back inside the house, Bob and I looked at each other. Dylan still hadn't emerged from his room. We felt awful. Thanks a lot, federal government. Fuck you.

Saturday
August 4, 2001

In the last six months I have lost twenty-five pounds. I am thinking about losing twenty more, but I doubt I could keep it off. I am as healthy as I've ever been. But I'm still a little worried. Lately, I've felt like my heart has been beating out of rhythm again, but I don't want to race to the doctor's to get it checked. It is hard to tell what is just stress and what is actual atrial fibrillation, an irregular heartbeat, that could put me at risk for a stroke. Sometimes I am in atrial fibrillation and can't even tell. When I am under pressure, I often have chest pain. It feels like an elephant has one foot planted in the center of my chest. I wonder if meditation or yoga would help. Probably.

I started cooking for the boat this morning. A huge batch of goulash was in order. Rummaging around, I dug out all the miscellaneous packages of ground beef and Italian sausage from my two freezers in the garage, defrosted and cooked those, and then started on the sauce. First I sautéed onions and garlic and simmered that for a while, then added cans of crushed tomatoes, a little tomato paste, the ground beef and sausage, and lots of seasoning. I cooked up a big batch of elbow macaroni, drained it, and combined the whole batch—tomato sauce, meat and macaroni—for what I called goulash. Damn, it was good; my mother's recipe. I packed it into individual Rubbermaid containers, put a chocolate cake in the oven to take to the guys working on gear, then dashed to the shower. The guys would need the dinners for sablefish season.

We own 300 sablefish pots, which are made of steel with mesh, trapezoidal in shape, based on a design by fisherman Jerry Wilson that Bob has refined over the years. As with crab pots, the sablefish pots need to be reconditioned before the season starts; each one examined, checked for holes in the mesh and refurbished if necessary.

Rockey and Bob are working on the boat today, but the rest of the crew, Ben, Dylan, Ron, Javier, and Richard, are at the port repairing pots. I drove down to the port and dropped off a pressure-washer they will need to clean the pots. The crew was happier to see still-warm cake, slathered with chocolate frosting, than the pressure washer. I had a camera and took a few photos of the guys.

The crew is getting the gear ready for both boats. Ben and Dylan will start out fishing with Richard aboard the *Nesika.* Dylan has to get off the boat in eight days, to go to college at Whitman, in Walla Walla. Assuming the *Nesika* catches its fish before Dylan has to leave, and if we get a reasonable price for the fish, Dylan could earn about $8,000. Once the *Nesika* captures its quota, the boat will be parked at the dock and the plan is for Ben and Richard to rotate in on the crew of the *Michele Ann.* Because the *Michele Ann* is allowed to catch more, and hence, there would be more money earned, everyone wants to fish on the larger boat. The trick is to get all of the crew access to a reasonable amount of fish.

Bob and I sat down last night and hammered out the numbers. Last year, we'd been allowed to catch 164,000 pounds of fish between the two boats. So last year, it didn't really matter which boat you fished on. But in the last couple of years we'd bought three more permits. These permits cost $320,000 and allows us to catch about 65,000 more pounds of fish this year. All the money to buy these permits came out of our savings. Needless to say, it will take a few years for us to recapture the cost of this investment.

Our crew is getting a tremendous benefit through our investment. Increased access to fish means greater earnings. However, we need to adjust the crew share percentages downward to pay ourselves for some of the cost of the permits. The boat will need to be paid a share. Running some numbers, if all goes as planned, and even with a lower crew share percentage, each crew member will earn $15,000 to $18,000 for this year's sablefish season. Including preparation before the season, and cleanup afterwards, the season will be about six weeks long. Not bad.

Sunday
August 5, 2001

I spent this morning cooking chicken. Six whole ones, in fact. I found them all in my freezer. I planned to make enchiladas for the boat until I ran out of either shredded cheese, chicken, tortillas or sauce. It is a lot of chicken to cook and bone the meat from the carcasses. I thought about saving the broth, but decided not to. I don't have the refrigerator space to de-fat it all, even with two refrigerators. Whew. One less task.

In between boning chickens, I worked on figuring the crab bonus for the crew. Each fishing season we retain two percent of the crew members' share to make sure they finish the season. They need to retrieve, clean and put the gear away and do the boat maintenance; a necessary part of the crew's job. By holding on to two percent, there's significant incentive to stay until the work is done. For example, a bonus on the *Michele Ann* for crab season is worth about $8,000 this year.

Calculating bonuses took me all morning. I like doing it, though. It shows us where we are financially for crab and I can compare it to previous seasons. For the 2000-2001 crab season on the *Michele Ann*, Bob caught 188,955 pounds of crab, earning, after paying the Oregon Dungeness Crab Commission tax, $534,161.60. Whew. On the *Nesika*, Richard landed 57,192 pounds, for a net of $110,578.60.

I spent the rest of the day making the chicken enchiladas. Set out on the kitchen table was a dinner plate and a pie plate. The pie plate held enchilada sauce. I'd select one tortilla and dip it in the sauce in the pie plate, and shake loose the extra sauce. I laid each tortilla on the dinner plate, took shredded chicken, added a little grated cheese, sprinkled it all with chopped onions, rolled the tortilla with chicken, cheese and onion inside, and laid it into one of the many Rubbermaid containers. There were three enchiladas to a container. I garnished the tops with more cheese, chopped green chiles and a little more sauce. Then lids all around were tightly fitted, strips of masking tape applied, and a permanent marker declared their identity as "C.E." Fifteen filled containers will join the other dinners already assembled in one of the two freezers in my garage.

Saturday
August 11, 2001

Tuna, marinated in soy and garlic, Caesar salad, and Szechuan pasta is what I fixed for dinner last night in honor of Cindy Smith, Sea Grant fellow and fisheries aide to U.S. Senator Ron Wyden. Cindy is visiting the coast this week. She came to dinner at our house with Ginny Goblirsch and Connie Kennedy to meet us and talk about issues important to Newport Fishermen's Wives. It is important to know, on a personal level, the people who can advance our interests on a national level. I could have just taken Cindy out to dinner at a restaurant, but having the Sea Grant fellows to our home has been a tradition the last three years.

Cindy is funny and warm and knowledgeable, and the evening was enjoyable. Earlier yesterday, I took Cindy for a dock walk, explaining the different vessels and fisheries. We'd gone to the gear pile and visited with our crewman, Javier Espinoza, who explained to Cindy how the pots were constructed and how they fished.

After dinner, I took Cindy down to the fish plant, where the *Nesika* was tied up getting ready to go out for its 900-pound weekly trip limit of sablefish. The crew was making bait. We watched them stuff mesh bags with bait, stacking them thirty bags to a flat, with the flats stacked ten high, then "Hystered" into the huge walk-in freezers. The crew was getting ready for the opening of the sablefish season, due to start on August 15.

Richard, Ben and Dylan loaded the pots and bait aboard the *Nesika*. Richard planned to drive the *Nesika* back to the dock, before leaving to go fishing in an hour. Cindy joined Richard and Dylan on the boat for a ride aboard the *Nesika* across the bay, and then Bob gave Cindy a tour of the *Michele Ann*.

I drove from the fish plant down the bayfront to the docks, and walked out to the finger dock where our boats were now parked. Ben was hard at work in the wheelhouse of the *Michele Ann*. Bob had just bought a new IBM Think Pad for the boat. Ben was supposed to go out fishing when the *Nesika* left, but he was frantically trying to backup and transfer the data from Bob's old laptop to the new computer. There were some complications. As only a mom can tell, Ben was tired, and struggling to keep his frustrations with his father under control. Bob's expectations of himself are high, as are his expectations of those who work for him. The pressure to perform could be very difficult, to say the least, particularly in a family business.

As if the stress of getting ready for the season isn't enough, it is now apparent we will have problems with our market. We had conservatively projected that with permits allowing us to land 180,000 pounds of fish, at $1.75 a pound, we'd gross about $300,000. We thought the only issue would be whether we would sell to Bornstein's, as we did last year (and who had paid a very competitive price for the fish), or whether we would "buy" our own fish. For the latter, we would pay to have them hoisted off the boat, iced, cut, glazed, frozen, loaded and trucked to cold storage until we chose to sell them. We estimated we could make at least $50,000 more for the fish doing it that way, but we weren't certain we wanted to accept the risk.

Once again at the kitchen table, with nothing but a calculator and a yellow pad, we totaled up the costs for owning and processing our own fish. Bob thought it would be a good idea. I was hesitant. We already had to borrow $200,000 this year. I lined up the business credit line for another $100,000 so we had the funds available to pay the crew, buy crab pots, and carry us through the end of the year until crab money came in January. Or we sold the sablefish. Whichever came first. But I was worried about the details of selling our own fish.

"Honey, what am I going to do if the sablefish are off the boat, processed and you are at sea and then the truck to take it to cold storage doesn't show?" I asked Bob.

"Call another trucking company, Michele. You know how to

do that," Bob replied.

I was worried I couldn't manage it.

"Well, I'm going to talk to Bornstein's, see what price we can get for the fish. They treated us well last year. Maybe we'll just sell to them," Bob said.

August. A sunny afternoon. The height of tourist season. People spill off the sidewalks onto the street. The bayfront is so crowded that it takes half an hour to drive from one end to the next, a distance of less than a mile. I joined Bob for lunch at Gino's, and ordered our favorite, popcorn shrimp. It is a tradition of ours to eat together at Gino's around sablefish season. Sitting at the picnic-style tables in Gino's that look out onto the bayfront, Bob said he was sorry the boys were fishing with Richard on the *Nesika*. He really enjoys working with both of them, he said. "Ben talks all the time on the boat and often has good ideas. Dylan is asking more questions and wants to know how and why certain decisions are made, to have a better understanding of the whole picture."

Damn those Feds. The boys should be able to fish with their dad.

Sunday
August 12, 2001

Today is Bob's 50th birthday. "Good morning, honey," I whispered to him, in bed, at 5:30 a.m. "Happy Birthday."

Up and out the door he went. I got up to walk Sally. I'd been up at 2 a.m. Dylan had come home from fishing on the *Nesika.* Bob and his crew on the *Michele Ann* would meet at 7 a.m. as they had for the last few weeks. This is a work day, no birthday celebration now. Ben and Dylan will be going back out on the *Nesika* this afternoon, taking pots out in anticipation of the opener. For Bob's birthday, the boys made him a beautiful ceramic mug, suitable for the boat; very heavy and with a wide base for stability at sea. On the mug is a sablefish and halibut, in bas-relief. Perfect. Bob was delighted.

I spent the morning getting the medical kit for the *Michele Ann* refilled. A captain of a ship has to be prepared for all manner of emergencies at sea: treat wounds, suture, and administer CPR, for example. In order to do so, vessel captains are authorized to possess and administer prescription drugs on board the vessel. You can buy these medical kits fully loaded from an outfit out of Seattle, but those run about $800. For us, a local doctor calls in the refills to a pharmacy and I pick up both prescriptions and over-the-counter items.

That job done, I bought a carrot cake for Bob's birthday and put it in my car. Home again, this time to make a crab sandwich for Bob, and tuna sandwiches from fresh albacore for Richard and the boys. I dropped the sandwiches off at Bornstein's, where the *Nesika* is tied up and the boys are making bait. I took Bob's sandwich to the boat and sat down at the galley table to join him for lunch. He didn't really get any rest. The phone rang continuously, but we did get a few words in. "Let's go have a piece of birthday cake," Bob said.

We drove from Dock 5, where the *Michele Ann* was parked,

down the length of the bayfront to Bornstein's. Our grey diesel Ford truck, which Ben often used this summer, was parked in a green loading zone, with our flatbed trailer attached to it, suitable for loading sablefish pots and totes filled with line. The flatbed was empty. Bob went into the fish plant and got Richard and Ben and Dylan to come off the *Nesika* and onto the street, and we had a party on the flatbed truck. We sang *Happy Birthday* to Bob and ate pieces of cake while tourists walked by and smiled. I hugged both the boys and said, "So long," to Richard. Chances are I won't see them again before they leave to take more gear out on the ocean. I drove Bob back to the *Michele Ann*, and then headed off in search of the last of the prescriptions Bob needs for his medical kit.

I still have more cooking to do, but I don't feel up to it. I've made 22 Chicken Malibu dinners this past week, but I still have pot stickers and ravioli to cook and sauce. "I'd like pesto, please, instead of red sauce on my ravioli," Bob had requested.

Tuesday
August 14, 2001

Bob was up at 5:30 a.m. I stayed in bed. I'd done everything I could to help him get underway, and I needed an hour of sleep. He kissed me before he left the room and as I rolled over, I heard his diesel truck pull away from the house. Bye, honey. I thought.

Half an hour later the phone rang. It was Bob. "Michele, I've got all the crew contracts here on the boat. I forgot to bring our copies home last night."

"Mmmmmm," I responded. "I'll be right there." I needed to have one set of crew agreements at our house. I threw on my clothes and raced down to the boat. They were just about to leave. I climbed on board and grabbed the papers. Bob said Richard would be at the fish plant at 8 a.m. to put bait on before he left to go fishing. I figured I had enough time to go home, get a shower, get dressed for work and then get down to the *Nesika* for the crew agreement signatures from Richard and the boys before they started loading bait.

Meanwhile, I stood at the dock and waited for the *Michele Ann* to pull away. "Bye, honey," Bob waved at me from the window.

"Bye, Bob! Good fishing!" I waved back. He looked so small in the window of that beautiful boat. I always try to hide my anxiety and worry about their safety. Fishing is such a dangerous business.

I drove home and jumped in the shower. By then it was 7:45 and Dylan still wasn't up. Bob had said the *Nesika* guys were meeting at 8 a.m. "Dylan, get up!" I banged on his door. "Aren't you meeting at 8?" I yelled.

"Nine, Mom," Dylan muttered from under the covers.

"Oops. Sorry, honey. See ya later," and I slunk from his room.

While Dylan caught a bit more well-deserved sleep, I went to my law office to work. Just before 9 a.m., I drove the few minutes back to the docks. As I pulled into a parking space, I saw

Ben and Dylan walking down the boardwalk, and then turn down the ramp to Dock 5 where the *Nesika* was waiting. They each stand over six feet tall, Ben a bit broader in the shoulders, Dylan a bit taller. They are handsome men and I am so proud of them. I find it fun to watch them, especially when they don't know I'm looking. They have grown so, from the young and vulnerable children in the photos of our wedding; Ben with a hand on Dylan's shoulder, always protective.

I followed them down the dock, clattering in my high heels. The boys hoisted their duffel bags and knapsacks aboard the *Nesika* and then Ben gave me a hand over the rail onto the deck of the boat. In Ben's other hand was a plate with an omelet Phoebe made. Ben is clean shaven—surprise! Like his father, I think Ben looks good both with a mustache and beard and without. Dylan is still light in the facial hair department, although I am sure that will change in a year or so.

"Come into my office, the kitchen, and the boardroom," Ben joked. The inside of the *Nesika* cabin is tiny. Richard was already there, paging through his fishing notebooks. The *Nesika*, although a sleek and efficient fishing machine, was not designed for crew comfort. For years, Richard, has slept in the half bunk in the cabin, where you had to open a cupboard at the end of the bunk to be able to extend your feet when you laid down to sleep. "Time for contracts—start signing," I said.

"Well, these aren't worth the paper they're written on," Dylan joked.

"Just sign here, please, wise guy," I said to Dylan, and they all laughed. I pointed out their crew share percentages, and then had them start the tedious process of signing everywhere. Ben and Dylan had to sign their own contracts as crew, each others' contract, and then Richard's as owners of the *Nesika*. Then Richard and Ben had crew contracts to sign for the *Michele Ann*, since they would also be fishing on that boat, too. Because of his seniority, Richard received a higher percentage share while fishing on the *Michele Ann* than did the other crew members. Richard slowly paged through the agreement, then signed and kept a copy for himself. I grabbed a plastic bag full of empty Rubbermaid containers from past dinners, the signed crew agreements, hugged both my boys, and carefully stepped off the boat onto the dock.

As I walked back to my car, I remembered the summer of 1996, Ben's first sablefish season as a full crew member. He was 16 and the work had certainly made an imprint on him. Looking back, I'm certain the unusual nature of his life in a fishing family made Ben stand out from the crowd of other college applicants.

In the early winter of 1997, Ben wrote the following essay about a fishing season as part of his college application.

Describe the educational experience—formal or informal—that has had the most significant effect on your life.

I am the oldest son of a father whose profession is commercial fishing. Our family owns and operates two fishing vessels, fishing mainly for Dungeness crab and sablefish, also known as black cod, off the West Coast.

From early childhood onward, I have built and maintained equipment and fished with my father, but in the summer before my junior year I first joined the crew for a season fishing sablefish.

Two years prior, the season had been nine days long, the year before it had been seven, and this year we would have five days to catch as many pounds of sablefish as possible. In these five days, my family would make a full one half of our annual income, as would our crew, each of whom had a family depending upon our success and the decisions made by my father. Needless to say, there was a great deal of pressure to perform and produce. I was honored to be part of this team of seasoned fishermen, carefully chosen by my dad to fill each position necessary to the operation.

Among these men was a man named Roger Fry who worked the sablefish season every year. He had a great effect on me and taught me much about motivation and self- improvement. Roger had dropped out of high school in the tenth grade, but was better educated than most college graduates I have met. He read in all of his spare time, solely for the purpose of gaining knowledge and improving himself. My interactions and conversations with Roger were an integral part of my experience and education.

During that five day season the boat did not rest, nor did my dad, for more than an hour or two every fifty, while somebody drove the boat. The crew was on a rotation. One of us would be sleeping at all times, and the rest would be working. In the five hours we had off to sleep, we were also responsible for feeding ourselves and usually performing some mechanical maintenance or miscellaneous labor. The rest of our waking hours were spent working to our limits on the back deck, pulling gear, landing fish, setting gear, repairing broken traps, splicing line, sorting fish, and preparing bait. I learned many practical skills and techniques, but more importantly, I was educated on just how far the human body could be pushed. I also learned what was possible with teamwork and cooperation. Having worked together in the weeks of preparation time for the season, the crew was already very well acquainted. After only a matter of hours we were a finely tuned machine of five. Rank and responsibilities having long been established, no quarrels resulted from physical and psychological fatigue. Since everyone knew the process and was aware of current situations, verbal communication was minimal, with an expressive look being much more efficient amidst the hum of the hydraulics and grumbling of the main engine.

On one occasion as we were setting gear, a precise activity in which we dump sablefish traps overboard attached to a ground line, in a location where fish reside, a pot got hung up on the boat. The man closest by responded immediately, as tension built in the ground line. In a matter of seconds something would break. He hung suspended over the rail of the boat. Hanging over the violent seas, he drew his Victorinox knife from his knife belt and cut the pot free, sacrificing several hundred dollars worth of equipment and a dozen man hours for the sake of safety and efficiency. As he did this, no one was in his position, so I rotated from mine and continued work. The man preparing bait was slightly ahead and rushed forward to fill my position. We had not missed a beat, and when Roscoe, the man who had cut the pot pulled himself back onto the boat, he rotated into the position of preparing bait, which was less intense and would give him a chance to catch his breath. During all of this not a word was spoken except to inform the captain, my father, of a possible developing situation.

As I labored away in my respective positions, I knew that if I slacked off or lost efficiency that no one would give me a hard time or tease me, but I would not personally tolerate it. I knew that the success of the entire season depended upon me as it did upon every other member of the crew. I knew that if focus was lost or my end of the work was not kept up, bad things could result. People could get hurt or even lose their lives. "It takes only one mistake to get an 'F' for the day," the seaman's saying went.

We started the season with moderate yields in our sablefish traps. My dad was not fazed and just reacted the best he knew how, based on the conditions he saw before him and the historical data he kept. Soon his years of experience paid off, and we were catching unprecedented numbers of fish. He found the product and we, the crew, moved the gear and fished faster than I previously believed to be physically possible. By the end of the five days we had filled the boat to overcapacity three times, and in the process set a fish plant record for the largest sablefish delivery in their twenty-five year history. Many other very qualified captains with experienced crews had made only one or two trips and had not been nearly as fortunate. We were called "lucky" and "in the right place at the right time," but I knew otherwise. Hard work, experience, preparation, teamwork, a ruthless competitive spirit, and intense focus had paid off in the highest catch on the Washington, Oregon, or California coast.

I have learned many facts and concepts in my years of schooling, many truths in my years of contemplation and many rules in my years of social interactions, but no one event has compared to what I learned during the 1996 sablefish season. From that I learned what men are capable of, the power of cooperation, and what motivates different people.

Ben Eder

Wednesday
August 15, 2001

After getting signatures on the crew agreements from Ben, Dylan and Richard yesterday morning, I didn't see Dylan again until 9 p.m. last night. They had worked all day and into the evening. I fell asleep on the sofa, exhausted after getting only a couple hours sleep the night before. Dylan was tired when he arrived home. Still making lists of things he needed to take to college, the reality had finally dawned on him that he was not going to have any time between getting off the boat and going to school. I told Dylan he could give me a list of things I could do for him, but so far he hasn't delegated any tasks.

I awoke this morning to Sally's barking at 6:30. I jumped up feeling as though I'd overslept. The *Nesika* was leaving to go fishing at 6:30. Looking out the window, I saw that the Explorer was still in the drive; Dylan hadn't left yet. I grabbed a robe and raced downstairs. Dylan was in the garage, pulling homemade dinners from the freezer and stuffing them into a grocery bag to take to the boat. I hugged him goodbye, told him to tell Ben goodbye for me, and he was off.

A day of quiet. The sablefish season has started. As of noon today, they will begin to pull the pots and land fish on the boat. It's always quiet for me when my men are at sea. I worry most when the boys are not with Bob. Then, if they are with Bob, I worry that I will lose them all at once. Then I worry that if they aren't with Bob, no one will try and save them. Then I go back to worrying that if they are all with Bob, etc. I get blue with worry, then stop. There is nothing I can do.

I'm sitting at my desk now, at my law office, waiting for Congresswoman Darlene Hooley to show up. I'm still considering running for the Oregon House. This week, Willy Smith, the state director for Darlene's office called me. "Congresswoman Hooley would like to come and talk to you," he said.

"What about, Willy?" I asked.

"Well, she'd like you to run for the House seat—wants to tell you what the experience would be like, answer any questions you might have."

Oh boy. This was flattering. Last week, Deborah Kafoury, the Oregon House Minority Leader, took me to lunch. I really enjoyed talking with her. The rough part about this decision is that I genuinely like all the people I'm meeting. They are dynamic, intelligent men and women who know how to get a job done, and better yet, do it. My kind of people.

Hooley was charming. In the lobby at my office, she gave me the once over, literally looking me up and down. I was wearing my favorite Misook outfit; a hot pink jacket, over a black sleeveless top and slacks. Wash and dry acrylic knit. Accompanied by her district director, Willy, and a district aide, Jennifer Wagner, we went into my office conference room.

Congresswoman Hooley immediately said, "You're wearing my favorite line of clothing, you know."

I laughed. Now I understood the reason for her once over of me in the lobby. "Misook?" I asked.

"Yup," she said. And with that we began a discussion of its merits. It didn't wrinkle when you traveled, and it didn't need dry cleaning. Willy steered the discussion back to the politics at hand, and Hooley told me how important it was to have me run for the Oregon House seat and for the Democrats take back this district.

At times I think I should just call a halt to it all and stop meeting with people who wanted me to run. But I continue the discussions because the possibility of running for the Oregon House presents me an opportunity to carve out my own life, one separate from fishing. I feel like I literally have to physically get away to reclaim myself, even if it is only to Salem, Oregon, where the legislature sits in session.

Saturday
August 18, 2001

It's 5 p.m. and I've just come back from helping the *Nesika* do a quick turnaround. I knew they were coming in this morning, and I called Richard on the boat, offering to help. He had a list of groceries and if I had time, he'd appreciate it if I could do the shopping, he said. I was happy to help.

Driving down to the docks around noon, the bayfront was a madhouse. A glorious, sunny, warm August day, it was the height of summer season. The street along the bay was clogged with tourists, fish trucks, and workers driving Hysters loaded with totes of bait and fish. Standing on the back deck of the *Nesika*, Ben looked in pretty good shape. He was tan, and his beard and mustache were already growing back. Dylan's nose had peeled. I need to get that boy some sunscreen and zinc oxide. Working with their shirts off, both boys pooh-pooh my warnings about the sun, but Dylan doesn't say no to the zinc oxide.

Richard gave me a grocery list, with some additions and suggestions from Ben. Richard had a special request for Kettle Corn. Off to the grocery store I went. "Get them whatever they want," Bob reminded me when I talked to him this morning.

"How's the fishing?" I had asked Bob.

"Terrible," he said. "There's no price, no market and no fish." With four days of fishing under their belt, the *Michele Ann* was to come in tomorrow morning and Bob estimated they'd have only 20,000 pounds on the boat. In years past, they'd have 50,000 to 60,000 pounds on the *Michele Ann* by now.

"Well, how's the grade?" I asked, referring to the size of the fish. Big fish are worth more; they are classified as 1-2 pounds; 2-3 pounds; 3-4 pounds; 4-5 pounds; 5-7 pounds; and 7 "ups."

"The grade's shitty," Bob said. "We aren't finding any big fish. And Richard on the *Nesika* is keeping everything that's legal."

Oh, brother. That, too, is a bad sign. Usually we "high

graded," releasing alive the smaller fish, in order to retain larger and more valuable product. Because the fish come aboard alive, we are able to quickly return to the sea those fish we wouldn't keep. Their survival rate is very high.

Several years ago, we took an observer aboard our vessel to document how well we handled our fish. Watching for several days, the observer determined that any fish returned to sea was aboard our vessel for no more than 65 seconds, resulting in virtually no mortality. In addition, we voluntarily equipped our pots with escape rings, allowing smaller fish to exit the pots, minimizing the catch of any sablefish less than optimal size.

"Is anybody finding the fish?" I asked.

"Noooo," Bob said, "but Denny Burke won't answer his phone, so he might be in 'em. I wish he'd pick up his phone. Talking to Denny always cheers me up." Bob laughed.

I marvel at my husband's attitude. Such a good spirit. I am pretty impressed with the boys, too. Bob said the weather was going to get sloppy midweek, and Richard mentioned it as well. I hope it means they'll come in on Monday or Tuesday and Dylan could get some sleep and pack for college. We are supposed to leave for orientation at Whitman in Walla Walla, Washington next week.

My arms loaded with boxes and boat dinners from home ("More Chicken Malibu, please," chimed the boys), I went back down to the *Nesika*. The boys unloaded the boxes filled with food and bottled water, Gatorade, cranapple juice (Ben's favorite), cereals, breakfast rolls, fruits and vegetables. I ran back to the house where I put their wet gloves and clothes through to dry another time. Dylan had called to remind me that the only thing he asked was that the inside of their gloves be completely dry. Their hands suffered so, particularly Dylan's. Being in the water and wet so much, the skin on his hands dries, cracks and peels almost every trip. Ouch.

Wednesday
August 22, 2001

As predicted, a storm hit like hell yesterday about midday. Both the *Nesika* and the *Michele Ann* had come to port that morning, and I was glad everyone was home, safe, and off the ocean. Both boats tied up and the crew was let off to go home. Bob decided to unload the fish tomorrow morning. I am glad of that; they'd get a little rest and Dylan can start packing for college. I'd been so busy I was able to keep myself distracted. I'm ignoring the reality that my youngest son is leaving home for good. Bob and I are about to become the proverbial empty nesters.

Last night I got home from work at 6:30 p.m., after stopping at the grocery store. I was intent on preparing some of Dylan's favorite foods just one more time before he left for school. Dylan was home, but the light in his room was out and the door was shut. He was sound asleep. Bob had called me before I left work and announced he also was headed home to sleep, and not to wake him up, please.

So with both Dylan and Bob asleep, I cooked. I made spaghetti sauce from scratch, my mother's recipe, and homemade meatballs. I sliced strawberries and made biscuits for shortcake. And made stromboli, which is bread dough filled with meats and cheese, and then baked. Dylan, tousle-haired, got up at 10 p.m. and we had a meal together and talked and laughed. He ate a couple of fresh peaches and some warm sliced stromboli and went back to bed. Bob hadn't stirred, so I read until I was tired, then went to bed around midnight. Of course, Bob then woke, couldn't get back to sleep, and we both tossed and turned until morning. Bob got up at dawn, and went off to the *Michele Ann* to unload their fish. Dylan had already left the house to go to the *Nesika.*

Sunday
August 26, 2001

It's Sunday night, and I am alone. Another milestone in our lives. It all started last Wednesday night.

Dylan was packing for college. Allison and Leah arrived at different times to say goodbye to him. Steve Ganz, a childhood friend of Bob's was visiting, on his way back to his home in Bellingham. Bob had been blown in from fishing on Tuesday morning, then when he heard from Steve that he'd be coming through town, Bob decided to stay home through Wednesday night. The weather was still crummy Wednesday morning, but by midday Wednesday it was good enough to go back out. But Bob chose to stay in to see Steve and say goodbye to Dylan before he left for college.

We had a great dinner together. I served the special request from Dylan: spaghetti and meatballs with sauce, salad, garlic bread, strawberry shortcake. We had a good evening with Steve, but I was having an anxiety attack about Dylan leaving for college, and the fact that Bob was going back out fishing. Bob wasn't coming with me to take Dylan to college.

By Thursday morning I was an emotional mess. Bob and Steve were having a leisurely breakfast. Both the boats were loaded with fresh bait and ready to leave the dock at midday. Dylan had been up most of the night packing, saying goodbye to friends, and he and I planned to leave at midday, too, to drive to Whitman.

I'm having a harder time with Dylan leaving than I was prepared for and the fact that Bob isn't coming with us upset me. After breakfast, I dragged Bob off into the living room for a talk. I asked Bob to come with me to Walla Walla. I broke down and sobbed about how upset I was and how I wanted Bob to change his fishing plans to come with me. Bob was astounded. First, sablefish season was underway, the weather has improved and everyone is ready to go back out. Second, we'd all known for weeks that Dylan was leaving for college in the middle of the fishing season, and that I would take him to college. "What is wrong with you?" Bob asked.

Pacing the room, I apologized to Bob for my last minute demands. "I simply didn't realize how hard this would hit me; Dylan's leaving," I said. "Yes, I'm capable of taking him to school. That isn't the issue. I'm tired of acting like we are single parents taking turns, as opposed to mom and dad. I want Dylan to go to college with his mom and his dad. Both of us. He needs us." Truth be told, I needed us.

"Okay," said Bob, "if that's what you need."

It meant getting the fresh bait that had been loaded on the boat in anticipation of going fishing, taken off the *Michele Ann* and restacked in the freezer at the fish plant. Bob made some phone calls, and Ron and Ben agreed to do it for him. It meant contacting all our crew about the change in plans. It also meant Bob would be tired as soon as he got back to Newport from the trip to Walla Walla, and would have to go full tilt on the ocean to make up for lost time. I shouldn't have asked him to do it, or at least I shouldn't have asked at the last minute, but goddamn it—I just can't go by myself and pretend that it is okay.

Dylan was royally pissed off at me. "I don't need him to come, Mom. I thought this time this trip was about me—what I want. I don't want to inconvenience him," Dylan said.

"Well, Dylan, you are right," I said. "This time it is about you, and my wanting Dad to come with us is about my needs. I need him to be there. I just don't want to go by myself. I can't handle it."

Dylan barely spoke to me for the rest of the day. I cried. Now Dylan is mad at me, too.

To his credit, Bob came with us. We took two vehicles. Bob rode all the way with Dylan in the boys' pickup that barely ran, and I drove Bob's diesel truck. That was part of the deal of Bob's coming, that I would do the driving so that he wouldn't tire any more than necessary. Bob offered to switch vehicles halfway so I could spend time with Dylan, but Dylan was still pissed at me. I passed on the opportunity. I didn't want to get the cold shoulder from Dylan for the remaining three and a half hours of the trip.

We arrived in Walla Walla, Washington, late that night, found a hotel near campus, and went to bed. As it so often does, everything looked brighter in the morning and after breakfast at the hotel, making our own waffles, we drove to campus.

I was totally relieved as soon as I saw the college. During Dylan's college selection process, unlike most parents, we stayed out of the college visiting circuit, helping Dylan only when he asked for it. As a result, I hadn't been to Whitman before, and neither had Bob. In the style of East Coast colleges, Whitman was set up in quadrangles with brick buildings and ivy; an oasis in the midst of eastern Washington wheat fields. "Oh, Dylan, you made a great choice!" I exclaimed. Dylan was full of smiles that morning, grinning broadly.

We helped Dylan move into his room, met lots of parents, went to some of the group activities, saw the campus, had a picnic dinner on the lawn, and made the run to Wal-Mart for those items we had forgotten. We were there long enough to see Dylan settled in. Our goodbye to him late Saturday night was very sad for me. We hugged in the parking lot behind his dorm, and he walked away with his head down, turning to wave once again and watch us leave, the sound of our truck, the only diesel engine around campus, chugging away. I cried and cried.

On Sunday morning, Bob and I left Walla Walla at 6:30 a.m. and made good time on our drive home. The route along the Columbia Gorge was, as always, beautiful. The river is so wide, and the steep walls of the Gorge changed from dry golden hills to sharp evergreen slopes as we progressed from the east downriver toward the sea. Bob, who so often crossed the mighty Columbia River bar, had rarely, if ever, driven upstream. Seven hours later I parked the truck in front of our house in Newport. Bob grabbed some clothes, went to the boat and loaded the bait on the boat with his crew, while I shopped for groceries, took boat food dinners from the freezer and carried them in boxes down to the boat. They left port. I went home.

I try not to cry as I wander around the empty house. We have done our job. We raised two healthy, happy, humane young men, well adjusted and well equipped to deal with their lives. It is time to let go, and for me to move on.

From: **Dylan**
To: **Mom**
Date: **August 26, 2001**
Subject: **alarm clock**

Mom, hey, I never turned up that alarm clock you and Dad bought me. I don't know whether you left it in the car or it got lost before I even saw it. Anyway, if you could please, send my old one. I hope you guys had a good drive back home. Thanks for coming up here with me and for everything else you have done for me since you began the long hard journey, which was raising a couple of hooligans into fine young men. Take care. Love, Dylan

Wednesday
August 29, 2001

Monday morning. I am back at work in the office. There was a phone message from Ginny Goblirsch. "Please call. Good news." I reached her on her cell phone.

"Are you ready for this?" Ginny asked. "I got a call from Jerry Fraser…."

"*National Fisherman.*" I finished her sentence for her. He was the editor of the magazine.

"Well," Ginny said, "I've been named Highliner of the Year. I'm going to be on the front cover!"

I started to shriek and holler. What an incredible honor! Highliner of the Year was a national award in the commercial fishing industry, made by the magazine to fishermen throughout the United States who were not only "kick ass" producers, but who had contributed significantly to the improvement of the industry. For Ginny to be so recognized, it simply acknowledged the truth; that she had worked long and hard for many years on behalf of fishermen. She has earned national respect.

Both the boats were out today. Ben is "two-manning" it on the *Nesika* with Richard; and Bob is at sea as well. Last night, back on the ocean, Bob reported the fishing was still poor.

Ben called me at work yesterday. In from fishing, he was at the apartment in Newport he shares with Phoebe, but wanted to come over to our house to do laundry. "Well, of course, honey!" I told him. "Leave it there on the floor, go to sleep, and I'll finish it for you." Having said that, I realized I was anxious to see him, so I darted straight home after appearing in court. His short reddish brown hair was tipped with gold. It looked like he'd spent a few hours at the salon getting it streaked, but of course, he hadn't. His neck and face and arms were dark brown, but like his father and everyone else on the boat, he has that endearing fisherman's tan: his brown skin stopped abruptly at the shirt-sleeve line. Ben sat at the kitchen table, pouring over his favorite magazine, *The Economist.* I laughed. He was so smart. I rubbed his head and massaged his shoulders as we talked.

"It was a pretty good trip, Mom," Ben said. "And Richard's cool. Steady. Just keeps going. If you make a mistake, he just looks at ya—doesn't say a lot, you just move on. He's pretty tough for an old guy." Ben wolfed down a thick sandwich I made for him. "I miss Dylan, though," Ben said. "I'd gotten him to go in the fish hold all the time and do the icing of the fish. 'Earn that bonus, boy!' I told him."

I laughed at Ben's description of him ordering Dylan about. There is a hierarchy everywhere.

Bob called last night, when he had a phone signal. They would be in early Wednesday morning to deliver a load of fish. Bob told me to expect a call from Devin Hanson. One of the crew members on the *Michele Ann* needed a trip off. Devin would rotate in on the *Michele Ann* as a crew member, at least until Richard and Ben on the *Nesika* caught their quota. Once the *Nesika* caught their fish, Ben and Richard would rotate in as crew on the *Michele Ann.* Ben said they still had another 10,000 pounds to catch on the *Nesika,* which would take at least two trips; one more "big" one, and another trip to clean up the poundage and to bring in the rest of the gear.

I was glad Devin was coming to work. Bob has known Devin for what seems like forever. Devin's family was from Charleston, Oregon. His grandparents had owned a local marine store there, since bought out and renamed Englund Marine, one of several Englund stores along the coast. The area where Devin grew up was called Hanson's Landing, after Devin's grandfather, Emory Hanson.

Devin is as fine a fisherman as has ever been on the boat. He'd fished since he was a kid. He and his wife, Frances, live in Charleston, and take care of Grandpa Emory. We hope that when Richard no longer wants to fish the *Nesika,* that Devin will take it over. In fact, I hope we sell the boat to Devin. If our boys don't want to fish, then the next best thing would be to partner with Devin.

The phone rang this morning as I was getting ready for work. Bob was in from fishing and he wanted me to pick him up at the fish plant and drive him to the other end of the bayfront where his truck is parked. I made a run down to get him. The dock was busy; a shrimp boat was unloading, two tuna trollers were tied up, and Bob. As exhausted as he looked, Bob is a handsome guy. He stood on deck, giving Rockey some last minute instructions as I watched, from above, standing next to the hoist.

"Come home with me?" Bob asked, after we got into my car.

"Mmmm, no, honey. I need to work, too," I said.

"Well, how about lunch?" he asked.

"Okay," I cheerfully agreed. Actually, he smelled so good to me, it would be fun to go home and roll around with him for a while. But duty called.

Phoebe is leaving today to drive back to college in Ohio. I fixed her a box of treats and necessaries: a U.S. road atlas, a camera, a big bag of M & M's, a couple of good books, and a flashlight. I dropped them off at the Whale's Tale, a restaurant where she was working one last shift as a waitress before leaving. Big hugs all around, and I wished her well.

Ben, Dylan and Bob

SEPTEMBER 2001

Saturday
September 1, 2001

I'm in mourning. All my men are gone. Ben and Bob are out fishing again. Dylan is away at college. Why do they have to grow up and leave home? Bob was in on Wednesday, unloaded his fish, came home and watched *West Wing* with me, falling asleep in his black leather chair. He turned the boat around on Thursday, getting the ice and bait loaded. That day we ate lunch together at The Coffee House down on the bayfront. Bob had the "numbers" on the cut fish processed by Bornstein's.

The fish plant provides us with settlement sheets for the gross number of pounds of fish delivered. The fish are then "J-cut," meaning it was headed and gutted in a manner our Japanese buyers prefer. After cutting, the fish was sorted into sizes: 2-3 pounds; 3-4 pounds; 4-5 pounds; 5-7 pounds; and 7 pounds and up. We are paid a higher price per pound for the larger fish. I poured over the information, sipping a latte, Bob with an iced coffee.

"Hey, the recovery rates on the fish look pretty good—62 percent," I said.

Finally, something to be cheerful about. The recovery rate was the percentage of poundage of the fish remaining after processing. Not only was the recovery rate important, but the grading of the fish into the poundage categories was crucial. Up until the last year, during the month of August, when the season for sablefish fishing was still very short, I spent days inside the fish plant, watching every single sablefish come off our boats and then iced and loaded into hard plastic totes, four feet square. Up the freight elevator the totes of fish went, to the cutting room floor. The totes were emptied onto a conveyor belt, where, rinsed of ice, a crew of 10 men and women cut, weighed, and sorted our fish. I stood on the cement floor in the cutting room, in a hairnet and rubber boots, for hours and hours, until all our fish were processed. Being present in the fish plant, I was able to ensure that all the fish we caught were actually processed and accounted for. Mistakes happen. For example, when multiple boats unload at the dock and totes of fish are everywhere, totes can get "lost" or mislabeled. We had an agreement with Jerry Bates, when he still owned the plant, that if a fish weighed 5 pounds, it went into the 5-7 pound category, instead of the 4-5 pound. Because we are paid a higher price per pound for the larger fish, this could mean a difference of 50 cents or more for every pound that particular fish weighs. My role in watching our fish graded into poundage categories often meant we were paid several thousand dollars more for our product. Vigilance pays off.

Now that the sablefish season stretches out over two months, it isn't practical for me to watch the unloading and processing of every fish anymore, and still try to practice law. Getting up from the table, Bob gathered up the fish tickets. "Prices still aren't so hot, and I don't know what we should do. We are supposed to get a better price at Bornstein's than Frank is paying at Pacific—and we're not." Bob was really irritated. "That was the reason I decided to sell the *Nesika's* fish to Bornstein. Hell, if the price is going to be the same, I might as well have sold all the fish from both boats to Pacific," he said.

"I feel so stupid," Bob continued. "We spent over $300,000 buying sablefish permits, and the Feds are gonna cut the sablefish quotas in half next year. Man, it's time to get out of this business. Everything we've worked for is gone, and as far as I'm concerned, it's the fucking draggers and Council's fault. They let the draggers discard and waste the sablefish for years, and now, nobody can catch 'em." Bob was over-tired, I knew, and would feel better after getting some rest. But he just turned 50, and his perspective is changing.

Wednesday
September 5, 2001

It's the first day of school, and the first time in 13 years that I haven't sent at least one child out the front door. I have a collection of photos of the boys, each taken on the first day of school, standing on our front stoop. "Oh, Mom," they'd groan, "Do we have to?" But they liked the tradition, I know. Even after Ben left for college, Dylan continued to humor me with a "first day of school" photo.

I called the House Minority leader, and the House PAC, to tell them I decided not to run for the House seat. I am bummed.

I'm pissed off at myself. I don't have the courage to do work I know I would be really good at. Instead, I fit my life around Bob's life. It doesn't matter how much Bob thinks he needs me and my help; the reality is it wouldn't be good for our marriage to be separated more than we already are. For me to choose to engage in a career move that would take me out of emotional and physical range isn't a risk I am willing to take. I can't believe how much anger I am feeling. But it is important for me to recognize that even though Bob doesn't support my desire to run for a political office, the responsibility for the decision not to do so is mine alone.

Yesterday, both the *Michele Ann* and the *Nesika* delivered fish. I went down to the docks and ran a couple errands for Bob and Richard.

Bob got off the *Michele Ann* and climbed up the ladder to the dock where I stood. "Well," he blurted out, "Richard quit."

"What?" I asked, astounded.

"Richard quit. Gave notice. Just like that. He is pissed off that I hired Devin, and is pissed he isn't going to get in on as much fish on the *Michele Ann* as he expected."

I feel sorry for Bob. No matter what he does, someone is always pissed at him. And what will we do without Richard? Not only is he a good skipper, he is a family friend. We feel terrible.

Speaking of crew, I ran into Tony and Connie Kennedy today at the dedication of the Fishermen's Memorial Walkway, down on the bayfront. The Port and the Newport Development Commission have worked together to create a sidewalk from the Embarcadero Resort, at one end of the bayfront to the Coast Guard Station at the other end. Thanks to Don Mann, the Port Manager, and crew, the newest part of the walkway is beautifully landscaped. It gives the tourists and residents better access to the commercial docks and port property. As part of the walkway, memorial tiles are inscribed with names of fishermen and vessels lost at sea.

I felt weird, walking along, looking down at tiles with all those names. It was like walking on graves.

Our Fishermen's Memorial Sanctuary is at the Yaquina Bay State Park, near the jaws of the jetty where vessels enter the ocean. An open gazebo, it has a stark black marble podium. The names of fishermen from the Newport area who were lost at sea since 1920 are inscribed in the marble. There are rows of wood benches where you can just sit, and be quiet.

Ben came over for dinner last night and brought a fresh loin of tuna he caught on the *Nesika* while they were sablefish fishing. I poured a bottle of Yoshida sauce over it, threw chopped garlic on top, added a couple of handfuls of sliced green onions and placed it in the oven for twenty minutes. It tasted so good.

Bob staggered into the house at 9 p.m., exhausted. He sat down at the kitchen table and I fed father and son Szechuan pasta and salad in addition to Ben's tuna. I listened to them talk about fishing. I ran a load of laundry. I listened. Did dishes. Listened. After dinner, Ben headed back to the *Nesika* to finish cleaning the boat, having agreed with his dad he could have the morning off to go to Eugene and find a place to live near campus. Bob and I went to bed.

Tuesday
September 11, 2001

Life, as we know it, will never be the same. Our country has been invaded, its security violated, by insane terrorism. I have cried all day for those people who cannot find their families. I am glued to the TV in my office. My chest aches and pounds. Today, for the first time in years, I went to Mass. At noon. I prayed and cried. As usual, I disliked what the priest said, but at the end, we sang *America the Beautiful* and then I sobbed. One Nation, Under God, Indivisible, With Liberty and Justice for All. Well, I'm not sure about the "Under God" part.

All I could think to do was call family. I called my parents first. I called Bob and Ben on the ocean, but couldn't get a signal, and had to leave a message. I called Dylan and left a message saying I loved him. I called my brother and his wife. I called Edie, Bob's mom. We talked about the tragedy, but it was clear she wasn't processing it too well, either.

Bob called me back. "Should I get the money out of the banks so we have cash?" I asked. I expected more terrorist attacks and financial collapse of the markets.

"Don't bother," Bob told me. "Only if you have gold will it matter. Getting paper dollars won't help, Michele. Gold, and then fish, is what we'll need."

He had a point. If the nation's economy collapsed, access to food would have more value than paper money. At least until the fuel ran out.

I wish I had confidence in George W. Bush as President. He's supposed to address the nation this evening. I called to give blood, but there is no collection site in Newport. I am astounded at how normally people are functioning. I suppose the best thing any of us can do, we who are not trained medical personnel on site in New York, is to continue with the life of America -- that no act, no matter how horrific, will in any way tear at the fabric of our spirit as a free nation.

I have much to write, but I feel frozen, shut down, unable to respond. Issues that inflamed me a few days ago now seem trivial.

Saturday
September 15, 2001

The devastation continues. I watch the TV, the faces of those who wander the streets of New York with photos of their loved ones, looking in vain for their people, not giving up hope. It is heartbreaking, just heartbreaking.

The day after the tragedy, I had to go to a Pacific Fishery Management Council meeting in Portland for three days. I was enormously relieved to get home last night. Bob had raised the flag outside our house. He'd held a moment of silence aboard the boat. At the Council meeting, a moment of silence was observed, but otherwise it was business as usual.

The Council meeting had many agenda items. We are affected by management measures for sablefish for 2002.

I arrived at the meeting on Wednesday night, after 9:30 p.m., astounded to find the Groundfish Advisory Panel (GAP) still meeting in the basement of the hotel. The GAP is one of the five or six panels that advise the Council. Bob served on it for two terms. I continue to attend and occasionally substitute when the fixed-gear representative can't make it.

My arrival at the meeting was greeted with smiles, cat calls, and good natured teasing about "Where the hell have you been all week while we've been working?" It was good to see the fishermen with whom I'd attended the baseball game in San Francisco in June. Barry Bonds had now hit 63 home runs and was still on track to break the record. When the meeting ended, our good friend and fellow fisherman Jim Ponts and I adjourned to the bar for a tonic and lime.

"Good thing you're here," Ponts said.

"Why?" I asked.

"Trawlers are trying to steal 200 tons of our fixed-gear quota for sablefish for themselves."

"What!" I exclaimed.

"They say they need more fish to get to the end of the year—or else they are shut down," Jim said.

"That's bullshit! Not again!" I was red-faced angry. Ponts was a veteran of the sablefish allocation wars from way back in the 1980s—long before I became involved in the Council process.

Each year, the federal managers set a quota of how many total sablefish could be caught by the commercial fleet. Trawl fishermen, who drag nets along the bottom of the ocean, catch a mixture of species, including sablefish. Because sablefish have a high value and are caught in conjunction with other deepwater fish, it is a high priority for the trawl fishermen to maintain or increase their share of the quota. If trawlers exceed the amount of sablefish they are allowed to catch in their nets, they discard it, dead, back to the ocean. The trawl fishermen, buttressed by the processors, are afraid that if they don't grab for a chunk of our fixed-gear sablefish quota when they exceed the monthly trip limits that regulate the trawl fishery for species caught in conjunction with the sablefish, there might be a shut down in their fleet's fishing as early as October.

I was up early the next morning as I am for every Council meeting. At 7 a.m. the "Oregon Meeting" took place. Present were Oregon Department of Fish and Wildlife staff, Oregon Council members, and people from the fishing industry, like myself. The purpose is to review the Council agenda for the day, see what the "Oregon position" is on specific issues, get information from the industry, and try to convince Oregon Council members to support our position. It is an incredibly difficult struggle. As long as fixed-gear interests don't conflict with trawl gear, I can occasionally count on support from the Oregon delegation. But generally, I fight an uphill battle all the way.

To be fair, I am always given an opportunity to speak, but the political reality is that Council members from Washington, Idaho and California are often far more supportive of our fixed-gear sablefish fleet than the management people from our own state. I can't understand it. Although the trawl interests dominate Oregon, of the three coastal states, the majority of the fish in the fixed-gear sablefish fleet are landed in our state. It blows my mind that often I can't get political support from our own people.

This morning, as we went over the agenda, I spoke briefly to the group and told them I was opposed to the attempted grab of 200 metric tons of the fixed-gear sablefish quota by the trawlers.

As soon as the meeting adjourned, Hans Radtke, an economist and Council member from Oregon, approached and told me he would support the trawlers' request for additional sablefish, to be taken from the fixed-gear allocation. I was livid. "We can't close down the processors, you know, Michele," Hans said.

And Burnie Bohn, a fisheries manager with ODF&W (Oregon Department of Fish and Wildlife), he wouldn't even talk to me about it. He was going to give the trawlers 200 tons of our sablefish quota so fast it would make my head spin. I walked up to Burnie in the hotel lobby.

"Burnie -- this is important to us," I said. He nodded, then walked away. I knew he wouldn't help us.

That afternoon, the issue came before the Council. In a cavernous ballroom, Council members sat at tables set up in an inverted V. The members from Oregon sat along the left side. Vice Chair Hans Radtke, Chairman Jim Lone, and Parliamentarian Dave Hansen were at the head table. Personnel from California and Washington were on the right. In front of the Chairman's seat was the "railroad light"; green when you started your allotted five minutes of public comment, yellow when you had a minute left, then red. It made me crazy to be limited to only five minutes when trying to explain our position on issues critical to the health of the fishery resource, and a difference of hundreds of thousands of dollars to our business. A decision of the Council could fundamentally change the business we'd built over 25 years. This is an insane process.

Trawl fisherman after trawl fisherman went before the

Council during public testimony and asked for the additional 200 tons of sablefish from our fixed-gear allocation. They said they had to have the fish. The trawl fleet couldn't be shut down. Processors would close their doors if the trawl vessels couldn't deliver fish to the fish plants, even when they exceeded the limits on the sablefish.

Then Jim Ponts got up in front of the Council and lit into the trawlers' bullshit. He talked about commitment, honor in the allocation process, and the millions of pounds of fish discarded dead by the trawl fishery each year. I just about applauded. He was great.

Next, Rod Moore, the Executive Director of the West Coast Seafood Processors Association, spoke. Rod told a story of fish processing plants up and down the coast that had already closed in the last 18 months; the result of the drastically reduced volume of groundfish allowed to be caught along the coast. He asserted that if the trawl fishermen didn't get the shift of sablefish quota from fixed-gear to trawl, more fish plants would close because trawl boats would be prohibited from delivering any fish. I couldn't believe what Rod was saying—that essentially, Newport was a dead port; that there were no processors receiving or processing fish with the exception of Pacific Seafood. Holy shit. I was on the edge of my seat, and my mouth was starting to water. Let me at him, I thought. Just let me at him.

It was my lucky day. The Council Chairman announced my name as next in line to testify. I used no notes; I forgot even to introduce myself. "Mr. Chairman, Ladies and Gentlemen of the Council. I can't wait for Jay Bornstein to hear Rod Moore describe Bornstein's Newport plant as "dead," processing nothing but one whiting boat. Let me tell you what's going on in Newport. Bornstein is buying a huge percentage of all the sablefish during this West Coast fixed-gear season. Then there's Corey Rock, a fisherman who's delivered over a million pounds of shrimp to Bornstein this season. For Rod Moore to tell us the Bornstein plant is dead—I don't think so. Tell that to Brian

Catton, who bought hundreds of thousands of pounds of crab in Newport last winter and this spring—and I should know, because we sold it to him. Regardless of what Rod Moore says, fish processing in Newport isn't dead and dying, and neither is it in any other port on the West Coast." I was on a roll.

"And now the trawlers propose to take 200 metric tons of sablefish that the fixed-gear fishermen are allocated, under the guise that processors need it to keep the plant doors open? I don't think so. Tell that to the 164 fixed-gear boats who want to catch that fish. Tell that to the thousand open access boats who depend on it. Tell that to those fishermen who range from Bellingham to San Francisco…" and so on.

I wasn't conscious of it then, but I was told afterwards that I pounded the table as I spoke. And that Rod Moore sat behind me, staring at his feet. It felt better than if I'd punched him in the nose and knocked him down. But for what? To keep 200 tons of an allocation of sablefish that no one should have been talking about taking from the fixed-gear sablefish fleet in the first place? It made me crazy that I would have to use so much energy in a defensive maneuver that was totally essential to maintaining our fishery. And besides Bob and Jim Ponts, no one much cared.

A trawler got up to testify after me and acknowledged I was a hard act to follow. The Council left our fixed-gear allocation for sablefish alone. And the trawl fishery was shut down for the year as of October 1.

Finally, I'm back home in Newport. The TV is turned on and I am glued to it. The video of Dr. Mark Heath, filming the collapse of the second tower of the World Trade Center, and the billowing ocean of gray dust, shocked me. What presence of mind he had, to continue to move forward to help other people after that terrifying experience! Then there was the bravery of the firefighters, who ran into the building to help, at the same time everyone else was trying to run out to safety. I heard estimates today of 1300 children who lost either a mother or father as a result of the attacks. That number is staggering.

The phone rang. It was a boat owner from New Jersey. A potential new crew member used him as a reference. The man was a scalloper, off the coast of New Jersey, from a town just north of Atlantic City. He was the mayor there, too. We spoke of the devastation. Tomorrow, he told me, his 90-foot boat would leave for New York City, filled with three truckloads of gear and supplies donated by fishing communities. I didn't get his last name or his town. I was just struck dumb as he spoke of the losses to their communities, and the generosity of others.

Tuesday
September 18, 2001

A week to the day after the tragedy.

Yesterday I got a call from Pete Fones, a friend for more than 20 years. Although he is retired from the state police and 51 years old, he is a reservist in the Coast Guard, Intelligence. He said he's been called up to serve. I am speechless. He tells me his estate plan needs to be updated. A husband, father of four children, I last prepared his will, with trust provisions, in 1990. "Things have changed since then," Pete says. I'll say.

I'm still glued to the TV most of the time. I have one in my office at the law firm as well. Some people say they can't stand to watch any longer, that seeing the destruction is just too painful. I have the reverse reaction. I am an information junkie. Today, Mayor Giuliani cast doubt on the likelihood of finding any more survivors at the World Trade Center site. Although he's probably right, the effect that statement has on the families whose people are still missing must be devastating. The count is now 5422 missing.

I remember the Oklahoma City bombing and when they began to remove debris using massive equipment. I can't stand the thought of bulldozers going into the crash site and shoveling out debris. Even if there's one person alive, they can't send in the bulldozers yet. People are still hoping. It's too early to destroy that hope.

The deaths have struck every corner of our nation. A man who died at the Pentagon crash and explosion, was the oldest son of a former next door neighbor. I met him once while he was visiting here. Lt. Commander David Lucien Williams. He left behind a wife and two children, ages 1 and 4. May he rest in peace.

Friday
September 21, 2001

Extraordinarily sad times. Yesterday on TV, I watched the funeral service for the pilot of the plane that went down in Pennsylvania on September 11. Thousands were in attendance. I think of that memorial service, then multiply it by 5422 more funerals for all those who have died. So immeasurably sad. The stories of the people who used cell phones to call their families from that flight, to report the hijacking—my God. The passengers who heard of the attacks on the World Trade Center, realized they were part of a suicide mission, took a vote and decided to take the hijackers down. Their courage renders me speechless.

I am amazed at how strong a feeling I have, to want to be back East, to be with my New York family. My people. Governor Pataki told a story, early in the aftermath of the devastation, of visiting a fireman in the hospital and commending him for his self-sacrifice. Governor Pataki said the fireman said, "Whaddya expect? I'm a New Yawkah."

And I'm a New Yorker. Even though I've lived in Oregon for 25 years, I feel like I want to go "home." I miss the bustle of the cities. I love the energy. I remember feeling high just walking the streets of Manhattan when I visited with the boys and my mom a number of years ago. The energy was so contagious and it felt so natural to me. One day Ben, Dylan, and my mom and I visited Ellis Island, the Statue of Liberty, and the Empire State Building. Near the end of the afternoon, Dylan and my mom, having run out of gas, took a cab back to the hotel. Although I was tired, too, Ben insisted I not miss the opportunity to go to the World Trade Center. It was a two hour wait to get to the top, but I've always been delighted Ben pushed me to go.

I haven't felt well lately. Really tired. I fell asleep on the sofa a couple of nights in a row. Bob had to wake me up to go to bed. I've had chest pain intermittently. I don't know if I'm tired, or depressed, or if it's my heart, or all three.

The fishing business is more and more difficult to manage. Even Bob is getting discouraged. This year, Tony Kennedy quit, and Richard Wood has quit. I cooked fettuccini last night, and tossed it with pesto and some feta cheese, while I thought about the problem.

"Are you sure that'll taste good?" asked Bob, peering over my shoulder at the kitchen counter where I worked.

"Trust me, honey," I told him.

I told Bob it would be a good idea to do exit interviews with former employees. Did they leave because of too much work? Not enough money? Difficult working conditions? Better offer? Didn't like co-workers? Didn't like supervisor? That kind of stuff. If it was something we were doing wrong, and could change, it would be helpful to know.

Bob said he'd had a good talk with Ben that day.

Ben had said, "Dad, anyone who's ever set foot on the deck of the *Michele Ann*, even if they've been fired, they're going to get a job on another boat. The fact that they have fished on the boat for you is a permanent good reference."

I told Bob, "I know it's difficult to think in this manner, but consider the fact of how many men you've taught and made into good fishermen. That's a tremendous contribution to the industry, and an important legacy." He thought about that and, I think, found some solace.

Monday
September 24, 2001

From: **Mom**
To: **Dylan**
Subject: **Hi Honey!**

Call Grandma Edie. It's her birthday—she's 75!!

Hope you had a nice visit with Ben and friends! He said he was glad to see you and he made it home ok. He left last night to go to school in Eugene. Now both my boys are gone. Boo hoo.

Let's see, what's new? After I dropped Ben off at Peter's in Portland on Friday, I went to Powell's and bought books.

Dad and I are fine. I spent yesterday working on our finances, then trying to do a budget for our personal expenses, ha ha! He may lease the *Nesika* to Devin, but a guy called this morning and he wants to skipper it. Someone with experience. So that is another option.

Marcel is 16 on Saturday. Give her a call if you get a chance.

That's the news from here. Hope you are having fun, that classes are interesting, and you are getting to know new people. Eat well and get your rest!

Love,
Mom

Tuesday
September 26, 2001

From: **Dylan**
To: **Mom**

Mom and Dad—

Everything is fine here. I have been pretty busy with studying. This weekend my intramural football team had two games and we won one and tied the other. I play wide receiver and cornerback and in this league, I actually get to catch passes and have a lot of fun. We are reading Euripides' *Bacchae* right now; it's pretty good. I took my first test in History this week. I studied like mad for it. My fish is still alive but my tropical plant died because it is too dry up here. It did rain here yesterday for the first time. It was great. I really miss the rain. I took an English test on grammar and got an A. We are almost done with Buddhism in religion and my class in music theory is moving right along, too. I had a good brief visit with Ben and his friends and I talked to Grandma Edie on her birthday. By the way, I wanted to send a thank you to Grandma Betty and Grandpa Joe for the cookies, but I don't have their address, so could you please send it to me?

Love,
Dylan

October 2001

Wednesday
October 10, 2001

I'm home. From the best trip of my life. New York, New York.

Over 950 Oregonians went on the "Flights for Freedom," sponsored by corporate and civic groups, and led by Portland mayor Mayor Vera Katz and Oregon Democratic Congressional Representatives Darlene Hooley and David Wu. The purpose was to show we were not afraid to fly in the aftermath of 9/11, to help New York City emotionally and financially in its time of need, and to live our lives as free Americans. As the principal organizer of the trip, Sho Dozono said, "If you have a message and it rings true, people will follow." And indeed we did.

I left Portland on Thursday morning, October 4. Arriving at the Waldorf Astoria in Manhattan, security was tight. I was graciously ushered into the hotel by an elegantly uniformed bellman, after my bags were discretely scanned for bombs. My identification was rigorously examined. My room, resplendent in down pillows and feather bed, was perfect. Tired from the trip, I snuggled in and slept. Up early the next morning, I met with other Oregonians to make an appearance on *The Morning Show* on CBS. After making my contribution to the group effort, I struck out on my own.

First stop: the Museum of Modern Art. The museum is being remodeled. The collection was limited to its highlights and there was no access to the sculpture garden. Damn. Evidently the museum has bought the entire city block and it is undergoing a significant expansion. I look forward to returning in two or three years. Nevertheless, the art I did see thrilled me.

The collection at the Frick Mansion was the highlight of my visit. The paintings roared at me, making me tear up with joy. In contrast was the Metropolitan Museum of Art, where I saw but a small portion of the collection: the Impressionists and the pre-1700 European paintings. My senses were assaulted at the Met, too, but it was by the noise and commotion this time. The contrast of viewing art in the Frick, a private mansion, and the vast galleries of the Met, was striking. I am so excited I was able to see three Vermeers during my stay. I bought art books everywhere I went.

And the music. I went to Lincoln Center and heard the New York Philharmonic conducted by André Previn. The program that evening had such contrasts. A well-known favorite, *Eine Kleine Nachtmusik* by Mozart, then a piece by Benjamin Britten, which included a soloist with a French horn and an operatic tenor. Weird!

I went to the Dance Theatre of Harlem. I loved that. There wasn't one other white person in my row. I had a similar experience in Chinatown; all Asian, no Caucasian. On Saturday, early in the morning, I walked in and out of the produce and live seafood stands, their offerings pouring from storefronts out onto the sidewalks. Many languages were spoken; and none I could understand.

Theatre, too. I saw *Proof*, a Pulitzer prize-winning drama. Traveling alone, I had no problem getting tickets to anything. I sat next to a woman from London, out on her own as well. We spoke of the support from England during this time of crisis. She told me how the English would never forget the Americans, what we did to help them in World War II, and that England would always stand by our side. The play was great, but I will always remember the English woman.

The food. I ate more hot dogs and sausages from street vendors in this short visit than I have eaten in the entire previous year. In the truly magnificent Grand Central Station, just a few blocks from my hotel, I sat at the counter in the Oyster Bar and ate raw cherrystone clams, which reminded me of the ones my father served during my childhood. I ate a dozen raw Duck Point Oysters from Long Island.

I went to Little Italy, lingering in a small grocery, inhaling the smell of hard parmesan and real prosciutto. A man was speaking

Italian with the grocer, and when he left, I followed. He held the door open for me and I said *Grazie.*

He turned around, looked at me and asked, "Who is the lucky man? You are so beautiful!"

I laughed, and said that the lucky man was my husband. This silver-haired fox handed me a card, kissed my hand, and said, "Come and see me." He owned a café in the district, and the restaurants were all starved for business. But New Yorkers, especially Italians, starving or not, know how to treat people. I returned to his café, named Sambuca, a couple of hours later. Seeing me enter, the owner jumped up from his table where he was paying bills. Despite the fact that there were few customers in the restaurant because of the Twin Towers destruction, he still had a full complement of staff on hand. He ushered me into his "home," gave me a tour of the kitchen, introduced me to everyone there, sat me down at a table and ordered for me. I was served a wonderful appetizer of hard parmesan and prosciutto and fabulous bread. Then an antipasto of red peppers and fresh mozzarella, perfectly grilled. And then a plate of several pastas—gnocchi, tortellini, rigatoni, all with different sauces. I had to stop there.

"*Tutti bene*?" he asked, as he swept by my table.

"*Tutti bene*," I replied. I was in love. With the city, the food, the people, the feelings.

I went to Mass in St. Patrick's Cathedral on Fifth Avenue. The only other time I'd been there was for Easter Sunday when I was 10 years old. Back then I was dressed in a spring-green coat, black patent-leather shoes, white gloves and a hat. Today was Columbus Day, an occasion that for New Yorkers means a parade. With 500 other Oregonians, and thousands of New Yorkers, I marched up Fifth Avenue, holding one end of a banner that said "Oregonians Love New York." At the corner of 46 Street and Fifth, in front of St. Patrick's, stood a couple of bishops and a monsignor, dressed in magenta vestments, watching the parade. These, after all, were their people: Italians,

Catholics, New Yorkers. One bishop, atop his raiment, wore an "Oregon Loves New York" t-shirt that one of us had given him. Perfect.

The people of New York were so happy to see us, surprised mainly that we would come so long a distance, to affirm our support for them, to help them emotionally and economically. I tipped busboys, maids, waiters, bellmen, cab drivers; those people so dependent on a volume of visitors to make their living. I had brought with me 200 Oregon crab emblems, courtesy of the Oregon Dungeness Crab Commission, and I handed those out. I wished I'd had 10,000 of them. The Newport Chamber of Commerce had given me a hand-blown glass ball, part of a selection of gifts for the General Manager of the Waldorf Astoria, who provided so generously for his West Coast guests.

In addition to eating seafood, I priced it. Although I didn't get to the Fulton Fish Market (it was moved to a parking lot in the Bronx as a result of the devastation), I went into restaurants and delis, open air markets and live tanks in Chinatown to see what I could find. Smoked sable sold for $30 per pound in the famous Dean and Deluca's delicatessen; cold smoked albacore loin, vacuum sealed, was $23 per pound. Live Dungeness crab sold for $19.95 a pound at City Crab, a restaurant on Park Avenue South. At City Crab, the Dungeness crab shared a tank with lobsters. "Hmmmmm," Bob said, when I told him about it, "I wonder how the crab liked that!"

Though I went to Union Square and Washington Park, I stayed away from the site of the bombing. It was, I felt, a mass grave, a place I ought not to go. Instead, I took a boat tour around the southern tip of Manhattan, and for me that view was enough. The destruction of the Twin Towers left a massive breach in the skyline. Smoke plumes still rose from the site. Our boat went under the Brooklyn Bridge, up the East River, turned around, and came back again. I took a city bus back to Grand Central Station, then walked back to the Waldorf. I was done in. Time to pack and then, in the morning, head home.

On the streets of New York City, in less than 24 hours, I was asked for directions by visitors four times, and once, by a Frenchwoman! In French! Once again, I was a New Yorker, albeit a saddened one, my heart breaking for the loss and the destruction.

Friday
October 12, 2001

I am trying to keep the positive energy of my New York experience alive.

It isn't easy.

We continue to lose, and then replace, crew. In the last two months we lost Tony Kennedy, Richard Wood, Rockey Green, and Ron Brandberg. The guy we hired to run the *Nesika*, to replace Richard, quit while I was in New York. Richard is going to skipper Jerry Bates' *F/V Chelsea*; he and Ron are working on gear at Jerry's gear shed. Tony is running Ginny and Herb Goblirsch's fishing vessel, the *EZC*; he's just back from a tuna trip and selling fish off the dock. Rockey quit and is going to work for Shawn Bertini, who skippers the *F/V Jaka-B*, a shrimp, crab, and halibut boat. Rockey says he just doesn't want to work as much or as hard as we do. Bob tells Rockey he'll do well with Shawn. Shawn worked with Bob for years on the ocean, and Shawn skippered the *Nesika* for Bob, before Richard had the job. Tasha, Shawn's wife, took care of Ben and Dylan when the boys were small, before we were married. We have family ties.

So. We have Devin Hanson and Javier Espinoza. A new guy, Steve Britt. Other new guys are Anthony Veach and Jared Hamrick. And we're still looking for more crew. Devin would like to buy the *Nesika*, we think. At least he says so. But what should we do about the permits, if we sell the boat? The boys aren't likely to fish for a living, nor do we want them to. And we need to lighten the load on Bob.

Congresswoman Darlene Hooley called me. She is still twisting my arm to run for the seat in the state legislature. Bob asked me later if my ego hasn't been sated enough just by the sheer volume of the people who are asking me to run. I say "almost."

Crab pot limit meetings are taking place in Oregon. Bob

attended the first meeting of the coast-wide committee and also the local meeting on the issue. Bob and a number of other crabbers think all the pots should be counted and everyone take a proportional decrease. In every other scenario proposed by the ODFW so far, some people end up with more pots than they currently own. Now where's the sense of equity and fairness in that? There's an Oregon Fish and Wildlife Commission meeting this week in Seaside. Will I go? Probably not. It's on the same day as Dylan's Parents' Weekend in Walla Walla. But I should probably draft a letter in support of our proposal, and get some other guys to sign on, too.

I'm tired.

Sunday
October 23, 2001

I'm at home now, back on a Sunday evening from visiting Dylan at Whitman College for Parents' Weekend. Bob couldn't get away to go with me. Too much uncertainty relative to the *Nesika*, and too much to do to get ready to take the *Michele Ann* crabbing in California. It's okay, though. Dylan and I had a good time. I watched him play intramural football all day yesterday. He caught a touchdown. I'm glad he didn't play football in high school, though. I like watching the sport, but it's so dangerous. Dylan and I went out to dinner, toured the campus. Met his friends. Saw a talent show.

And today is Dylan's 19th birthday. Happy Birthday, Dylan!! I can still picture his cake and party when he turned six; the first birthday celebrated in our home on Cherokee Lane where we first lived together as a family.

Wait a second. As a family? Now there's a romanticized memory! Bob was sablefish fishing and he and the boys were living in a large three-story house in Newport when we married. The bottom floor of their home was a combination garage and shop, filled with tons of Bob's fishing equipment and gear. I don't know what Bob thought I was going to do, but I'd hired movers. That was the first big "issue" of our new marriage.

"Can't you just round up some friends with pickups and get all this packed and moved?" Bob asked me, shocked.

I simply had to laugh. "Now let me get this straight," I said to him. "I work full-time, we have two small children, this is your home with four years accumulation of stuff, and I'm supposed to pack up everything myself and move it? While you are out to sea fishing? I don't think so, buddy!"

Bob had never heard of such a thing. "I've never known anyone who hired movers," he said, his jaw still on the ground where it had fallen in dismay and surprise.

Well, get used to it, honey, I thought.

Movers bid on the job. I hired a local outfit, signed a contract, and they came, packed, and then drove a couple of miles to our new home, a sprawling oceanfront 1940s beach house, with so much old-growth cedar and tongue and groove paneling inside that it reminded me of the interior of a yacht. When the men were unloading the truck, the owner of the moving company came to our house and announced that his men wouldn't finish unless I paid more money. Holy Christ! I stood in the middle of the road and yelled at him and his crew.

"You get in that truck and finish this job, you son of a bitch!" I sounded just like the stereotype of a fishwife. "I'm all by myself, I've got two small children, and my husband is out to sea. Don't you dare try to pull this crap on me." At this point I was shrieking. I'm sure my new neighbors were very impressed. "Get back on that truck and unload our stuff right now," I howled.

Well, they did. Nothing worse than an angry fishwife!

This past summer, Rockey, one of our crewmen, had to move out of his old house before the end of sablefish season. Rockey told Bob he needed a trip off the boat to move his family to their new home. Bob was astounded.

"Well, just do what my wife did," Bob said.

"What's that?" Rockey asked.

"Hire movers," Bob said.

Tuesday
October 25, 2001

Press Release:
Coast Guard to Check Crabbers for Safety

Thirteenth Coast Guard District personnel will again be conducting vessel safety spot checks, fishing vessel safety training, and voluntary dockside exams in various Northwest ports during the week prior to the opening of the Oregon and Washington state Dungeness crab fishery. The coastal dungie season is currently scheduled to open on December 1, 2001. Coast Guard fishing vessel safety examiners will be conducting training in safety, damage control, stability, and port security, as well as offering voluntary dockside exams for interested vessels. In addition, there will be spot-checks of primary lifesaving equipment and crab pot loading practices for vessels at the dock. These spot-checks of survival suits, EPIRBs and liferafts are meant to insure that these critical safety items are ready for use should an at-sea emergency occur.

Similar checks last year of 266 crab vessels revealed that 28% of EPIRBs had missing or incorrect registration information, and that 22% of vessels had an incorrect raft installation. Most of these problems are easily corrected on-the-spot. Fishermen are advised that extremely serious discrepancies, such as overloading, missing or expired primary lifesaving equipment, or nonfunctional EPIRBs may result in the vessel being restricted from operating until the problems are corrected.

The Coast Guard will also discuss port security issues with crews: fishermen are often in the best position to act as observers to protect America's marine transportation system.

Any questions about "Operation Safe Crab 2001," or about specific vessel requirements can be directed to Mr. Ken Lawrenson at the Coast Guard Marine Safety Office in Portland

November 2001

Saturday
November 1, 2001

Well, the crew situation is finally settled. Whew. Someone else's misfortune is our good luck.

Gene Law, owner of the *F/V Ms. Law*, a 60-foot crabber and shrimper, let go his skipper of 10 years, Rob Thompson. Gene announced that his son was coming back from Alaska to run the boat, and Rob was out of a job. What a total shock for Rob and his family. As soon as Bob heard the news, he called Rob. "A skipper for the *Nesika*?

Rob knew how to run a boat, manage a crew, and he was a good communicator and a really nice man. Rob was happy with the offer, Bob told me. Rob thought about it for an afternoon and accepted.

Bob is restored to his usual cheerful self—well, almost, given the pressure of trying to get ready to go to California to crab and leave in less than 10 days.

This morning Bob and I decided we would have our traditional crew Thanksgiving, before Bob and his crew left on the *Michele Ann* for California. With the changes in crew, we all needed to know everyone, to meet each other, connect as families working together. We invited everyone, crew and family from both boats, for Sunday night dinner.

Thanksgiving dinner for 25! I need to buy the turkeys right away. Let's see: we'll have turkey, gravy, dressing, mashed potatoes, creamed onions, pumpkin bread, rolls, orange Jell-O with mandarins, pickled green beans—what else? Oh, pies! Pumpkin, pecan, and apple, I decided. I need to get busy. Tables, chairs, tablecloths, centerpieces, candles, silverware and dishes have to be found.

Tuesday
November 6, 2001

I slept 12 hours last night from 6 p.m. to 6 a.m., straight through. I was bone dead tired with a killer headache and I just collapsed. Wish I had Bob's stamina, but I don't. I was so tired I was in tears by the time I fell into bed, half-clothed, lights still on.

I've knocked myself out the past few days, between work and helping Bob get ready to go to California, and, of course, "Crew Thanksgiving." What a blast! I shopped last Wednesday and Thursday and started cooking on Friday. First, I made the orange and strawberry Jell-O salads, with Mandarin oranges. Made cranberry sauce and the pumpkin bread, the favorite recipe given to me by my sister-in-law, Linda. Picked up tables and chairs, on loan from the Extension office.

On Saturday, I made dressing and cooked one of the two turkeys I would serve. A 23-pound turkey won't yield enough meat to feed the 20 to 25 people I've invited, so I cooked two smaller turkeys and then ordered a sliced ham from JC Market, and scheduled to pick it up Sunday noon. As I have done for years, I called my mother in New York while I cooked and we talked and laughed. I miss her so much.

Made pies that day, too. Two apple, two pumpkin and two pecan, Bob's favorite. Then I peeled potatoes, 20 pounds worth. Boiled the potatoes, then mashed them with sour cream and cream cheese and put into casserole dishes to bake, after the turkey came out. Brown crusts formed on the bottom of the potatoes and they were so delicious. I debated about making a green bean casserole, complete with crispy fried onions, but realized space in the ovens was at a premium. I made a great big green salad instead. We would eat turkey, ham, dressing, potatoes, gravy, creamed onions, cranberries, green salad, Jell-O salads, pumpkin bread, pickled green beans. Yum.

Bob figured out how to set up the tables in the living room to seat 23 and still have enough space to maneuver. He is good at that, considering how he can stack 540 crab pots in the hold and on the deck of the *Michele Ann*. But we laughed, recognizing that Ben was the best of all of us at it, recalling Ben's early skills loading and unloading groceries from the car and stacking the dishes in the dishwasher. We miss both our boys. This "Crew Thanksgiving" is the first "holiday" without our children at the table.

Eastern Washington, where Dylan is at school, is too far to hope that he will appear for the occasion, but I secretly wish that Ben would surprise us and come from Eugene, only two hours away.

Instead, Ben called at 5:30 p.m., just before guests arrived at 6 p.m. He knew he would catch us both home then, he said. He'd earned all A's on his midterms, with the exception of biochemistry. He had a raw score of 81, but didn't yet know where that would be on the curve, as the median score was in the low 60s. He'd been working hard, but was well and happy and had enjoyed a wonderful visit from his girlfriend, Phoebe. Dylan, that scamp, hasn't written or called us in two weeks, or responded to any of my chatty emails. Whatever is up with that boy? Establishing himself as an independent young man, I guess.

So, Sunday night everyone arrived. There was Javier Espinoza and his girlfriend Andrea and her family. There was Jared Hamrick, and his girlfriend Kelly, still a high school senior. Tom Ramsay and his girlfriend Ryann. Listening to their chatter made me miss our boys all the more. Then the Retherfords arrived; Bill, his wife, Sandy, and two of their children. Sandy is fun and warm and pretty and I was glad to meet her. Come spring, and the arrival of shrimp season, Bill would be the skipper for the *Michele Ann*, so I want to get to know them both. Then the Thompsons: Rob, who would skipper the *Nesika*, and Trish, his wife, a hairdresser, and their three children, one in middle school and two in high school. I sat with the Thompsons and talked a lot with their daughter, Katie.

I remember when I first met the Thompsons. It was on the *Nesika* in the early spring of 1988 for the Blessing of the Fleet. Rob and Shawn Bertini were Bob's crewmen. I'd made a big batch of fried chicken and deviled eggs that blustery day. With all of our families on board, we fell in line with the other boats in the bay and received the ritual blessing.

This evening, Bob was sitting further down the table with the Retherfords. Two of the crewmen, Tom and Jared, are very funny. Their joking around together reminded me of Ben and Dylan and I felt even more lonesome. Outside of work, Tom and Jared are friends and talked about working out together at Big Bear gym. I was amazed at that—after lifting crab pots all day long, they still had the energy to go to the gym? Ah, youth!

Everyone stayed three hours, and that was a good sign. Now everyone had met and talked, put a name to a face, and I hope, when things get tough, as they are certain to get, that the human connections established this evening will help carry everyone through. Take care of my husband, please, I thought, and we will take care of you.

This morning, toasting a bagel for Bob's sandwich, I suddenly realized I needed to get crew agreements signed. We have so many new crew and none had seen the contracts before. So, off I went, in the rain, to the boat, the gear shed and the gear pile, with sample crew agreements, explaining the provisions to the guys, urging them to read them before the final agreement was presented.

Today, I need to print out the contracts for each person on each boat, nail Bob down on the percentages that each man is to be paid, and get all the agreements signed, or at least the ones for the crew on the *Michele Ann*, before they leave to go crabbing in Bodega Bay, California.

From: Mom
To: Ben & Dylan Eder
Subject: Hello my sons
Date: Wednesday, November 7, 2001

Dear Ben & Dylan –

Just a note to say "hello!" Hope all is well with you both. Miss you. Am anxious for Thanksgiving to come! It will be so good to have you both home. Dylan, when are you coming? And you, Ben? Grandma Edie is arriving on Tuesday, two days before Thanksgiving. Let's have sushi out at Sada's together; maybe Wednesday night? Yum.

Crew Thanksgiving went well, though I missed you both. It was weird to have other people's sons in our house, but not our own. We had 23 for dinner, including ourselves, and it was fun.

Dad is getting ready to go to California. There are still some crew challenges on the *Nesika* (last crew man hired tried the old "submit someone else's pee" trick for his drug test, which didn't work), so now we are in earnest search again for another crew member. Life goes on. Dad is trying to get out to go to California by Sat or Sun

Love you all. Write me when you can. We think of you both every day.

Love,
Mom

Thursday
November 8, 2001

Hog rings. I'm on an errand to get 500 to 1000 of them. "Number 3s," Bob tells me.

I have no idea what a hog ring is for, only that they are at the Feed and Seed store and Bob needs a lot of them. Okay. "I'll get 'em," I say. I go to the Newport store first, then out to the store in Toledo to get more. I've been on the *Michele Ann* for the past three hours, working on crew contracts and Bob's boat computer.

The boat is a frenzy of activity. Bob tells me he is leaving tomorrow, Friday, not Saturday or Sunday as he'd said yesterday, and I am somewhat surprised. When they break for lunch, Bob and I eat on the boat. Warmed up leftover Szechuan pork and Kung Pao shrimp from the local Chinese joint from the dinner I had delivered to the boat the night before.

Bob tried to doze as I handwrote the percentages and changes on the crew contracts and then printed instructions for each crew member on the outside of the manila folder: 1. Read. 2. Initial handwritten changes on both copies. 3. Sign both copies and fill out "instructions" on the last page. 4. Return one copy to Bob/Michele. Keep one copy for your records.

Besides being required by law, crew contracts define the owner's, skipper's and crew members' responsibilities while on board the vessel. In addition to defining the manner and method of payment, the owner promised a seaworthy vessel, and the crew member warranted he was capable of doing the work.

The clock radio's alarm has been going off at 5:30 a.m. for about a month now. Bob is already exhausted because they've been working until 11 p.m. the last few nights.

Yesterday was the first meeting of the season of the Newport Crab Marketing Association. Local crab fishermen organized into a group to discuss and negotiate price with processors. Bob was elected president, by default, he says. No one else will do the job.

Bob Spelbrink agreed to be vice president, at least while my Bob is in California.

I loaded 70 homemade dinners on the *Michele Ann* tonight and stacked them in the freezer: chicken enchiladas, pork loin with orzo, beef chili, turkey with dressing and gravy, Chicken Malibu, and goulash.

Saturday
November 10, 2001

Finally, Bob's gone. It's Saturday morning and I'm at the office, sending letters off to my parents, Ben, and Dylan. Luxuriating in the fact that for one solid week, until Dylan comes home for Thanksgiving, I will be living alone. I always feel guilty about the relief and delight I feel when I'm alone. What if something happened to one of my beloveds and they were gone from me forever? But I push those thoughts away, and revel in the quiet.

This morning I got up and looked at my immaculate kitchen, vowing not to dirty any dishes all week. I scrambled eggs, wiped the non-stick pan clean with a paper towel, ate off a paper plate, drank orange juice straight from the plastic Tropicana jug, leaving a red rim of lipstick. Perfect. No dishes to wash. I would eat fruit and raw vegetables this week. And I would eat out.

Yesterday was a whirlwind of activity. Up at 5:30 a.m., I assembled Bob's clothes, gathered last minute items, and off he went to the boat. They were to leave mid-day, maybe later. I had a client coming in at 9 a.m. After that, Bob wanted me to go grocery shopping with him. Around 10:30 a.m. I went down to the boat. It was unusually warm and the sun was shining. This time of year I am accustomed to standing on the dock, wearing a hooded gore-tex jacket, trying to hide from gale force winds. Instead, I was in a sweater and jeans, dressed too warmly for the day.

The boat, parked along Bornstein's dock, was at its most colorful. Freshly painted, royal blue hull and white wheelhouse and mast; it was the prettiest boat in the harbor. There were 540 crab pots on board; the stacks of pots tied down from every angle with bright yellow woven nylon straps four inches wide. Seven stacks across the deck of six pots high. Twelve rows from the stern up to the wheelhouse, plus 92 pots in the hold. The straps were tied in the middle of the stacks of pots in a big yellow bow—someone's sense of humor. A huge Christmas present.

Topping off a load of crab pots on the *Michele Ann*, Newport

***Michele Ann* loaded with crab pots to go to Bodega Bay, November 2001**

"Whose idea was the bow?" I asked.

"Bob's," said one of the crew.

It figured. With yellow and orange buoys, and turquoise blue shots of line tucked inside, the pots looked like brightly wrapped gifts. On top the wheelhouse were large blue plastic totes filled with more shots of line, and stuffed alongside them were bright orange "chew bags" to be filled with bait and put into the pots. The boat was a veritable rainbow of colors.

I had brought a big Pyrex dish of chicken enchiladas. The guys wolfed those down for lunch while Bob and I left to do the grocery shopping. This would be our last "date" together for a while. We loaded boxes of goods into the truck and went back to the boat, where the crew and I unloaded and stored groceries. I visited briefly with each of the crew, wishing them well, good fishing, and to be careful, and asking a couple of them to take care of Bob, too. Bill Retherford, the oldest, and a skipper himself, told me how the work I did took some of the pressure off Bob. It was good to be acknowledged, and I thanked him. As the boat got underway, I took pictures and waved goodbye.

After making arrangements to get the truck and gear trailer back to the shop, I went down to the docks to talk to Rob Thompson on the *Nesika* about getting him another crewman. Guys are looking for jobs, but some aren't qualified and some would stay a couple trips and then leave. We need a steady, reliable crewman. I gave Rob a couple of names. Rob said he thought he'd found someone, but he hadn't had a chance to check his references yet. The fellow's name was Steve Langlot. I offered to make the phone calls and Rob was glad for the help. I think.

Late afternoon. The *Michele Ann* has left port. Will Bob be home in two weeks or two months? Will they fish or will they strike? Were there crabs to be caught in Bodega Bay, or will it be a bust? I have no idea. I grabbed the local paper, and went into Gino's Deli on the bayfront and quietly ate a big order of popcorn shrimp and chips.

Tuesday
November 13, 2001

I thought things would be quiet with Bob gone, but I'm still hopping around. Yesterday I baked cookies for the annual Fishermen's Appreciation Day, sponsored by Don Mann, the port manager for the Port of Newport, and the Coast Guard. While the guys are down at the port, working on stacks of crab pots, the celebration gives them a chance to get in out of the rain.

Fishermen's Wives provide coffee, donuts and cookies for the morning, and Don Mann sets up his barbecue and cooks hamburgers at noon. The Coast Guard comes by, gives a safety talk and encourages everyone to get a dockside safety inspection for their vessel.

After dropping off my cookies, I headed out to the gear shed to see Rob and the guys; crew agreements and drug policy forms in hand. I always try to get these to our crew well before the season starts, so that if they have questions or need advice they can get it. I also wanted to meet our new crew member, one that Rob hired, Steve Langlot. Steve had a lot of experience and fished on a king crabber in Alaska. I had called his former employer, a good friend of ours, Gary Painter. Gary gave him a good reference. We are lucky to get Steve.

I pulled up to the shop and was glad I wore boots. The recent rains left the grounds surrounding the shop buildings awash in mud. Rivers of water ran in truck ruts. I slid the shop doors open and enjoyed a few minutes chatting with Rob, Jared and Steve while they worked on gear, before leaving for the law office.

Sunday
November 18, 2001

Strike. Or is it a "tie up"?

Bob sits in Bodega Bay, unable to fish. The boat arrived there on Monday, November 12, just missing the bad weather that blew in after them. Safe. The sigh of relief I felt was momentary, and the agitation of whether they would actually fish began.

Bodega Bay is a town of 1500 people, just north of San Francisco. Notable as the film site for the Alfred Hitchcock film *The Birds*, it is a beautiful harbor and the home of a small-boat crab and salmon fleet. Across the bay is Spud Point Marina, where most of the commercial fleet is docked. Bodega Bay is generally a small boat fleet. When "big boats" start showing up, it often causes significant resentment among local fishermen. Yes, we are from out of state, but when limited entry was implemented in the California crab fishery, we were issued a California crab permit due to Bob's history of fishing in the state. Bob had paid his dues in the fishery and had every right to be there.

Bob first fished out of San Francisco in 1980, taking the *Nesika* there. Crab boats the size of the *Nesika* generally don't travel up and down the Pacific Coast while crabbing. The logistics of getting all the gear moved is a nightmare, and more work than most folks want to do.

In recent years, it was rumored the local fleet tried various tactics to discourage out-of-state boats, such as vandalizing gear, even after it was legally set in the water. In the early 1990s an incident took place where a non-local went fishing during a "tie-up" of the fleet, and came back to discover his car had been overturned and set on fire. Another favorite tactic of the local fleet was to strike, and refuse to fish for the offering price from the buyer, tying up all the boats in port. Although not unlawful, Bob felt it was simply unethical for him to fish when other boats "tied up." The local association knew that virtually no boat would fish in the face of a tie-up, and so their strategy was to strike and wait out the boats from other areas, until they gave up and left. Once the "big boats" left, the locals would immediately reach a price agreement with the buyer, and everyone would go fishing.

The opening of the Bodega Bay fishery supplied an important market: the San Francisco Thanksgiving market for whole cooked crabs, a many-generation tradition in the homes and restaurants of that city. Prices were routinely 50 cents to one dollar higher per pound for crab caught in the small Bodega Bay opener than when the larger West Coast season opened two weeks later, on December 1. But this year the local crab association in Bodega Bay seemed determined to shoot themselves in the foot.

"I can't believe they are this stupid," Bob moaned into the phone. "I thought they'd gotten used to the outside boats coming in. I can't believe they'd be so self destructive as to trash the Thanksgiving crab market. What short-term thinking!"

Bob was miserable. Since arriving in Bodega Bay, the local crab association had a couple of meetings. The crabs were in fine condition, the fishermen were asking a reasonable price, $2.25, and our buyer, Mike Lucas, had offered a reasonable price, given the markets and the aftermath of 9/11. Two bucks per pound was on the table from the buyer, Mike Lucas, and the Association wouldn't accept it. No one would say it to directly to Bob's face, but other fishermen said the locals wouldn't fish until he, and other boats, left. Last night we spoke, as we have every day this week. "I can't believe I'm down here," Bob said. "We aren't fishing, and everyone's going to be there in Newport for Thanksgiving."

Dylan had come home from college, Bob's mother Edie was arriving on Tuesday, and Ben would be home from the University of Oregon on Wednesday. Phoebe would likely join us for at least part of the day. Dylan's friend Leah would be coming, too. For all that Bob was willing to travel, if necessary, to optimize his fishing opportunities, he hates being away from home, particularly, when our family was gathering under our roof. He is miserable, and our daily conversations show it. I have to work very hard to maintain my equilibrium; to be supportive, but not feel totally miserable after every phone conversation with him.

Thanksgiving and Bodega Bay will forever be inextricably linked in my mind, and in the culture of our family. Back in 1991, we celebrated Thanksgiving in Bodega Bay. Bob and the boat and crew were there, on strike as usual, so the boys and I decided to go and see him. Ben was in the sixth grade and Dylan in third. I shopped and cooked just as if it was a real Thanksgiving at home and made up as many side dishes in advance as I could: mashed potato casserole, pumpkin bread, and cranberries. Ben found a flat compartment underneath the cargo space of our old Volvo station wagon and loaded my homemade pies in there, carefully shutting the lid. In went bags of groceries, the turkey and all the rest of the goods. While Ben and Dylan slept, I drove 12 hours through the night, to arrive in Bodega Bay on Thanksgiving morning.

The boat was tied up at Lucas Wharf. After hugging and kissing Bob, I put the turkey in the oven in the galley, and as a family, we left to go hiking in the dunes around Bodega Bay. When we came back to the dock, the aroma of the turkey emanated from the smoke stack of the boat, overwhelming even the smell of the fish plant. Bob had been so happy to see us.

So far, it seems his crew is coping in Bodega Bay this year. The younger guys took trips into San Francisco. Bob and Bill Retherford went hiking in the dunes. We paid our crewmen draws on their future earnings, so their families' bills were paid, which relieved some pressure, but also made them realize that their net pay, once they do start fishing, is going to be significantly reduced.

Meanwhile, the draws are coming out of our pockets and we are paying interest on the money we advanced. I had to tap into our credit line to get us to the end of the year. We aren't going to "take" any crab money until next year, to reduce our taxable income, so right now we are short of funds. Things aren't looking so hot.

November 16, 2001

The San Francisco Chronicle

Expect pricier crabs – if you can find them
Dungeness dispute may limit supply
by Larry D. Hatfield

Bay Area consumers will face higher prices for Dungeness crab for Thanksgiving no matter how a 2-day-old dispute between the Bay Area's crab fleet and processors comes out.

The fleet remained in ports for a second day today in what fishermen say is a dispute over price.

A primary marketer of Dungeness, however, said he thinks Bay Area crabbers may be stalling until big crabbing boats from farther north leave when their season opens Dec. 1.

Whenever and however the dispute is resolved, it almost certainly means higher prices, if Dungeness can be bought at the market at all. The prized crab, taken commercially in bay waters since the Gold Rush, is a mainstay of many Bay Area Thanksgiving menus.

In the absence of a local catch, Mike Lucas, owner of North Coast Fisheries, said he is buying crabs from out of state but supplies are limited.

What that means is higher prices for Thanksgiving.

"It's going to be harder to get crab for Thanksgiving," Lucas said. "We do have product. We're buying from a tribal source out of Washington, and we're taking everything they can produce. But the supply is limited.

So will they (supermarkets and other outlets) have enough to meet demand? "Probably not. Thanksgiving crab is going to be hard to come by, and the price is going to be higher."

Fishermen belonging to the Crab Boat Owners Association were meeting at Fisherman's Wharf this morning to try to resolve the price dispute. Similar meetings were being held by crabbers in Half Moon Bay and Bodega Bay.

But a resolution did not seem at hand.

"There's really not much going on," said Chuck Wise, president of the Bodega Bay Fishermen's Marketing Association. "I talked to the buyers again this morning, and there doesn't seem to be any wiggle room for them to come up to our asking price of $2.25 (per pound). But frankly, the move is up to them. I don't expect any movement today, to tell the truth."

The Dungeness season along the Central California coast opened yesterday morning, but the fleet did not go out.

Fishermen were demanding $2.50 a pound, since lowered to $2.25, while processors are offering $1.75 to $2. Last year's opening price was $2.25.

But Lucas, who owns the region's biggest processor, said he thinks the dispute has less to do with prices and more to do with competition with bigger crab fishing vessels from the north.

"It's a ploy to keep the big boats out," Lucas said. "There are more boats than ever this year."

Traditionally, the local fleet and "out-of-town boats" from the North Coast don't start operations until prices are set between fishermen associations and buyers. Lucas suggested that if the local fishermen stall long enough, the northern boats will leave when their own season starts Dec. 1, thereby substantially reducing competition.

There are more boats than usual from the north this year, Lucas said. "If they (fishermen associations) stall past Thanksgiving, these boats will take off and go back home to be there for the important opening day. That's what it's all about, stalling the thing more than the price."

Lucas also said he didn't expect the matter to be resolved at today's meetings. "It's not a price issue. It's a matter of do they want to go fishing with all those big boats around."

Wise said that was nonsense. "It would be suicide for us to try to freeze the northern boats out," he said. "As soon as they thought we'd do something like that, they'd go in and start fishing and we'd all be fishing for peanuts."

He also noted that boats from the Bay Area go to the North Coast during its seasons, and it's important to both fleets to maintain good relations.

Lucas said the $2 buyers are offering "is a very fair price, a realistic price." He also said, "The economy has forced a situation upon us that we just can't pay $2.50."

Wise countered that fishermen also faced increased bait and fuel prices, making it impossible for them to accept the buyers' offer without ending up losing money.

There are 584 crab permits for California-registered boats and 68 from out of state, according to the state Department of Fish and Game.

Tuesday
November 20, 2001

Midnight. I was in bed. The phone rang. It was Bob. He and his crew are getting in his truck, all five of them, and coming home. A twelve-hour drive. Bob doesn't expect the strike to break before Thanksgiving. He said they should arrive midday Wednesday, the day before Thanksgiving.

How long they'll be home, I don't know. But Bob will be here to see Dylan, Ben, and his mother Edie for Thanksgiving.

Dylan had driven to the Eugene airport to pick up Grandma Edie, who'd arrived from Los Angeles. Ben was still busy with classes in Eugene and he wasn't sure when he'd arrive in Newport. I am anxious to see Ben. I haven't seen much of him this fall. After Thanksgiving, he'll be home again for Christmas break and wants to get some crabbing in during the month of December.

I am in full Thanksgiving mode, although admittedly, this will to be a scaled down event in comparison to "Crew Thanksgiving," two weeks ago. There will be only six of us: Bob, Ben, Dylan, Edie, Leah and me. I made all the same dishes, just not quite as much quantity, but I did make plenty of pies. Whatever we don't finish, I figure, Bob could take back to the boat for our crew.

For dinner Wednesday night, I announced I wasn't going to cook. We went to Sada's, a sushi place on the bayfront, and a favorite of Ben's. Sada's was crowded. We ate sushi, sashimi, bento boxes. On our way out, we saw Judy and Denny Burke, good friends and crabbers, too. Denny was worried about the start of the season: the price, the weather, the uncertainty, the pressure to make a living. Denny, usually cheerful, looked grim.

"Somebody's gonna die," said Denny, shaking his head.

"God almighty, what a thing to say," I said to Bob, out on the sidewalk when we left.

"Yes, but he's right," said Bob.

Saturday
November 24, 2001

Thanksgiving was fun. Ben finally arrived from Eugene at 11 a.m. and I was a little upset because he had Phoebe in tow. Well, like I said, who could blame him? Girlfriends are more important than family at this point in a young man's life. We all sat around and talked and ate and took family photos, Bob and I standing on the living room sofa, with Ben and Dylan standing on the floor in front of us. Our boys are so tall!

We went for a walk on the beach. It was a good day. Leah was with us, and she is such good company, setting the table with my mother's silver and lighting the candles for me. After we'd all stuffed ourselves, Phoebe came back from her family's celebration to eat pies with us. By then, Bob was getting agitated to leave. He wolfed down his pie, looked at me and said, "Let's go." I had agreed to drive him back to Bodega Bay; the 12 hours would have wiped him out completely.

He'd brought home a load of dirty clothes and I had them washed, folded and ready to go. I packed pie and food for the trip. Two of the crew arrived to drive Bob's truck back to Bodega Bay. We loaded Bob's gear in my car and said our goodbyes. At least I got out of doing the dinner dishes!

"Tank of gas?" Bob barked at me.

"Yes, dear, the car's tank is full," I said. To myself, I laughed and said *Aye-Aye, Sir*, but with the mood he was in, I didn't think Bob would find my comment funny. Still, I don't like it when he talks to me as if I were a crew member instead of his wife.

We picked up the other crew members at their homes and headed south on 101. It would be a straight shot all the way down the coast. Everyone took turns driving and keeping the driver awake. After I drove for a few hours, I slept in the back seat, waking to find us parked at Safeway in Sebastopol, California, just a half hour outside Bodega Bay.

"Come on, honey, get out," Bob said. "We've gotta get groceries and be ready to leave the dock, in case the strike settles."

I stumbled out of the car and into the grocery store. It was 6 a.m. We filled a cart, grabbed some rolls for breakfast and drove over the hills to Bodega Bay.

In the harbor, none of the boats had gone out fishing. We got coffee at the local hangout and Bob introduced me to a couple of the Bodega Bay crab fishermen, grizzle-faced and flannel-shirted. We chatted with the men and the owner of the dock, Richie, who would unload Bob's crabs if the season ever got underway. I was tired, but wanted to get home. I kissed Bob, got in the car, and headed north on 101 for Eureka. I spent Friday night there and made the rest of the drive home to Newport today.

This afternoon the phone rang. It was Bob.

"I'm coming home," he said.

"What?" I said.

"These fuckers aren't going to move," he said. "Mike Lucas has offered to pay the price that the Bodega fishermen demanded, and they still won't untie their boats and leave to go fishing. I'm not going to sit here until January again. I'm coming home to Oregon to fish."

December 2001

Newport News Times
Friday, December 7, 2001

Crabbers Stay in Port, No Move on Price Dispute
by Joel Gallob

The price for crab being offered by West Coast buyers is $1.40 per pound; the crab fishermen are asking $1.75.

That disagreement kept the crabbers in port opening day Dec. 1 up and down the West Coast from Bodega Bay, California through Oregon and into Washington state.

They were still in port as of Thursday afternoon, according to local crabber Bob Eder.

Eder is the president of the Newport Crabbers' Association. The local group and similar ones in ports from Brookings to Astoria, north in Washington and south into California, are negotiating with buyers for what they hope will be a better price.

Newport crabbers met this week and took part in a coastwide conference call with their counterparts.

"We're holding with the rest of the coast at $1.75 a pound," Eder said Thursday. "We feel we have an outstanding product, and it's a dangerous and labor intensive fishery. We got $1.40 a pound back 20 years ago. Costs, payments for vehicles, homes, all have grown since that time, and we'd like to see the price of our product do so, too."

"We're all anxious to go to work and generate income for our crews and for the people working at the processors, and stimulate the local economy," Eder concluded. "But it's possible the boats may not move for a while."

Saturday
December 8, 2001

Too much to do. Ben's coming home tonight, sometime, hard to know when. Spent the day putting the outdoor Christmas lights up, always a task. First, I went to Fred Meyer to make sure I had plenty of spare bulbs and correct fuses.

Returning home, I dragged the ladder outside, climbed up top with my trusty staple gun, and attached the cords to the shingles, outlining the garage, the doorways, and the railroad ties that delineate my garden. Pow, pow, pow; I love the sound of my staple gun. Bob, on the other hand, dislikes my method. The residual staples leave rust marks in the shingles.

I told Bob that when he retired, he could put the Christmas lights up the way he wants, but while he is at sea and it is still my chore, my way rules.

Went looking for a Christmas tree today, too. Checked the usual spots: Fred Meyer, the Boy Scouts, and Jackson Hill Tree Farm, but didn't find one that jumped right out at me. It is more fun to get the tree with at least one of the boys with me: we'd select one, turn it in every direction, ask for the other's opinion, make a decision. I'm worried. It's just a couple of weeks before Christmas and the supply is going to dwindle.

Dylan, Bob and Ben with halibut aboard the *Nesika*
summer 1988

"Got 'em!"
Knee-deep in crab after *Nesika* fish hold was full, 1988

Michele, 1994

Christening of the *F/V Michele Ann*
Michele, Bob and Roger Fry, 1996

Ben and Dylan rowing on the Siletz River, 1996

Dylan and Ben, 1997

Michele and Bob on the beach in front of our home in Newport, just south of Yaquina Head, summer 1998

Dylan with halibut on the *Michele Ann,* 1999

Bob in the *Michele Ann* engine room, 2000

F/V Michele Ann crabbing off Point Reyes, Northern California

Ben getting sablefish pot ready for the season, summer 2001

Ben and Ron Brandberg sablefishing on the *Michele Ann,* summer 2001

Bob, Dylan, Michele and Ben, Thanksgiving 2001

The *Nesika* beached with Coast Guard personnel aboard
December 12, 2001

From: **Mom**
To: **Dylan**
Date: **Monday, December 10, 2001**

Hi, Honey—

Light your candles, pretend you are Judah Maccabee and you will get through this week of exams. Good luck! I will make you latkes when you get home.

Looks like the price for crab settled today (your father has done an excellent job as a leader of the fishermen's association), but weather is keeping them in port, for the moment. Ben is home. All is well. See you soon.

Get chains for your car before you drive home. They are prohibiting vehicles from traveling without them in some areas of the Columbia Gorge.

Love ya!
Mom

From: **Dylan**
To: **Mom**
Date: **Monday, December 10, 2001**

Hey Mom—

Happy Chanukah, and thanks for the rugala and cd's. I have my first final exam tomorrow.

Love,
Dylan

U.S. Coast Guard
Group North Bend
December 11, 2001

COAST GUARD SEARCHING FOR NEWPORT FISHERMEN

At 10:44 a.m., Coast Guard Station Yaquina Bay received a call from the fishing vessel *GARY LEE* reporting the fishing vessel *NESIKA* had capsized ½ mile west of Yaquina Head. At 10:53 a.m., Coast Guard Group North Bend received a signal from *NESIKA's* emergency radio beacon. *NESIKA* is a 40-foot fishing vessel with four men on board. Arriving rescue crews located the *NESIKA* inverted, and have not located any of the crew.

Three motor lifeboats from Stations Yaquina Bay and Depoe Bay, and one Dolphin helicopter from Air Facility Newport are searching the area for the men. Fishing vessels *GARY LEE* and *JAKA B* are assisting the search.

As of 6 pm, rescue crews have not located any signs of *NESIKA's* crew. Coast Guard crews will continue to search the area throughout the night with a motor lifeboat from Station Yaquina Bay. A Dolphin helicopter from Air Facility Newport will complete two search flights tonight followed by a first light search tomorrow morning.

U.S. Coast Guard
Group North Bend
December 12, 2001

COAST GUARD SUSPENDS MASSIVE SEARCH EFFORT FOR MISSING NEWPORT FISHERMEN

The Coast Guard has suspended its two-day search for the crew of the fishing vessel *NESIKA* which capsized off Yaquina Head yesterday morning.

Capt. John Miko, Commander of the Coast Guard rescue crews searching for four missing Newport fishermen, suspended the intense search today, but not before personally contacting the men's families to express his condolences.

"I am confident that if there had been someone there to find, we would have found them; if there was someone there to be rescued, we would have rescued them," said Miko. "I extend my personal condolences to the families for their loss."

Coast Guard crews responded with three motor lifeboats and a helicopter after receiving a distress call from the fishing vessel *GARY LEE* reporting they had located a capsized fishing vessel. The Coast Guard also received an automated distress signal from *NESIKA's* emergency radio beacon, but never received any transmissions from *NESIKA's* crew.

Fishing vessels and rescue crews located *NESIKA* upside-down ½ mile west of Yaquina Head within 20 minutes of the alert. One of the first fishing vessels on scene reported seeing two unresponsive persons in the water, but was not able to recover them. There has been no further sighting of the four crewmen.

The three motor lifeboats and one helicopter searched until 9 p.m. Tuesday. Two motor lifeboats searched throughout the night and the helicopter rejoined the search at daybreak this morning. Fishing vessels from the crab fleet have also been assisting with the search. The search was suspended at 11:08 a.m. this morning due to the unlikelihood that a person could survive more than four hours in the 50-degree waters.

NESIKA is a 40-foot fishing boat home ported in Newport, Oregon. The master of the vessel is Rob Thompson, age 40. The crew consists of Stephen Langlot, age 34; Jared Hamrick, age 20; and Benjamin Eder, age 21, all from Newport. The families of the crew have been notified of the tragedy.

The Oregonian
Thursday, December 13, 2001

Newport grieves for men with fishing in their blood
The skipper and crew of the crab boat *Nesika* chose a life friends call "a very noble occupation"
by Matt Sabo

NEWPORT—Three weeks ago, Rob Thompson considered getting out of fishing. He spent four hours debating whether to build cabinets for a living before agreeing to skipper a boat for Newport fisherman, Bob Eder.

The boat was the *Nesika.*

Fishing gets in a man's blood, Newport fishermen say. For Thompson, who leaves behind a wife and three teenage children, it's a way of life he couldn't give up, even knowing the hazards he faced at sea.

The 36-foot *Nesika* capsized Tuesday morning while Thompson and his crew were dropping crab pots in the ocean.

Lost at sea with Thompson were Ben Eder, the 21-year-old son of the boat's owner; Stephen Langlot, 34 of Newport, and Jared Hamrick, 20 of Waldport.

On Wednesday a salvage crew hefted the *Nesika* off Beverly Beach, where it had come to rest early that morning. No bodies have been recovered.

"It just hits everybody right in the heart," said Ginny Goblirsch, wife of a fisherman and a friend of the Eder family.

Fishermen are well aware of the risks inherent in commercial fishing. Twenty-five Oregon fishermen have died since 1992 and of those, 16 were lost when boats capsized at sea, according to the Occupational Safety and Health Administration.

The crab fishery is one of the most dangerous because boats head out in the turbulent winter seas. To compound the risk, crab boats are all in a pell-mell rush to get out to sea fast, get the biggest crabs and the best loads, and get back to port to sell their catch. The season opens in early December, and the best fishing is usually in the first month.

"It is a derby sort of fishery, where they ring the bell and everybody sort of goes," said Ken Lawrenson, a Coast Guard investigator. "It is the mostest and the fastest."

Fleet keeps crabbing

The 36 crabbing boats operating out of Newport when the season got under way Tuesday continued to navigate the treacherous Yaquina Bay bar throughout the day.

"It isn't just a job," Goblirsch said. "It's in your blood, it's a way of life, it's a culture. It's also a very noble occupation."

Thompson was an outdoorsman who liked to hunt deer and elk. He loved commercial fishing, said his brother-in-law, Perry Garrett.

"It was different every day," Garrett said. "You could go out and get a haul in one day or you could go three months and get nothing. Once you get it in your blood, you can't get it out."

Thompson was uninsured. Garrett said he doesn't know what will happen to Thompson's wife, Trish; sons, Josh, 18, and Tyson, 13; and daughter, Katie, 15.

"It's hard," Garrett said. "It's just going to be so hard. It's the holidays, it's Christmas. And now we have to bury somebody."

Ben Eder graduated from Newport High School in 1998. He was home from the University of Oregon on winter break. A high-school classmate, Matt Harner, was on a crabbing boat Tuesday that set its load of pots and returned to port safely.

"We were going to get together (Monday) night, but we kept missing each other," Harner said.

Boat was in good condition

The *Nesika* had a full Coast Guard inspection in June, said Lt. Bob Beck. The only problem found was a ring buoy – a kind of life-saving ring – and that was quickly remedied. The Coast Guard inspected the vessel again Nov. 27 as a part of a pre-crab season program. Only an expired license for a safety beacon was discovered. That beacon worked after the capsizing Tuesday.

Beck is part of a team investigating the capsizing. He said no witnesses saw the boat overturn but that he boarded the boat Wednesday after it beached north of Newport and saw no open hatches.

A second Coast Guard investigator, Ken Lawrenson, said he thinks the boat was in good shape to be out on the ocean.

"My gut feeling on this is, without completing the investigation, it is not a boat issue," Lawrenson said.

Coast Guard investigators inspected the *Nesika* on Wednesday before it was loaded onto a tractor trailer and hauled to a dry dock in Toledo.

Bodies seen on water

The boat was discovered overturned a mile off Beverly Beach at 10:44 a.m. by crewmen aboard the nearby *Gary Lee.* Two people in typical fishing rain gear were spotted bobbing in the sea but were unresponsive, and the *Gary Lee* could not reach them before they disappeared, a Coast Guard spokesman said.

A survival suit and other personal items washed ashore at Beverly Beach.

Goblirsch, the wife of a commercial fisherman, said the *Nesika* was a "well-kept boat" and that Thompson was a competent, experienced skipper with a capable crew. Thompson was in radio contact with Bob Eder, who was aboard a crabbing boat south of the *Nesika,* shortly before the boat overturned, Goblirsch said.

"No mayday was sent out, which means whatever

happened, it happened quickly," she said.

"It just reminds you that none of us are immune. It could happen to anyone."

Community Memorial Service
Saturday, December 15, 2001
2 PM
Newport Church of Nazarene
227 NW 12th Street

To honor and remember. . .
Rob Thompson
Ben Eder
Jared Hamrick
Steve Langlot
Our beloved friends and family
Lost at sea
F/V Nesika
December 11, 2001

Reception to follow
At Best Western Agate Beach Inn
3019 N. Coast Highway, Newport

Tribute to the Men Lost in the Capsizing of the *F/V Nesika*, 12/11/01

The Oregonian
Sunday, December 16, 2001

Newport honors four lost fishermen
The community holds a memorial service for Rob Thompson, Ben Eder, Jared Hamrick and Steve Langlot
by Matt Sabo

NEWPORT – On a stormy Saturday that kept the crabbing fleet in port, four fishermen who were lost at sea Tuesday were tethered to a community's memory.

Rob Thompson, Ben Eder, Jared Hamrick and Steve Langlot died when their 36-foot crabbing boat, the *Nesika*, capsized about one mile offshore near Yaquina Head. Their bodies have not been recovered.

Saturday's community memorial service drew a somber crowd of about 500 people who laughed occasionally at speakers' memories of the men. Such services are an all too familiar ritual in this coastal town. Since 1900, 105 Newport fishermen have died at sea.

Jeff Feldner, a commercial fisherman who was asked to speak on behalf of the Newport fishing community, said he was at sea Tuesday along with about 200 other fishermen when word came over the radio that a boat had capsized. Later he learned it was the *Nesika.*

"It got colder, the skies got darker, and the seas got bigger," he said. "It felt like I got hit in the chest with a crab pot. It always does."

He said it is impossible to verbalize the pain, fear and awe fishermen feel when someone goes down at sea. Still, men are drawn to the fishing life for its independence, the lifestyle and the "purity and comfort of doing something real," he said.

"It's a sense of absolute rightness about what we do. It's inside, it's visceral."

Nesika skipper Rob Thompson, 40, shared Feldner's

passion for fishing. He had sea sense, said Eric Conrad, Thompson's brother-in-law.

Thompson, who leaves behind a wife, two teenage boys and a teenage girl, told good stories about the sea, Conrad said. He also was a wizard at a troubleshooting, whether it was repairing mechanical, electrical or plumbing problems aboard a boat, or rigging his television to get a clandestine satellite feed.

Thompson also loved to hunt, and when he couldn't find deer or elk, he went after what he could find. Thompson once lugged a washing machine out of the forest, disassembled it and turned the drum into a barbecue, Conrad said.

"I would buy the tools because I could afford them and give them to Rob because he could use them," Conrad said.

Eder, 21, was majoring in biochemistry and international relations at the University of Oregon. He enjoyed traveling and had boundless energy and enthusiasm, said his uncle, Alan Eder.

The UO student was a deep thinker who brought a thick paperback book titled *Islam* onto the *Nesika.* He had an ongoing skepticism about God, and the book was part of his attempt to solve the perplexing puzzle of who we are and why we are here, Alan Eder said.

He followed his father into commercial fishing and loved the work and the occupations that went with it, including electrician, plumber and weatherman.

"Ben understood well his father's joy and connection when it all went together," Alan Eder said.

Hamrick, 20, was making his first trip to sea. He had a genuine smile and was generous, willing to give anyone the shirt off his back, his friends and relatives said.

"He was just a force for joy," said his uncle, Mike Rolf. "He always had a positive outlook and a good sense of humor, and he will be dearly missed.

Langlot, 34 was engaged to Dawn Davis and had three young children. Langlot's uncle, Louie Modrano, said his nephew liked to smell his daughters' hair and was comforted by their sweet smells.

"Steve loved life, every moment of every day," he said. "His children were his life, and he will always be the best father anyone could ever have."

In the summer, Langlot would head to Alaska to fish, always returning with great stories. Better yet, he always came back with king crab for a feast, Modrano said.

Like all Newport fishermen, the four men aboard the *Nesika* were considered brothers to the men who made their living at sea, Feldner said.

"They're our brothers in arms," he said, "and that's why it hurts so much to lose them."

Bill Wechter
Commercial Fisherman

On Tuesday, December 11, 2001, I left port about the same time everybody else was streaming out around 8 a.m. There was a group of about 40 boats that all trickled out. Everybody had waited until daylight, except for the bigger boats that had left earlier. I was on my boat, the *Gary Lee*, which is 58 feet long; it's a wood troller and crabber. I had two people on the boat: Mark DeBrall and Red Coberly. Red was on the boat just to steer, he wasn't a crabber. I was actually setting the pots; I wanted to make sure the pots were laid correctly and the buoys were trailing.

The *Nesika* was a few boats ahead of me leaving to go fishing. As you leave the jetties, the whistle buoy is about three-quarters of a mile west of the jetties. There's a green can that's a marker that's about halfway between the end of the jetties and the whistle buoy. I turned north at the green can and was headed toward the lighthouse. I was going to begin setting gear around Little Creek Cove. Rob, on the *Nesika*, started to set gear at about 20 fathoms. Rob had gone out to the whistle buoy and headed north. I was setting gear in about 17 – 18 fathoms off of Little Creek Cove – that's on the beach, and I came upon the *Nesika*. Well, I saw a boat upside down, I saw the aluminum and at first I thought it was a sport boat.

I called the Coast Guard right away and I asked if they had an overdue sport boat or vessel charter. They said no, and I said, "Well, we've got one upside down. We've got an overturned crabber." Then when I got closer, I saw it was the *Nesika*. It was laying flat in the water at that point with the stern pointing toward the beach and the bow pointing to the west. I gave the Coast Guard my latitude and longitude. When I got close to the boat, there was a debris trail that headed to the southwest.

There were two bodies in the debris trail just to the southwest of the boat, that were floating face down. There was also a rain boot floating on the water, a tote lid just south of the bodies, and a couple of five-gallon buckets just north of the bodies, but generally the debris trail headed to the southwest.

The body, well, the body I called "number one," was the one closest to the *Nesika*. That guy was in orange rain pants and a sweatshirt, arms extended, face down. Short hair, reddish brown, cut straight across the bottom. The other body had full raingear on, yellow, with dark black hair, long. I wasn't surprised that the bodies were still floating, as there was air in their chest, and air in the raingear would act as flotation. There was no "natural" movement of the bodies; a wave would wash over the bodies and then they'd go down and then they'd pop up 15 seconds later in a different location.

The *Lillie M* and the *Jaka-B* arrived on the scene to help search. I think the *Lillie M* showed up first and then the *Jaka-B*. Then the Coast Guard showed up; first of all the 52-foot *Victory* and then the 47-foot boat appeared and the chopper got there after the lifeboats. I don't know why it took so long for the helicopter to arrive; they must have taken the time to do a preflight check before they left. You'd think they'd have been ready to leave as soon as they got the call, given that it was the first day of crab season.

Once they were all there, the *Lillie M*, the *Jaka-B*, the two Coast Guard cutters and me, we were all looking in the debris field. I still had 200 pots on the boat and given there were four vessels there, and the swells were pretty rough, I decided to leave and get the rest of the pots off my boat. I had seen the bodies maybe for only five minutes before they disappeared for good, and then I could no longer locate them. I was going to try and buoy stick them, you know, grab the bodies with a buoy stick with a hook and drag them to the boat, but they were gone. I was in the Coast Guard as a swimmer. I had the ability to go in the water, but I didn't have anyone on board the boat who could safely maneuver the boat while I was in the water, and trust to get everybody back on.

Shawn Bertini on the *Jaka-B* went "up" the debris line, meaning Shawn headed southwest from where I found the *Nesika* upside down. Shawn found the tangle of pots where the *Nesika* had turned over. You know, from where the tangle of pots was found, and from where I found the *Nesika* – the accident must have just happened. The current was moving at about 2 miles an hour, and they were only a short distance away from where the pots had dumped. Those guys weren't in the water very long.

All afternoon, still in the search were the *Lillie M* and the *Jaka-B* and at least one of the Coast Guard cutters, plus a private helicopter showed up, too. By this time, the *Nesika* had drifted north of the lighthouse on Yaquina Head.

You know, there should have been a "bird" in the air immediately. The chopper should have been there before the Coast Guard boats got there. I had an interview with the Coast Guard a couple of days after the accident. I really laid into them. I told them there were 50 crab boats on the water that day, heavily loaded with pots, and that it was ridiculous not to have a Coast Guard helicopter in the air.

Chief Warrant Officer John Dodd
United States Coast Guard

For Stations Yaquina Bay and Depoe Bay, December 11, 2001 started out as many winter days on the Oregon Coast. Boats were moving, setting crab gear for the new season. The Yaquina Bay Bar was actually not too bad, considering the offshore winds of 20 to 30 knots, and the swell running anywhere from 10 to 14 foot.

The day started early with a "bar standby" for the 82 foot *F/V Grumpy J* around 0140. If the conditions are severe enough for these proud fishermen to ask us to "standby," we will be there. If a situation does arise during the crossing, then my folks are already on station, ready to assist. It is just a little better way to do business.

The Motor Lifeboat *47266* and the Motor Lifeboat *Victory* were on station at 0300 waiting to stand by for the *F/V Grumpy J* as she came across. During the standby, the condition of the bar is checked several times by making passes in and out bound along the buoy line, and then just sitting at the tips of the jetties. The tips of the jetties are called the "Jaws," because if you mess up in this area or something goes wrong, there is not a lot of room. Those rocks can close down on your vessel real quick, just like teeth. The *Grumpy J's* crossing proceeded without incident, and all vessels were inside the bar safely.

With the oncoming of sunrise, the Motor Lifeboats returned to the station, quickly shifted out crews, and returned to the bar. Many boats, the *F/V Persistence*, *Captain Andy*, *Lillie M*, *Nesika* and the *Footloose*, to name a few, were transiting the bar that morning, due to the fact that an agreement on the crab price had been reached.

You watch the boats cross the bar and you watch every aspect very closely. Sometimes I am sure the local fishermen would say we watch too closely. But we live with these men and women. I have received confidential calls from worried wives as to the whereabouts of their husband's boats and asked me to make sure they get home safe. I take this charge very seriously. The boats and the people here in Newport are very special to me; they have welcomed my family and me very warmly.

At 10:44 a.m., the *F/V Gary Lee* reported seeing the hull of a capsized vessel approximately one nautical mile off of Yaquina Head Lighthouse. When a report comes in like this, many things happen in a short amount of time. First, the search and rescue (SAR) alarm is pushed: This activates the first and second boat crews to launch the "ready" boats. A motor lifeboat can be launched in under five minutes, usually under three minutes. The second is to notify the next higher Operations Center of the reported situation, in this case the Operations Center located at Group North Bend, Oregon. With this type of notification, a helicopter is automatically requested to assist in the search. The third is to assume your watch station. On this particular day BMC Mike Mahoney had the Command Duty Officer and assumed control of our Operations Center to coordinate vessels and response efforts at the local level. When multi-resources respond from several different units, the Group Operations Center in North Bend assumes the role of Search and Rescue Mission Controller. They are very well versed in planning and coordinating all aspects of executing a search.

By this time we had vessels responding from Station Yaquina Bay in Newport, Station Depoe Bay in Depoe Bay, helicopter support from the Aviation Support Facility located at the Newport Airport, and rescue beach vehicles from both units. I knew Chief Mahoney had things well in hand; SK2 Hanson and I took my truck to the Agate Beach area, just south of Yaquina Head, to conduct a beach search for any persons that might have washed up. When we arrived, a squall was passing through, visibility was reduced and the cold rain driven by the wind stung at our faces as we made our way to the water's edge. This initial search revealed nothing, not even debris. We discussed possible drift scenarios as we worked our way up the beach back to my truck. I requested a confirmation on the direction of the nearshore currents. We were informed the "set" was to the northwest and were directed to move to the Moolack and Beverly Beach areas.

As we moved north along Highway 101, we caught glimpses of all the rescue units and the local fishing vessels assisting in the effort. Bits and pieces were heard over the radio about possibly seeing a person in the water and debris being recovered. I knew with this many resources responding so quickly it would be just a matter of time before we found the men. My heart would jump and fall at every radio report. There is nothing better then rescuing a person in peril and returning them safely to their loved ones. It was just a matter of time.

Approximately one hour had passed, and BMC Mahoney called and requested me to return to base. By the sound of his voice there was something happening back at the unit. It was becoming rapidly apparent to me that this case was not going to be concluded as soon as anticipated, but I still believed it was just a matter of time before the first person would be located.

When I entered the Operations Center BMC Mahoney gave me a look that told me "We need to talk in private." Curious, I knew the Search and Rescue aspect was being taken care of. The unknown comes into effect when you are dealing with families and high interest news issues such as the *F/V Nesika* case. Chief Mahoney and I had already established who would conduct which duties in a major case such as this. He would control the Search and Rescue units and I would assist the members of the family and field any outside media requests, as well as work with the Group North Bend Command and Control, discussing the case status and where we were heading. I was told family members were starting to arrive.

Every Commanding Officer handles these types of situations differently. There is a remarkable struggle that takes place as to how much you are going to open yourself up to this type of situation. The easy way out is to isolate yourself, tell everyone to go home and they will be notified when situations change. Cold, but, easy. The other side of the spectrum is to completely become involved in the families' grief and forget your responsibilities. That's very nice, but you lose your focus on the situation as a whole. I had to determine where in between those extremes I would allow myself to go. How would I want to be treated?

There were several people from the Newport Fisherman's Wives Association who were indispensable to me. The first was Ginny Goblirsch. She knew who the families, friends and support people were. The second was Connie Kennedy, also invaluable in helping me to understand the dynamics of this close community. I appreciated their assistance so very much. They made it clear; they were there to do whatever was needed, not to take over, but to assist and assure that everyone was being taken care of, including me.

As the minutes passed by and there was no change in the situation, it was becoming very evident we were now working against time and the cold waters of the Pacific Northwest. What we did not know was how the fishermen were dressed when they went into the water. Were they wearing exposure coveralls, dry suits, or jeans and a T-shirt? All gave you a different answer to the question that was on everyone's mind: how long. . . . . .

Part of my role was to watch and evaluate others, deciding what I needed to let them know about and when to let them hear it from me. Knowing the news I might bring could invoke a myriad of responses, I had to be ready, but not overreact to their response. I could be sympathetic, but I could not let my emotions out of hand, or interfere with the execution of this case.

I watched Michele Longo Eder closely, a very strong and dedicated woman making phone calls, "handling it."

She was ensuring all was being done that could be, but I could see that inside of that hardened exterior was a woman whose family was in peril. Her husband, Bob, was on the *F/V Michele Ann* on scene, assisting in search efforts, and she was as scared as the others. She did not have the luxury to let her feelings show then. A very impressive person.

As I dealt with the families and reporters, I also had a station to run. It was obvious this case was going to last through the night, if we did not have any new developments soon. At this time we conducted an "all hands" recall of all station personnel. After everyone had reported back onboard, I informed them of the current situation, the families we had here, and the current security level as to any new persons found onboard. The food service staff went straight to work, ensuring everyone had meals. The boat crews made sure they knew their scheduled underway times and settled down to make sure they were properly rested. I was very proud of the crews of Depoe Bay and Yaquina Bay Stations. They worked together very smoothly, checking and rechecking that proposed search patterns were correct, and would not place our boat crews in hazardous areas. The people that were not on watch played pool with some of the kids of the families waiting for news. Our people made them feel welcome and watched over them.

The hours went by and there were still no new developments. I had several conference calls with Group North Bend as to the expectations of this search effort. The system we used was one of checks and balances. Group North Bend ensured I knew the real expectations of the search efforts, and I assured Group that they knew the real time situation I had with the local community I served.

The helicopter crews would be hitting their maximum allowed time for flying shortly after dark, but the Motor Lifeboat crews would continue searching through the night. The case would be re-evaluated in the morning. This information was presented to the families from the group Commander, Captain John Miko, during a conference call later in the afternoon on the 11th. Captain Miko was a good mentor for me. He allowed me to express myself passionately, explain my feelings about the case, and then gave me his views of the situation as he saw it. He and his staff were very compassionate with me as the senior Coast Guard representative on scene, and supported me in all my decisions. I knew I was not alone in dealing with this situation.

After the phone conference with the Group Commander, the families departed. I made them the promise that if anything changed, I would personally call them. And then there was silence. I sat and looked around my office and tried to understand what had just transpired for the last several hours. I replayed the scenes I had witnessed throughout the afternoon in my head and started to allow myself to get pulled in to it all. "Stop it!" I said to myself. I did not have that luxury. I still had other crab vessels working. I still had a case going on and associated issues that went with it: personnel and logistics. I still had to talk to the press; three TV interviews to conduct and two phone interviews.

I busied myself reviewing back over all the search patterns that had been executed. I contacted Group North Bend to verify their intention and discuss issues to ensure nothing was being missed. Everything was working as planned. Boat crews were swapping out, people were getting fed and people were sleeping. As I walked through the halls at the station I could perceive the mood changing from my crew. They now knew that time was against us. Most of these young adults were new to the Coast Guard. They had never had to face the reality of how serious and what it is they do for a living. For some, they also had to face the fact that we are mortal and sometimes we lose. That is a very sobering thought to an 18 or 19-year-old.

Heck, it was a sobering thought for a 40-year-old.

I discussed the situation with the Group Commander and Group Operations Officer one more time. Our feeling was we would continue to search until all aspects had been covered. After that time the Group Commander, with the concurrence of the Operations Center located in Seattle, Washington, would make the unenviable decision to suspend the search pending further developments.

Through out the night the Motor Lifeboats came and went. The cooks kept the coffee and food hot. I made several trips to the beach to watch my boats through the dark squall-filled night, and to search for whatever might come ashore.

Shortly before sunrise, the beach crews and helicopter crews launched again for a first light search. Two things had happened: the beaches were being searched again, and through the black night, the position of the *Nesika* had been lost. Debris was quickly found. An empty survival suit and the hull of the *Nesika* were approximately 50 yards off Beverly Beach. A representative from the Coast Guard Marine Safety Office in Portland was on scene to assist, once the vessel came ashore. The *F/V Nesika* came ashore around 0700. A search of the vessel was conducted and none of the crew was found on board. As most of the fuel had been expelled during the time it took the *Nesika* to drift north, I was not overly concerned about a pollution problem. Once the Marine Safety Office representatives were on scene, they would do the boarding of the beached vessel to assess the risk the vessel posed to the environment.

The first light crews were finishing their searches. I knew that the Group Commander was coming to the station to address the families of the lost fishermen. Due to the time that had elapsed, I knew the search was no longer a search for survivors, but a recovery mission.

Captain Miko and Commander Martino arrived at the Yaquina Bay Station and we met in private. The Captain explained the process that he has to go by, one that I had been involved with several times over 22 years of service, but it never was easy. As Captain Miko prepared to meet the families, Commander Martino asked how we were holding up. I think being tired and the overall realization that this was not going to turn out the way we wanted was weighing heavy on my heart. My eyes welled up. "Stop it," I told myself. I now had to be especially strong. I turned and looked out the window, but the Commander knew.

Captain Miko addressed the families eloquently, in a sympathetic but business-like fashion. "This search is being suspended pending any further developments." It was said. I believe everyone appreciated his willingness to be there in person and his honesty. On behalf of all the families, Mrs. Eder thanked Captain Miko for the exceptional efforts and support by the men and women of our unit. Overcome with emotion, I had to leave the room.

The Motor Lifeboats and helicopters were stood down and ordered to return to base. The families left the station, as did the Group Commander and Operation Officer. As our motor lifeboats and Search and Rescue vehicles returned, they were fueled, rinsed and re-stocked. I met the crews on the dock around 11:15 a.m. on the 12th of December and thanked them for the great job.

Ginny Goblirsch
Oregon Sea Grant Marine Extension Agent
President, Newport Fisherman's Wives

Tuesday morning, December 11, I was driving down the bay front. I had been at Englund Marine at a meeting with some fishermen. As I left Englund's, my cell phone rang. It was Don Mann, the Manager at the Port of Newport. He said, "Ginny, where are you?" And I said, "Well, just driving down the bay front." "Come over right away," Don said. I went over to the Port office and walked in. They had the marine radio on, turned to the Coast Guard channel. I heard conversations between Coast Guard cutters and the station regarding a search underway for a vessel which had capsized. "What boat?" I asked. And Don looked at me and said, "The *Nesika*." "My God!" I yelled. "Does Michele know?" And of course, they didn't know.

I raced out to my car to go directly to the Coast Guard station. I tried to call Michele at her office as I was driving. The receptionist said that she was unavailable, so I said, "Please tell her I'm at the Coast Guard station." My assumption was that Michele had heard the news and that she had friends or colleagues with her.

I went to the Coast Guard station and went into the communications room. The Station Commander, John Dodd, was not there. I was told Dodd was out helping with the search on the beach. I got a quick update that the *Nesika* had capsized, that they were running search patterns now and nobody had yet been found. Bob had been notified and he was on his way north to the site with the *Michele Ann*. I didn't know how far away Bob was. I asked if I could please stand there quietly and listen to the search in progress and they said "Of course." So I did that. The person in charge was a young officer.

About 15 minutes after I arrived, Michele came in. Michele walked up to me and said, "What's going on?" I said, "Michele, it's the *Nesika.*" Her face paled and she said, "My God – Ben's on the boat." At that point, it hit me even harder because I hadn't known Ben was on board. Michele became quite agitated. I took her down the hall away from the communications area, because seeing Michele was upsetting the Coast Guard people that were trying to coordinate the search. Mike Mahoney, in charge at the station, came in and said he felt it would be helpful if family members stayed out of the communications room. While it was difficult, because I knew Michele wanted to be right there, listening to every minute, I also knew that the first priority at that time had to be the search, and hopefully the rescue, that was going on. So I told the Coast Guard guy that I would talk to Michele and I did.

She went down on her knees at a desk in one of the offices and prayed momentarily. Michele and I then talked a little bit. At that time we did not know when the boat had capsized. For some reason, I was under the impression that it had just happened. The report I had heard was that a boat had come upon the *Nesika* capsized in the water, and it sounded like the accident had happened a very short time ago. I though that the chances of retrieving Ben and the others in good shape seemed fairly good at that time, but as the morning wore on, of course, the reality sunk in with every passing moment that they would not be found alive.

Other family members started coming to the Coast Guard station. I don't know how they were notified. I don't believe I called anybody else besides Michele. At that time I wasn't aware of who else was on the boat besides Ben, and then Michele told me. Trish, Rob Thompson's wife, came in and her sister and her sister's husband and some of the kids. The vice principal or one of the counselors at the high school brought Rob and Trish's daughter over. Commander Dodd's office was made available to us and all the families. The Coast Guard did a great job that day and night, giving us regular updates on how the search was coming.

Michele asked me to call some people, which I did. Return phone calls for her came on my cell phone. I essentially began acting as the "go-between" for the Coast Guard and the families. We wanted to limit the people in the station to just immediate families. The Coast Guard felt they had somebody in me that could help make decisions and give the okay on who was appropriate to come in and who wasn't, and handle the incoming phone calls.

I remember early on that Michele wanted very much to get another helicopter there on scene. Connie and I helped coordinate hiring Evergreen Helicopters to come and be a part of the search. Initially, Michele wanted to go on the helicopter. I kept thinking I wasn't sure that was such a good idea, but maybe more eyes looking would be an asset. Michele was trying to be rational and make good decisions and I admired her for what she was trying to do. Ultimately, the helicopter did join in the search, but to no avail.

The Coast Guard supplied the families with food all during the day, and during the evening gave regular updates on how the search was going. Other members of Fishermen's Wives helped out—Maria Rock, Chris Carley and so many others. Connie Kennedy contacted several clergy members, some at families' requests, some at our own. Mitch Watney, the pastor at the Atonement Lutheran Church, came over to the station and just sat with the families, to provide any kind of emotional or religious support they might want. I helped Michele make some phone calls. I answered lots of incoming calls, giving out information to family members as we knew it. All I could say was "The search is on and nobody has been found." All day and into the night, that was the answer: "The search is still on, but nobody's been found."

Early in the evening, right after dark, Bob came to the

Coast Guard station. The *Michele Ann* had come in to port and I was very glad to see that Bob was off the boat. I was worried about him being out there at sea in that state, and what he must have been feeling. And I'm sure it was a huge relief to Michele to have him there. Then Michele and Bob went home and the other families went home and I went home around 10 or 11 p.m. that night.

The next morning, on the 12th, the commander from the North Bend station came up to Newport to be with the families, to give them a briefing, and to say that the search was officially called off. It was hard to take. The enormity of it all, while it was kind of sinking in, it really hadn't with any of us. I think we were all in shock. I went back to my office after Michele and Bob and the other families left and had many calls from the media waiting for me to call them back. I thought about it. I didn't want to talk to the media, but then I thought maybe I should call, because somebody needed to give them an account of what had happened in a reasonable and balanced way. I didn't want the media to get their story by grabbing somebody from the tavern or just cruising the docks. So I did that. The papers reported accurately that the crew were highly qualified, and that the was boat well-maintained. So that's one of the big lessons I learned, too. The first lesson was having somebody at the Coast Guard station to help the families and be the go-between with the Coast Guard. The second lesson was to have somebody to talk to the media. Talking to the media that first day was just not something that I could do.

Kim Lehmann

On December 11, 2001, I was at work at the travel agency I own. Ginny Goblirsch called me. She said that the *Nesika* was down, lost, I think she said, and that Michele had asked that I be called before I heard it on the radio. When I asked where Michele was, Ginny said Michele was at the Coast Guard station. I hung up the phone, got in my car and I went over there.

When I went to the door, they let me in. A Coast Guardsman came through with me and made sure that I was "okay." I went back and in this room were about three or four women. There were some family members out in the waiting area sitting around. When I came in the room, Michele was in "attorney mode," pacing the floor, on the phone. She was trying to get another search helicopter down to the Newport area. We hugged as she was talking on the phone. I asked her if Mary had been called. Michele said she hadn't been able to get through to Mary, her line was busy. I wanted to know if there was anything I could do. Michele told me to go to her house and get her address book and the personnel files for their crew men, because she needed phone numbers to notify their families and crew member's families.

And so that is what I did. I went to her house. When I went into the garage, where everyone always went in and out of their house, I thought, I know I have seen her take the key from someplace, but what if I can't remember? And I couldn't remember. And then I walked in the garage and all of a sudden I just had the answer; it was just there. And I got the key and went in and found her address book and the crew files. I took Sally their dog for a walk, because she'd been in the house all morning, and I worried she might not get out again that day. I went back to the Coast Guard station, and brought the address book and crew files back to Michele.

Michele was still pacing up and down. She was talking

on two phones at the same time, a cell phone, and a Coast Guard phone. She tried to reach Mary again and this time, Mary answered. Michele told Mary briefly, gently, what had happened and then handed the phone to me. Mary said to me, "'We think we lost Ben?' Is that what Michele thinks? Please, give me a break, here." And I said, "Well, she's in 'attorney mode,' and when she goes in 'mother mode,' she is going to have a complete breakdown. But she's doing what she needs to do now." Mary asked, "Should I come down? What should I do?" I told Mary, "I think you should be prepared to spend the next day." I got off the phone and Michele said, "Would you go back to our house? Somebody needs to be at the house all day to handle the phones." So I went back to Michele's house. It was about 1 p.m. then. At first I thought she was just giving me something to do, so that I could feel like I was helpful. Otherwise, you just stand around; you just wonder "what can I do?" And so I went to her house and I paced.

I started washing the dishes in the sink and picked up the living room. The living room had a blanket on the sofa and you could tell somebody had been laying there. It was so hard to see that—a reminder of when their life had been peaceful, and would never be again. I started getting phone calls. One man called and asked for Michele, and I said she was at the Coast Guard station. He said, "Well, I understand that they can't find the *Nesika*." And, I said, "Yes, the *Nesika* went down." And he said, "So, have they pulled it out? Is it on the beach or where is it?" And I said, "Well, they're still searching for it." And he said, "You mean they can't find it?" And I said, "No, it went down." And then he said that he was the brother of the captain and that he heard that it was just lost, that they had only lost communication or something. And I said, "No, they know that it went down. I am really sorry." And he said, "Well, would you tell Michele to call me?" I assured him that I would.

Bob's cousin, Mark, called and was distraught, of

course. And then I got a call from a woman up in Seattle. She said that she heard that the boat went down and her son was on it. She said she heard that there were two of the crew that were saved, and she wanted to know if her son was one of them. About this time I started looking out the kitchen window. I told the woman I was really sorry to have to tell her this, but so far they hadn't found any of the crew, and that they were still searching. Now I realized Michele had a reason for sending me back to the house—and it wasn't just to make me feel useful.

As I looked out their kitchen window that faced out on the ocean, I saw there was Bob and the *F/V Michele Ann* and a Coast Guard boat and they were going back and forth. At first, I thought, it looked like it was a frantic back and forth and back and forth. And then as I watched, I realized they were in a set pattern, that one boat would go up and come back and then the other would, and the boats searching kind of wove back and forth. It was an eerie, frantic dance. And it was so painful to watch, it just felt so desperate. You wanted to run out there and try to help. I picked up the binoculars that were there on the window sill. I kept watching, waiting for them to pull somebody up out of the water, but the boats just went back and forth and back and forth all afternoon. I don't know how long I watched them.

You know, it was a sunny day. It wasn't a stormy day; it wasn't what you would expect the weather to be when you hear a vessel has capsized.

And then Michele called and said that Dylan was driving home and that he should be there soon. I don't even know what time it was, but I know that it was later in the day, maybe 6 p.m. Michele said she and Bob were going to be coming home. She asked me if before I left, would I please close all the blinds on the ocean side of the house. I thought, What a stroke of brilliance. She didn't want Dylan to see the Coast Guard out there doing the search where the boat went down. I was astounded that she could think such clear thoughts, that you would protect your son from this kind of an experience, and try to buffer him from any of the pain that you could possibly spare him. I knew that when she got out of "attorney mode," it was going to be devastating for her, but it was amazing to watch her. I don't think it was just her attorney training. I think that's just Michele. You hear about people that rise to the occasion, but she was so clear and so businesslike, taking care of all the details. And it was incredible to watch.

I'll never forget the boats, ever, doing that search. First of all, I was in shock when I realized what they were doing and then I realized there was such a rhythm and a purpose to it. Maybe that's part of what they learn being in the fishing industry and the Coast Guard, certainly. But to have this big Coast Guard boat and then the smaller *Michele Ann* be perfectly in tune, back and forth, weaving back and forth.

I don't think that there was any time that day that I believed that the men could be lost, really lost. I looked through the binoculars and every single second I expected to see a boat stop and see Bob throw life jackets or pull people up out of the water. I never for a minute thought that they wouldn't find them. I had no idea how long you could realistically even expect people to be alive after being in the water. But I knew that Bob knew, and that really, really was upsetting to me, and probably Michele knew, too, but Bob really knew and he was out there. Watching the *Michele Ann*, going back and forth, you could just feel a father searching for his son and he wasn't going to give up. Bob kept going long past when he had to know there was no hope. But then you think that maybe the men got washed up on the beach. The other thing that was crazy was that where the *Nesika* capsized it was so close to shore. Where the boats were searching wasn't miles out to sea. You just think, "Why couldn't they swim in?" It's ignorance, on my part, I know, because you hear about hypothermia and how fast that happens. Watching Bob search was the most heartbreaking thing I have ever seen.

How many things I learned from that day. Things I didn't want to know; things that scare me; things I may end up having to use some day. And yet I'm grateful that I had the opportunity to hopefully share some of their burden, share some of their pain. Something like that is too much for anybody to carry alone.

Newport News Times
Ben Eder

Benjamin Alan Eder was born in Coos Bay, OR on March 22, 1980. He died on December 11, 2001, lost at sea along with three other men, Rob Thompson, Steve Langlot, and Jared Hamrick, while fishing for Dungeness crab aboard the *F/V Nesika.*

Until 1986, Ben lived in Port Orford, OR, after which he moved with his family to Newport, OR. Ben attended local schools and graduated from Newport High School in 1998 as a salutatorian.

For his freshman and sophomore years, he studied at Reed College, in Portland, OR, taking a leave of absence during the 2000-2001 school year to travel for six months in South America. Upon his return, he enrolled in September 2001 as a junior at the University of Oregon in Eugene, with a double major in biochemistry and international relations.

Dedicated to life-long learning, Ben signed all his letters to family and friends "Learn, learn, learn!" At the time of his death, on his nightstand was a biochemistry text and *A History of Knowledge.* In his backpack, salvaged from the hull of the vessel, was a copy of Barron's *Islam* and a recent issue of *The Economist.*

Ben loved to travel and did so extensively. In addition to traveling across the US several times and to Brazil, Panama, Chile, Uruguay, Argentina and Bolivia while in South America, Ben had traveled to Israel, British Columbia, the Dominican Republic, Mexico, Costa Rica, and Venezuela.

He is survived by his parents, Bob Eder and Michele Longo Eder and his brother Dylan Eder, all of Newport, OR; his grandparents Edie Eder of Los Angeles, CA and Joe and Betty Longo of Worcester, NY; his aunts and uncles Lorna and Alan Eder and Harvey Eder of Los Angeles, CA and Linda and Marc Longo of Milford, NY;

his love, Phoebe Morris; many cousins and innumerable friends.

Memorial services were held on December 15 in Newport, Oregon.

Newport News Times
Rob Thompson

Robert "Rob" Thompson, 40, of South Beach died as the result of a boating accident on Dec. 11, 2001.

He was born in Portland on Feb. 3, 1961 to Carl and Sharon Thompson. He married Patricia "Trish" Garrett in Siletz on July 25, 1993.

He was a commercial fisherman, working for 10 years as a skipper aboard the *F/V Ms. Law*, for four years as skipper and deckhand aboard the *F/V Cap Elza*, and most recently, as skipper of the *F/V Nesika*.

He was a member of the All Nations Lutheran Church and enjoyed fishing, picking mushrooms, cabinet making, creating, inventing, and cooking.

Survivors include his wife, Trish Thompson; sons Tyson Burton and Joshua Thompson, both of South Beach; a daughter, Katie Burton of South Beach; his parents, Carl and Sharon Thompson of Vancouver, Wash.; and brothers John Thompson of Gresham and Tom Thompson of Beaumont, Texas.

Newport News Times
Jared Hamrick

Jared Allen Hamrick, 20, of the Newport area died as the result of a boating accident on Dec. 11, 2001.

He was born in Eugene on Sept. 9, 1981 to Elizabeth Rolph and Calvin Hamrick.

He enjoyed drawing, skateboarding, sports and playing the guitar.

Survivors include his mother, Elizabeth Rolph of Newport; his father, Calvin Hamrick of Washington; brothers Jacob Hamrick of Newport and Aaron Rolph of Salem; sisters Jessica Hamrick of Eugene, Lisa Johnson of Springfield, Danielle Hamrick of Rainier, Wash., Courtney Parrish of Lake Oswego and Tawnee Rolph of Salem; a nephew, Devon Johnson; nieces Kayla Johnson and Sara Hamrick; grandparents Beth Rolph of Salem and John and Cathy of Hawaii; a great-grandmother, Wilma Rolph of Eugene; his fiancee, Kelly Tryon of Waldport; and several aunts, uncles and cousins.

Memorial services were held.

Newport News Times
Stephen "Steve" Langlot

Stephen J. "Steve" Langlot, 34, of Newport died Dec. 11, 2001, as a result of the capsizing of the fishing vessel *Nesika* off Yaquina Head. He was lost at sea.

He was born in Seattle, Wash., on June 21, 1967.

He was a commercial fisherman.

He graduated from Inglemoore High School in Bothell, Washington, in 1985.

He began working as a chef but soon began fishing out of Kodiak, Alaska, which he pursued for the past 14 years. He was an avid skater and played for the NW Americans in Lynnwood, Wash.

He leaves two daughters, Breigh Justine and Stephanie Rayanne; his fiancee, Dawn Davis, and a son, Mason, all of Newport; his parents, Vicki and John Langlot Jr. of Kenmore, Wash.; sister and brother-in-law, Carol and Shane Scott, and nephews Blake and Derek, all of Wichita, Kansas; a brother, Brian Langlot of McPherson, Kansas, and numerous aunts, uncles and cousins.

Memorial contributions may be made to the Newport Fishermen's Wives, P.O. Box 971, Newport, Ore. 97365 for the children of Steve Langlot.

Tuesday
December 25, 2001

It's Christmas morning.

Two weeks ago today, our son, Benjamin Alan Eder, died. I sit on the sofa in the living room of our home, looking out on the ocean where the *Nesika* capsized on December 11, 2001.

What do I remember of Ben's last days? Ben came home from Eugene very late the evening of December 8, driving two hours to Newport, having finished his final exams at school. I can't remember what we did on Sunday, December 9. Did we all sleep in, eat a leisurely breakfast? I think not. Crab season was about to start, and both Bob and Ben probably went off to work. That evening though, I do recall, because it was the first night of Hanukkah. I grated potatoes and an onion, added a little flour, an egg, and a pinch of fresh parsley to make latkes, as my mother and grandmother had in the generations before me. Ben loved applesauce with his latkes, but we didn't have any, so he went to Safeway and bought some.

I had taken the menorah out from its red velvet case, where I store it on a shelf in the linen closet throughout the rest of the year. It is silver. The "Tree of Life" it's called, with nine branches. Eight branches are for each night of the holiday; the ninth branch, the "shamas," holds the candle that lights the others. As he had done each year, Ben unscrewed the brass candleholders of the menorah and cleaned the wax out. He carefully folded a large square of aluminum foil to place on the kitchen table to catch any drippings from the candles as they burned. Together, we sang the blessing in Hebrew and lit the "shamas."

Ben and I cleaned up the dishes and were about to watch *The Simpsons* at 8 p.m. when Bob entered the house. He was exhausted, but still had to do the grocery shopping to be ready to leave to go crabbing on the *Michele Ann.* Ben and I volunteered to go to the store for him—but not until we watched *The Simpsons*, of course. Ben and I went to Safeway in Bob's truck, taking the list Bob had carefully prepared. Pushing a grocery cart down the bread aisle, Ben stopped and pointed out Richard's favorite kind of bread—country potato. Ben remembered that idiosyncrasy from fishing sablefish with Richard on the *Nesika* this past summer. I laughed, thinking it funny how they all knew each other's preferences. We loaded the groceries in boxes into the back of the truck, drove down to the bayfront to the *Michele Ann*, which was loaded with crab pots and parked at Dock 3.

On the *Michele Ann*, the crab pots were stacked so close to the bulkhead of the cabin that I had to climb six feet up on top of the pots and then jump down onto the deck to get to the door of the cabin. Ben, who was far more nimble than I, climbed up to the wheelhouse. From the dock I handed Ben boxes of groceries and from inside the wheelhouse, he carried them down a ladder into the galley. I then got on board and we both unpacked the boxes. Ben was a whirlwind. Everything was put away efficiently and in its right place. I chuckled, remembering him as a child, doing the same thing for me, coming home from the grocery store. We left the boat, job done, and drove home.

I went to bed, but Bob and Ben stayed up for a while.

The next day, Monday, December 10, I know that Bob and Ben went to work, but I think I left the house after they did. I went to the office, then came home around dinner time. Then Ben came home. He had been out at the shop most of the day, and told me he'd been working on welding a menorah, a gift for his father for Hanukkah. Ben had bought sourdough bread and hummus at the store. I was cooking dinner, making a big bowl of pasta with olive oil and parmesan cheese, and a salad. Ben and I dipped the bread into the hummus and talked while I cooked. We also nibbled on Goldfish crackers, agreeing that they were addictive. We polished off a small bag. Bob wasn't home for dinner. After dinner, I laid on the floor in the dining room and Ben gave me a back rub. I remember yelping with pain and pleasure when Ben hit on a particularly sore spot, and he laughed.

Ben and I watched TV in the living room that evening. He was seated in Bob's favorite black leather chair. We were watching *Boston Public* when Grandma Edie called. Ben talked with Edie a bit, then handed the phone to me. It was so cheerful, I remember, and relaxed; me laying on the sofa, and Ben sitting in his father's chair. When I went to bed, Ben was reading his biochemistry text from college. I was upstairs and was already in my nightgown when Ben yelled up the stairs to me. He asked if it was okay for him to drive my Ford Explorer the next morning. He said he didn't trust being able to get his car started and didn't want to be late for work. I leaned over the upstairs rail to see him and told him it was fine—go ahead and take the Explorer.

That was the last time I ever saw or spoke to my son.

Bob came home sometime after 10 or 10:30 that evening. When he came to bed, Bob told me that he and Ben had sat at the table and talked, eating the rest of the pasta.

Bob was up very early, around 4 a.m. It seemed we had barely been asleep. Bob was checking the weather and making phone calls. I got up to help him get ready to leave. I remember seeing him sitting at the computer, looking at the NOAA weather site. The phone rang; it was another fisherman who, having crossed the bar, gave Bob a report. I think it might have been Mike Retherford. When Bob left the house around 5 a.m., I went back to bed.

Around 6:30 that morning, I heard Ben leaving when he started up the Explorer. It was parked in the carport, close to our bedroom window. I didn't get up to say goodbye.

Two weeks ago today, I had an appointment at my law office with a client at 10 a.m. I was finishing up with the client an hour later when our receptionist handed me a message that Ginny Goblirsch had called and that she was on her way to the Coast Guard Station. I didn't understand the immediate significance of the call. I walked into my office and looked at the phone, knowing one of two things: either a vessel close to us had gone down or one of our boats had gone down. My mind went blank. I didn't know the Coast Guard Station number and I couldn't think of Ginny's cell phone number, but I called the Extension Office where Ginny worked and spoke with Patty Mann. Years ago, Patty had filled in as a substitute legal secretary for me, and I knew and liked her well. I told Patty that I'd just gotten a message from Ginny that she was on her way to the Coast Guard station. I asked Patty if she knew what it was about. Patty said a boat had gone down. I asked her if she knew which boat it was, and, after a pause, she told me it was the *Nesika.* I remember thinking to myself, Oh, Patty, I'm so sorry you had to be the one to tell me. But I didn't say it out loud.

I hung up the phone, got in my car, drove on autopilot to the Coast Guard station, and pulled into a space near the door. I walked in and saw Ginny headed for the Communications Center, which is down a short hallway to the left. Ginny said, "You can't get hysterical, Michele, you can't get hysterical." I wasn't hysterical. I just wanted to know what happened.

The next thing I remember is that I was in a room with phones. I don't know whose office it was. My old friend, Bev Divis, was already there. Trish Thompson, Rob's wife, arrived. Ginny, Becky Leake, Chris Carley, and Connie Kennedy were there. I gave Ginny my parents' phone number and Edie's number so she'd have the contact information. Instead, Ginny called my parents and Edie immediately and told them what happened. I was surprised she'd done that, but I guess, in retrospect, that was okay. I was focused on finding out what had happened, locating Dylan at Whitman College in Walla Walla, Washington, and talking to Bob.

More people began arriving at the Coast Guard station; family members and friends. Coast Guardsmen came in and periodically updated us as to the status of the search. I spread out my "operation" to a couple of offices, had cell phones going, and was making phone contact lists. Another friend of mine arrived, Kim Lehmann. At my request, Kim went to our house to retrieve my folder with all my crew personnel files so I could call their family members. She returned to our home to answer phone calls there. I called our crew's parents, and girlfriends, and talked to them. I had clicked into some space outside of myself that allowed me to deliver such horrific news.

It was probably about an hour after I arrived at the Coast Guard Station before I talked with Bob. I waited for him to call me, but finally, I called him on his cell phone on the boat. Bob said simply, "I couldn't call and tell you." I told him I'd talked with his mother and family, my parents, and that I was trying to locate Dylan. Bob was on the *Michele Ann*, 30 miles south of Newport, and was steaming north to participate in the search, trying to get there as fast as he could.

Although the people at Whitman College were very helpful, from the secretary in the Dean of Students office, to his residence assistant, locating Dylan was a nightmare. They finally found Dylan on campus.

There was nothing worse than my telling Dylan his beloved brother Ben was gone. There's nothing worse I will ever have to do.

School personnel promised to get Dylan on a plane and fly him home, but Dylan insisted on driving instead. His friend, our friend, Leah Brooks, drove and met Dylan halfway, at Woodburn, where he left his car. Leah drove him the rest of the way to Newport, arriving at our home around 10 p.m.

During the day, the Coast Guard station was awash with activity. Periodically, Chief Dodd showed me maps with the grids of where they were searching. I looked at the papers and nodded solemnly. Intellectually I understood what I was looking at, but emotionally it was just a blur of cross-hatched lines on paper. They had everybody out there: the lifeboats, the helicopter, other crab vessels. Bob was on the scene by early afternoon. There were only a few more hours of light, and then after that, the likelihood of finding the men, or even the likelihood of their survival in the water, was severely diminished. The vessel, upside down, floated north, moved by the current. I asked Connie

Kennedy to call Evergreen Helicopter, and when she got them on the phone I hired a private helicopter to join in the search, even though by the time they arrived there was only a couple of hours of light left in the day. I just didn't know what else I could do, except coordinate matters from the Coast Guard Station, and make the phone calls to the families. I never sat down, I never stopped calling, and I never stopped directing people as to how they could help. To stop my activity would mean to acknowledge the reality of what had happened, and that I could not do.

TV cameras arrived, and to my surprise, there seemed to be no security at the door of the Coast Guard station. People came and went. The Coast Guard was very sensitive to making sure that the families had everyone around them that they needed to support them during the search, but the flip side was that any Tom, Dick or Harry could come in and out of the station, including news people. At one point, I saw Dave Campbell, one of Ben's teachers from Newport High School, standing outside the Coast Guard station. Dave had been such a good friend and mentor to Ben. I ran out the front door to talk to him. I didn't realize it, but until Dave saw me, I don't think he understood it was our vessel that was involved, and that Ben had been on board. The names of the men on board had not been publicly released. I was so glad to see him. Dave was the closest person in connection with Ben that I had yet seen. And I realized when I saw Dave, and the enormity of his shock and grief, that seeing people that Ben loved and that loved Ben would be the hardest.

Amber Morris had called her daughter, Phoebe, at Antioch College in Ohio, and explained what happened. Phoebe called me. I gave her my credit card number and told her to get herself a ticket and get on a plane and to get back here right away. She was in disbelief and shock, but she was on her way.

At each juncture, I asked the Coast Guard to let me have input as to the level of search going on. Bar conditions had been getting worse, and there was a possibility that the Coast Guard would have to "draw a vessel" off the search to protect other fishing boats still crossing the local bar. However, bar conditions improved and the "assets" involved in the search for Ben and our men remained the same. That evening, we had a phone update from the Commander out of the North Bend station who was in charge of the rescue operations. We all gathered around the speakerphone in Chief Dodd's office to hear his grim update. I spoke on behalf of the families, thanking the Coast Guard for their efforts.

By the time Bob came in off the ocean, it was 6 or 7 p.m. He parked the boat at Bornstein's and walked up the hill to the Coast Guard station. As he came down a hallway toward me, his eyes were so devoid of life that I thought, My God, I've lost him, too. Bob talked with some of the families with me. We thanked Jake Albinio, the skipper of the motor lifeboat *Victory*. He was white-faced and speechless. We stayed at the station for a while, and then left, going home where we wept and waited for Dylan. Chicken soup, from our neighbor, Bette Ouderkirk, sat on the counter; the first of quarts to arrive. Bob opened all the wood blinds on the ocean side of the house.

"Why are these blinds closed?" he asked me.

"I shut them because I couldn't stand to watch the Coast Guard search," I said.

"They're doing what a civilized society does, Michele."

I had no idea what he meant. "Bob, what do you mean?" I asked.

"We look for our dead," he said.

Dylan arrived home. We heard the garage door open. We went into the night to meet him, and Leah, who had driven him home. We unloaded his bags, which he had taken time to pack before leaving, not knowing if he would be home for a while. Perhaps for good? No. He had packed for just a couple weeks. Leah drove away. Dylan came inside.

It was the third night of Hannukah. The menorah sat on the kitchen table, on the same piece of foil Ben had so carefully folded for me, two nights ago. Before Dylan arrived Bob had said to me, "We'll wait until Dylan comes home. Then we'll light the candles and sing the blessing." I thought that Bob had truly lost his mind to think that Dylan would want to participate in a ritual that most symbolized family, on the very night his brother died. Perhaps Bob, in his grief, was reaching deep into that which has sustained people throughout centuries of sorrow: the maintenance of tradition.

The three of us went into the kitchen. "We waited for you to light the candles," Bob said. Dylan looked at him, then with one wave of his long arm, Dylan knocked the silver menorah off the center of our table. He hit the menorah so hard, it flew in the air, striking the wooden casing under the ocean-facing window, where it then clattered to the floor.

Dylan ran from the kitchen, screaming. His words were indecipherable. Huge sobs were mixed with guttural anger such that I had never heard emanate from his, or any other body. I heard furniture thrown, broken. I didn't intervene. What did a chair, a lamp matter? He ran from his room, out to the garage. I heard more things break. But those were only things. Dylan's heart was broken, and that I could never fix.

As Dylan, Bob and I sat in frozen shock, there was a knock at the door around 11:30 p.m. It was John Ball, father of Leah, Nathan and Johanna, and husband of Sarah. It took great courage for John to come and face us in our terrifying loss. John had loved Ben as a son. His palpable grief pulled me out of my immobile state and into the reality of what had actually happened. Our son was dead.

Bob, Dylan and I all slept together that night. With strength I didn't know I had, I pulled the mattress off our bed, dragged it downstairs and threw it on the floor of Dylan's room. Bob and I slept with Dylan. Bob eventually drifted off to a tortured sleep, but Dylan and I stayed awake, talking about college, his friends, his classes. Sally, our black Lab, slept atop of us. Bob's and Sally's snoring kept us awake and we laughed, but eventually Dylan drifted off, as did I, for an hour or two.

On the morning of Wednesday, December 12, 2001, I got up around 7 a.m., to take Sally out. The feeling of horror upon awakening, knowing that our beloved son Ben was dead, was so sickening that I cannot describe it. Standing outside, right in front of our house, I remember reflecting upon the absurdity of the everyday task of taking the dog outside. I pulled *The Oregonian* from its box, saw that there was a story about the *Nesika*, and I shoved the newspaper back in the box.

While I was standing outside in my flannel nightgown, a large pickup truck pulled in. I didn't recognize it right away and wondered who could be coming up to our house this early in the morning. Out of the truck jumped Shirley Welton, a local restaurant owner whom I had known for many years. She opened the back of her truck and began unloading big platters of food.

"Here," Shirley said, handing me a sliced ham, a platter of meats and bowls of salads. "You're going to need this."

As quickly as I walked into the garage and stored the food in our extra refrigerator, Shirley waved goodbye and left. I was struck dumb by her spontaneous generosity, but as I was soon to learn, it was the beginning of an outpouring of love and support from our family, friends and our community, the likes of which I could never have imagined.

I don't remember how or why we knew to do this, but Bob, Dylan and I got dressed and went to the Coast Guard Station. The gathering was to hear the official announcement from the Coast Guard that the search had been called off. Once I understood that it was a recovery mission, rather than a rescue mission, meaning retrieving dead bodies instead of possible survivors, my heart went stone cold.

When we arrived, the families of our men were already there. The Commander of the Coast Guard Station from Coos Bay was personally present to give us the news. I think it was then that we first learned the *Nesika* washed ashore at Beverly Beach an hour or so earlier. The boat had drifted to the north all night and then the current beached it.

Leaving the Coast Guard Station, Bob and Dylan wanted to go see the boat. Inside, I was horrified and didn't want to go, but mindlessly agreed.

We drove a few miles north along Highway 101, and as we came over a rise, saw what looked like a hundred cars parked on the beach side of the road, along with vans from TV stations equipped with satellite equipment. These people were gawking at our loss. What it is about human nature that compels people to want to see firsthand the deepest and most horrific tragedies of others?

We got out of the car, and in the pelting cold rain, walked about a quarter mile to where the *Nesika* was beached. I could barely stand to look. The bow of the vessel was smashed from bouncing along the bottom of the ocean. The mast was broken. Coast Guard personnel were aboard the vessel. We saw Tom Curry, hired by our insurance company, assessing the damage. We climbed in his truck to escape the rain and talked for a bit, although I don't remember what was said. After a while, we got out of his truck, walked back to our car, and drove home. We had seen what we came to see.

The *Nesika*, washed ashore at Beverly Beach, December 12, 2001

Connie Kennedy arrived at our home sometime that morning and stayed a couple of hours. Peter and Leah Fones from Eugene came, as did "Aunt" Mary Ridings, from Neskowin. Dylan's friend, Leah Brooks, who had driven to meet him the evening before, was there, too. Our friends answered the phone when Bob and I were unable to talk. They answered the door and accepted the massive amounts of food and bouquets of flowers that had begun to arrive.

Around 11 a.m. on Wednesday, that first day after the accident, Ken Lawrenson, from the U.S. Coast Guard Marine Safety Office in Portland, Lt. Tony Sellers, also from the Portland office, and Lt. Bob Beck, from the Coos Bay station, arrived on our doorstep. They had just come from Beverly Beach, where the *Nesika* lay.

We invited them in and sat in our living room; the men seated on the sofas and in the leather chair. I sat on the floor, close to Bob, as they asked questions about what had happened. Bob spoke slowly but clearly, giving detail after detail about the boat and its construction, how it was loaded, what he knew had happened and what he thought caused the accident. A fire burned in our fireplace. Pete and Mary had brought in wood from the carport, but nothing could take the chill from our lives. I served coffee to the Coast Guardsmen and offered them a plate of cookies and chocolates. I distinctly remember being aware that I was acting in a bizarre manner. My son and three other men died and I was pretending to be Martha Stewart.

I could tell the Coast Guard personnel were uncomfortable knocking on our door in the midst of our shock and grief; however, Bob and I understood the necessity for them being there and I didn't find their presence offensive. In addition, we are required to make this report.

As the men talked, all I could think of was that one of the Coast Guard officers was sitting in the black leather chair where Ben had sat reading his biochemistry book just 36 hours before. After what seemed to be an interminable time, and their questions answered and condolences given, they left.

The next day, Jon McKnight, our insurance agent for the boat, and Kurt Gremmert, our insurance company adjuster who had been assigned to the "loss," arrived at our home. They, too, were apologetic for intruding at such a time, but the families of our three crewmen had also suffered an incomprehensible loss, and whose financial needs had to be addressed. Again, we were in our living room, Jon nervously sitting and standing, Kurt perched on the foot stool of the old brown chair where Bob had cuddled the boys on his lap when they were small.

In speaking to Jon and Kurt, we emphasized how important it was to get money to the families immediately. Our crewmen had all been waiting for crab season to start and now, without any income, their families were going to be in a world of hurt. Kurt assured us he would get at least $10,000 to each of the families to meet immediate bills, but Kurt said if the families hired lawyers, he wouldn't be able to issue any more checks. I groaned. I could see the nightmare beginning to unfold: law suits, lawyers, claims. The complexity was overwhelming. Ben and Dylan owned the vessel, but all of us were named assureds on the policy; we would all be sued.

Although I'm sure I'll never know all that Jon had already done to help us, I asked him to do one more thing for me. Kelly, Jared's girlfriend had called several times. She wanted, if it could be found, Jared's blanket. Jared had carried it everywhere with him since he was a child; it was his one remnant of safety, of home, when indeed, at times, he had no home. He and Kelly had slept with the blanket and Jared had taken it aboard the *Nesika* with him.

Had it been found on the boat? Had it washed ashore? Kelly wanted to know.

Jon told me all the gear that remained aboard the vessel was diesel-soaked; that I would not want it; that even if he could find it, the blanket could not be cleaned. But I asked Jon to try and retrieve it for me regardless of the condition it was in. Kelly wanted it, and if I could, I would make sure she had it. Jon agreed to try, and I thanked him.

By Thursday, my mother arrived from New York. Kim had driven three hours to the Portland airport to get her, then driven the three hours back to Newport. Friends of Dylan's, and particularly Esther and Nikki, were the shuttle crew; they kept driving to and from the airport in Eugene, picking up Edie, Alan, Lorna, Harvey and our nephews, who arrived from Los Angeles. Our friends self-arranged shifts to take care of us; Mary took the mornings, Pete and Leah, the afternoons. Many others helped.

In the days after Ben's death, in the midst of all the frenzied activity, the person I was most isolated from was Dylan. He retreated to a place so far deep in himself, in his pain, that I could not reach him. I could feel his anger and much of it was directed toward me. I didn't know why. Dylan didn't want to talk, and Dylan didn't want to be held. He wanted to be left alone, at least by me. Sometimes Dylan wanted only to be with his friends, sometimes only with Ben's friends. Phoebe, having arrived from Ohio, moved throughout our home like a ghost.

Meanwhile, Trish Thompson, Rob's wife, frequently came to our house. Trish knocked on the front door and I would answer it. She was either by herself, or sometimes with one, two or all of her three children. I made sure her children were fed and sent them home with platters of food, passing on what had so generously been given to us. One time Trish came in, looked at me and said, "I am sorry. I just don't know where else to go." Most painfully, Trish also said, "Please don't be angry with Rob. He didn't mean to kill them." Sometimes, her sister, Maggie, was with her; and sometimes her brother, Perry. At one point, I remember Trish sitting on our sofa in the living room with her brother, and by way of making conversation, I asked him what they had been doing before coming over to our house. Trish's brother said matter-of-factly, "Oh, we have just come from the lawyer's office." Then I felt kind of funny. Here I was providing support and comfort as best I could in the face of my own grief, feeding her family and children, while at the same time I knew we were going to be sued. All I could do was the right thing, and that was to help Trish.

In addition to staying touch with Trish and Kelly, Jared's girlfriend, I spoke with Dawn Davis, the fiancé of Steve Langlot, and the mother of his children. I took her call, and in order to get some privacy, sat at the top of the stairs to talk, the half-walls of the tongue and groove fir stairway providing some refuge. Dawn asked if she should take the money from the insurance man. She asked me if she needed a lawyer.

I was in an impossible position. I couldn't give her legal advice, and gently explained why I could not. I told her to listen to me very carefully: "Do everything you need to do to take care of your family, Dawn. We have insurance and this is what it is for."

She pressed me. "What would you do, Michele?"

"I'd hire a lawyer," I told her.

Sometime that week, or perhaps the next, Bob and I took bags of groceries to her home, and sat and visited with Dawn and her children.

I don't know how we kept acting normally. Somehow the house still functioned: food was bought, the garbage got taken out. Mostly, I never left the house except to go to the store after 10 at night. I couldn't stand to see people. I was terrified to see people, just as many were terrified to see us, alternately attracted to, and repelled by our raw grief.

After realizing that the Thompson family hired a lawyer less than 48 hours after the accident, and that I had more or less told Dawn to do the same, I knew I, too, had to mobilize. Kurt Gremmert, the adjuster for our insurance company, recommended Doug Fryer, an attorney in Seattle, to protect us from our own insurance company in the event they tried to refuse us coverage.

So, in the week after Ben's death, other than late night forays for groceries, the only trips I made were to my law office to see Pete Gintner and Rick Diaz—friends of mine, and lawyers I worked with. Pete and Rick, on the day of the accident, frustrated by not having any way to help, had gone to Yaquina Head. They climbed the rocks and cliffs and beaches just to the north, searching against hope they would find one of our men, maybe injured or dead, washed ashore or pounded onto the rocks. "You should have seen Rick, Michele," Pete told me. "He did everything he could."

Pete had come directly to the Coast Guard Station the day of the accident. He looked as if he was about to explode, wanting to help. I knew he would be tortured watching me suffer, so I asked him to go out to our shop on the Bay Road. Our shop phone number was the only one listed under our names in the phonebook. Our home phone was unlisted.

One sane voice in all of the comings and goings was Ginny Goblirsch. After giving us a day alone on Wednesday, she came by on Thursday, December 13, to discuss a memorial service. Some of the men's families were from out of town; they were here now, and if a memorial service was going to take place, they wanted it to happen that weekend. Ginny did not want to push us into making decisions, but asked, "What do you think about a community memorial service?" We thought that was a good idea. Arrangements were made with the Nazarene church, the largest venue in town and with Mitch Watney, a Lutheran minister, to preside. A Catholic priest would be present for the Langlot family. Trish's sister, Maggie, worked at the Best Western, and the manager, Steve Cockrell, was our neighbor. They made arrangements for a reception to be held at the hotel after the memorial service.

Ginny launched the Fishermen's Wives into action. I really have no idea how she and Maria Rock, Chris Carley, Connie Kennedy, Heather Mann and many, many others did it, but they arranged for the church, got the announcements out, had programs printed, met with ministers, and asked several fishermen to serve as ushers for the service.

Each family wrote a short paragraph about their loved one for the program. Ginny asked that each family choose a song to be played at the service. When it came to choosing music for Ben, my mind went blank. I think it was Friday morning when Bob came downstairs after his shower and said he wanted the song "Comes A Time" by Neil Young. He asked if I was familiar with it. I wasn't, but I trusted that whatever Bob chose was right. And it was. When I heard the words, the song reminded me of Ben and Bob together, when Ben was very young and Dylan just a baby.

Comes a time when you're drifting
Comes a time when you settle down
Comes a light, feelings lifting
Lift that baby right up off the ground.
You and I, we were captured
We took our souls and we flew away
We were right, we were giving
That's how we kept what we gave away.

In life, as in death, the issue of religion is always troublesome. Here we were, Jews, about to memorialize our son in what was arguably the most conservative Christian church in the area. The pastor was the father of a good friend of Dylan's. But the thought of Ben being memorialized in a Christian church gave us the shivers, and we cast about for a solution.

On Friday at noon, Bob and his brother Alan, met with Pastor Mitch Watney about their concerns for an ecumenical service. Ginny was there, too, to act as mediator, if necessary. Since there was a Catholic priest, and a Lutheran minister on the altar, rather than trying to round up a rabbi, we decided that Alan would speak, representing the spiritual side of our family. Peter Jordan, Ben's best friend from grade school to college, also spoke. The depth of Peter's loss is so profound. Bob's grief is so raw; he is an open wound. But I am most afraid for Dylan. He has lost his anchor.

I depended on Alan for everything that I could not talk to my husband about. My grief, my worries, Alan shouldered it all. I still can't sleep, and stay up until all hours not wanting to go bed because I am terrified of waking up in the morning knowing that I will have to face the horror all over again. I'm in an unending cycle of grief and terror.

As friends streamed in and out of the house, one evening is particularly vivid in my mind: the night Ben's friends from Reed College came to our home. It was two evenings after Ben had died.

The Reed students had placed a journal in the college chapel, and many people wrote precious remembrances of Ben. Fifteen of his friends drove from Portland to Newport, all crashing at Rita and Warren Jordan's home. The Jordans had always been Ben's second home. Late afternoon on Thursday, Rita called, wanting to know if this would be a good evening for the kids to come and see us. I invited them all to come over at dinnertime.

Rita told me they had been cooking all afternoon to bring us food. They arrived with pans of lasagna and their great big hearts, full of their love for Ben. We sat in the living room that evening; young people wall-to-wall on the floor, sofa and in chairs. It was "standing room only." Other people stopped by: Tom Branford, Rick and Nicki Price. Everyone in the room told stories and shared memories of Ben. Someone mentioned "The Big Lebowski" party Ben organized in the Chem lab, which involved the drinking of many White Russians. Another girl spoke of Ben driving her to the coast to see her first ocean sunset.

The room vibrated with such warmth and love. By their sheer force of will, Ben was alive in that room again, and we could all feel him. It was good for Dylan and it was the first time I saw Dylan "come alive"; the first time I had hope that Dylan might recover.

People kept appearing from out of nowhere, to help us. I remember running into Mark McConnell in our front hallway. Mark's wife, Cindy, had been Ben and Dylan's Spanish teacher all three years in high school. Mark asked me what I needed. I blurted out the first thing I could think of: a couple of cases of bottled water. He said, "Okay," and within the hour brought me two cases of bottled water. Another friend, Rose, who lived down the street, said to call her if I needed anything. Someone sat on one of my mother's knitting needles that day and broke it; she was also out of cigarettes. I picked up the phone and called Rose. I told her I needed a No. 10 knitting needle and a pack of cigarettes. The only thing Rose said was, "Regular or menthol?" I said, "Regular." She said, "Okay," and hung up the phone. Within a half hour, Rose was at the door with the knitting needle and smokes in hand. She passed the bag to me, said goodbye and left.

At one juncture, I think it was Friday evening, I opened the door to the garage to come face to face with Jim Hanselman and Joann Ronzio. They were our "summer neighbors" and had just flown in from Ann Arbor, to help comfort us.

Saturday, December 15 was the morning of the Community Memorial Service. I'd been up until 2 a.m. Alan was up, too, working on his eulogy for Ben. He managed to weave a story of spirituality that included references to the religions of both grandmothers, the Nazarene Church, Judaism and Islam: an absolutely miraculous feat of ecumenicism. But the most inspirational phrase Alan came up with was a quote from Winston Churchill: "When you're going through hell, keep going." Perfect. It captured the inferno in my gut.

In the hour before the Community Memorial Service started, people began arriving at our house. Phoebe came over. Since the accident, she had stayed and slept at our house for a couple of nights, but then returned home to her own family. I had invited her to come with us, as family, and sit with us. Old as I am, I could still remember how powerful love is at that age, and I sensed she felt she was the one who really knew Ben best. To some extent, she's right. The loss of Ben to each of us is experienced differently—a brother, a son, a nephew, a grandson, a boyfriend, a friend—the loss isn't greater or less, bigger or smaller than anyone else's. It is just different for each of us.

I don't remember driving to the church for the service, but I do remember getting out of the car in the parking lot. When Ginny had been at our home planning the memorial service, I had asked her to mark off enough parking spaces close to the church for the families, and there were orange cones placed as I had suggested. Good, I thought. I'd also asked Ginny to make sure there was a private room where the families could gather before the service began, and then enter the sanctuary together. It was also important to be sure to mark off rows in the front of the chapel for family members. Ginny looked at me, somewhat stunned that in the midst of all this I was managing crowd control, but I knew the place was going to be packed.

I was right. We arrived early, but the other families were all already there. We gathered in the cafeteria. I was unprepared for the sheer number of family members present. There must have been over one hundred, although I'm sure that is an exaggeration of my mind. I murmured to Bob that we needed to introduce ourselves and talk to all the family members of our crew. And we did, moving from group to group. I recoiled in shock when I saw Rob Thompson's brother; they looked so much alike, it was as if Rob had come to life. I was comforted, though, by everyone's kindness, and in particular, the words of Steve Langlot's parents and Rob Thompson's parents, who understood that we, too, lost our son. I don't remember seeing Elizabeth, Jared's mother, before the service, but I know she was there. Kelly Tryon, Jared's girlfriend was there, and her family and friends, as well.

Holding hands, all of us, Dylan, Bob, me, Phoebe, the grandmothers Betty and Edie, we all went down the hall into a lobby already filled with the overflow from the chapel. Hundreds of people were bursting out of the seams of the building. I kept my head bowed. I couldn't make eye contact with anyone. I just wanted to get in there and sit down. I heard afterwards that to accommodate the overflow, the service was broadcast on closed circuit TV in rooms throughout the church.

I don't know how any of us got through the service. Edie, my mom, myself, Dylan, Bob, and Phoebe sat in one row. Alan, Lorna, Harvey and the nephews were behind us. You couldn't call it a funeral. There were no bodies, nothing to bury. Jeff Feldner, Alan Eder, and Peter Jordan, Ben's friend from childhood, spoke movingly, as did Eric Conrad, Rob Thompson's brother-in-law.

Family members and friends of Jared Hamrick and Steve Langlot spoke, too. I can't remember much of what was said. I knew, or thought, I was experiencing what I'd only read about before: disassociation. I was so out of touch with myself and my real feelings it was as if I was floating in a bubble. I kept up a running commentary in my brain. Our grandson, our nephew, our friend, our brother, our son hadn't died. It happened to someone else.

The service was finally over. I stood up and turned around. At the back of the church I saw Roger Fry. Oh God, Roger. His face drawn, Roger, who loved Ben so, and who Ben loved. Roger had known Ben as a baby, watched as he'd grown from childhood into a young man, and had fished with him. I wanted to get to Roger to hold him but I couldn't. We should have been able to leave first, and get to the reception before everyone else, but it didn't happen that way. We were mobbed by dear people who loved and cared for us and wanted us to know they were there, but didn't want to come to the reception afterward. I understood that, but it meant we didn't leave the church for what seemed like hours, and I knew I'd be receiving people at the reception for hours after this.

We finally got out of the church and drove to the Best Western. As we walked into the lobby, we saw more crowds. Dylan took one look at the crush of people, and said, "I'm not going in there, no way." He was ready to bolt, and I understood. He went with his close friend, Jordan King, to his home, where Jordan's parents, Barbara and Leslie, fed Dylan pancakes and took care of him, while we stayed and greeted those who came to remember and honor our men.

The hotel hallway was lined with people; we couldn't get into the room. Breathtakingly, there were massive funeral wreaths set up on easels from the Port of Newport and from ports and fisherman's associations all along the coast, from Bodega Bay, California, to Seattle, Washington, and from friends and families. I had never thought funeral wreaths beautiful before; I had thought them a waste of money. Now, I treasured each of them, so touched by the remembrance. Bob cried as he looked at the cards on the wreaths. He knew the men of these fishermen's associations. He had fished the same grounds, crossed the same dangerous bars, felt the same fears. He had stood in sweaty, crowded rooms, arguing about strikes and the price of crab and regulations with them. These were Bob's people.

Friends prepared the ballroom so it was warm and welcoming; the light had been dimmed low. The grandmothers, our mothers, Edie and Betty, stood with us for a while, but then sat at a table, stricken, so old. I was so angry, so angry. Why did these old people, our mothers, at the end of their lives, have to suffer this horrific loss? Hadn't they suffered enough? Couldn't the gods have left my parents and Edie alone, so their final years would not be suffused with this sadness? It seemed we all suffered more for each other than for ourselves. I guess that's love.

In high heels I stood for interminable hours. I felt as if we saw everyone we knew. It meant so much that people would stand in line for so long to talk to us. As always, I was as absorbed in the process as much as the grief, I had to gently remind Bob of all those who waited to talk to him. Bob would get intimately involved in a conversation with someone and I'd have to urge him to keep moving to the next person waiting so patiently. But that is the essence of my husband. He is incapable of small talk, or the superficial interaction. As impatient as I could be with him at times, what I love most about Bob is that he is real.

The Reed students were there, and Ben's friends from grade and high school; his teachers, coaches, old girlfriends, first loves. There were fishermen and fishery managers, their wives, husbands and families. Lawyers and judges, clients, and our friends, who came to say goodbye to the dead men and to comfort us. I remember looking idly at the buffet line, wondrous in its bounty, the generosity of all who had given food, but was struck that people had appetites. I don't know why I was surprised; as a cook, I know that everyone is always hungry, even in the most awful of situations. It is a fact of life. But it bowled me over. My son was dead and people were standing in line with plates in their hands.

The Fishermen's Wives set up several tables, each with a large piece of whiteboard that displayed photos of the dead men, and pens, so people could write remembrances. It was touching what people wrote. I was never so moved as when I read what Derick Staffenson had written. Derick is Ben's round-faced friend from childhood, grown into a handsome man. "I never had much in high school, Ben, but I always had you." Oh, God. Ben was the boy who remembered what it felt like to be excluded, to not be cool, and when he became popular, he didn't forget. Ben remembered everyone. And now, they remembered him.

Several hours later, it was finally the end of the reception. We were the last to leave, along with those fishermen and wives who had helped to set up and who would break everything down. Chris Carley, and her husband Phil, hauled all the wreaths to the Fishermen's Memorial, where, bathed in the cool air, they would remain fresh reminders of the pain.

We went home. We were grateful for everything that had been done that day, but we felt incomplete. All week long we had discussed whether we should have another service, just for Ben. In a sense, the Fishermen's Memorial service had been about community grief. Getting up the next day, Sunday December 16, we began to plan a memorial for Ben.

On Sunday afternoon, five days after the accident, once again we assembled on the sofas, chairs and floor of the living room. Logistics had to be addressed: the date, where, who would speak, music, food?

I called Jan Eastman at home. Jan managed the Performing Arts Center, and I asked her if we could have Ben's Celebration there. Jan's response was immediate and welcoming. "Of course, Michele," she said. I asked how much it would cost to book the facility and she kindly replied that they wanted to donate its use. I was, once again, so moved by the generosity of those in our community. People needed to do something to help us, to ease our pain.

We sat around, planning. Peter Jordan was there, as was Phoebe and Dylan, and friends of Ben. Under the direction of Alan, they put together a CD of music to be played at the ceremony. Ben was a great Bob Dylan, Neil Young, and Bob Marley fan, and the selections were oriented in that direction. Ben also loved the movie *The Big Lebowski*, and so music from that was included as well. The selections were heartbreaking: "Shelter from the Storm," "Long May You Run," "Redemption Song," and "Like a Rolling Stone." All the songs had a special meaning to Ben, and to our family. I had a moment of hope as I watched the compilation of songs come together. Dylan was actively engaged in the process, as was Alan. They were working together, communicating. Watching Dylan, I hoped he would begin to emerge from the black hole into which he had retreated.

Alan and Dylan located the appropriate songs, and copied them onto CD's. I stayed out of the process entirely. I realized how important it was for others, particularly Dylan, to have ownership in the many aspects of the memorial service to honor Ben.

One day, I am not sure which, Jon McKnight came by the house again, this time carrying Jared's blanket, which reeked of diesel fuel. Jon stood on the stoop of our home. "I tried to get the smell out, but I couldn't. I'm sorry," he said. I thanked him, deeply grateful for his efforts.

I called Kelly, and she and her mother, Shelly, came to our house. I remember Kelly and her mom sitting at the kitchen table. Kelly wrapped herself in the blanket. The room reeked of diesel, but in her happiness to be enveloped by Jared, it was clear Kelly couldn't smell a thing.

Even though we were so heavy with sadness, the days still marched on. Steve Ganz, a childhood friend of Bob's, drove down from Bellingham, Washington, to be with us. Monday, December 17 was Steve's birthday, and instead of my cooking dinner for him, he cooked dinner for us. I have learned that it is good to let people do things for you. Helping us also takes their minds off their own grief.

Steve made Mexican food for dinner: tacos, rice, beans and a salad. During dinner, the phone rang. It was Ginny Goblirsch, from Fisherman's Wives, for Bob.

Bob excused himself and got up from the kitchen table. I followed him through the swinging door from the kitchen into the dining room. Ginny had been contacted by Swede Pearson of the Oregon State Police. A body had washed ashore and been recovered. Ginny wanted to know if Bob could come to the funeral home to identify it. Oh, Jesus Christ, I thought. I don't know why, but I didn't want it to be Ben. I wanted him to stay at the bottom of the sea. I didn't want to see some half-eaten carcass that used to be my warm, live, flesh and blood child. I looked at Bob. "I can't do this," I said. "I am going to ask Steve to go with you to view the body."

Steve didn't hesitate. "Of course I'll go with Bob, Michele," he said. To some extent, the worst had already happened. Ben's tortuous death, and that of Rob, Jared and Steve—the nausea that swept over me, my fear of their pain and their suffering as they knew they were going to die—the trauma of viewing a dead body was infinitesimal in comparison. Thank God for Steve. Ginny arrived and Bob and Steve left with her. The rest of us pushed away from the table. We had all just been pretending to eat, anyway.

A half hour passed, then an hour. How long could this take? Then Bob and Steve came through the front door. "It wasn't Ben, Michele. In fact it wasn't any of them," Bob announced.

"What?" I asked, incredulous. "They pulled you into the morgue and it wasn't one of our guys?" I felt sick, from the anticipation, and dreading the news.

"Nope," Bob shook his head. I groaned. "They don't know who it is. They don't even have a report on this guy as a missing person. He was very fresh looking, not as if he'd been in the water for days," Bob said. "They unzipped the body bag for me to look at him. I stood there and looked at the body for quite a while. When I didn't say anything, Swede asked me, 'Well, is it anyone you know?' When I told him it wasn't, Swede said, 'Oh, shit!'"

On Monday, I designed a simple announcement of Ben's Celebration of Life for the newspaper, and made the deadline for the Wednesday and Friday editions.

We decided to serve Martinelli's sparkling apple cider. It was a favorite of Ben's since he was a little boy and it was a tradition in our family. I would buy the cider in preparation for Thanksgiving and we'd drink it through New Year's. Even when Ben, "all grown up," came home from college, he still looked for it in the fridge. I bought the cider by the case, given Ben's guzzling capabilities. And now, his favorite childhood beverage would be the one to send him off. His college friends would have likely preferred we serve bottles of vodka, cream and kahlua, the ingredients of White Russians and Ben's favorite "adult" drink, but I preferred to remember his boyish innocence and enthusiasm.

For Ben's obituary, we struggled to find a good head shot for the newspaper. Phoebe, bless her soul, came through with a perfect picture. It was a handsome photo of Ben, a black and white, she had taken just five months ago. He'd been working on pots with the rest of the crew at the gear pile at Port Dock 5, getting ready for sablefish season, and Phoebe had visited him. The photo was taken the same day last summer that I'd taken a cake to the guys.

We were all so exhausted that we decided the best way to

honor Ben was to keep it simple and meaningful. No buffet lines of food. Just tables in the lobby, with guest books to sign. A stage that was bare except for a microphone. A glass of Martinelli's cider for everyone. And a memento for all, something of Ben to take away for all who came: a copy of Phoebe's beautiful picture of Ben.

Alan and others went to the photo store and had several hundred copies of the picture made. I painstakingly hand-wrote the message I wanted on the back of the photos and Alan took it to be printed on labels at Lazerquick.

Benjamin Alan Eder
March 22, 1980 – December 11, 2001
"Learn, learn, learn!"
photo by Phoebe Morris

I sat on the floor of a variety store one evening that week, in the office supply section, looking at leather-covered albums. I bought albums for the guests to sign at Ben's Celebration. I also bought numerous G-2 gel pens; the kind Ben always used. Any gesture, no matter how small, that connected us to Ben through this frightful nightmare, gave me a small measure of comfort.

Still, more community members helped us. David Terry, of a local media production company, loaned Alan his equipment so the events of the evening could be recorded. Ron Miller, whose son, Morgan, was a fellow fisherman and friend of Ben's, ran the stage and music production at the Performing Arts Center, and helped Alan by working the lights and sound. I picked up tablecloths from West Coast Linen. They refused to let me pay, just as they had done for the Community Memorial Service; once again donating the linens. The generosity of our community is endless. Nikki and Esther, the girls who are our "jack of all trades," and Lorna, Dylan and Edie sat around the kitchen table, affixing the stickers with Ben's name and "Learn, learn, learn" to the back of the photos.

I don't recall what we did during the day of Ben's Celebration. It was held on Friday evening, December 21. I know that in addition to Harvey, Edie, Alan and his family, Bob's cousins, Mark and Craig and their wives, Margo and April had come from Los Angeles, and Steve Ganz was still with us. We visited the Fisherman's Memorial, adding more flowers, reading notes of condolence that both friends and strangers had left for all the families. Hundreds of cards had come to the house for Bob, Dylan and I, as well as a multitude of bouquets that we continually took to the Memorial, as our living room and dining room were filled to overflowing. We could only read the condolence cards a few at a time. The kindness from friends and strangers alike, made us awestruck. Contributions poured in from all over the country to Fishermen's Wives, for the benefit of all of the families.

We took the funds intended for Ben and put them in the bank. to be used as seed money for a scholarship in Ben's name for Newport High students going to college. Within a week of the accident, more than $20,000 came in to Newport Fisherman's Wives, donations large and small. Englund Marine contributed $5,000. I was simply staggered by their generosity. Another woman, a complete stranger from the Eugene area, sent $5. She wrote: "I can't do much, but I wanted to help." The Fishermen's Wives distributed the funds to each family. Combined with the advance from our insurance company to each of the families to tide them through the first month, at least Trish, Rob Thompson's wife, and Dawn, Steve Langlot's fiancée wouldn't have to worry about paying the bills and making a Christmas for the little ones.

On Friday evening, we went early to the Performing Arts Center to set up. I knew I was going to have to feed a ton of people afterwards. Our neighbors, Jan and Pat, took my list of menu items and went to the markets and restaurants and bought platters of food. More help from wonderful people.

For the Celebration room set-up, Dylan enlisted his friends and they positioned tables, laid out the white tablecloths and carefully arranged hundreds of the black and white photos of Ben for a stunningly simplistic effect. Each person who came would take away Ben in their heart, but would also have a photo emblazoned with "Learn, learn, learn!" The kids put together the plastic wine glasses, and made a dash to the store for the bottle openers I had forgotten. Alan worked with Dylan and Ron Miller to get the music system, lights, and mikes working. Dave Campbell, one of Ben's teachers from high school, was the moderator for the evening.

Although the Celebration was to begin at 7 p.m., people started arriving much earlier. Bob and I stood and received everyone as they entered, and each person brought with them both a wave of pain and love such that I had never felt before, not even the week previous, at the Fisherman's Community Memorial Service. I had been anaesthetized by shock then. Now, as I saw Ben's friends and ours, his teachers, just all those who loved him, I was overcome. I alternated between delight and surprise that they had come for the evening, and a depth of sadness I had never known existed.

Forty minutes after the evening was to have started, Alan came and took my arm and said we needed to go in and be seated. For once I refused Alan. I was sorry our friends already seated would have to wait, but we would not sit down until we personally greeted each and every person who came to honor and remember our son.

Finally, the line of people arriving ended, and we sat down in the front row of the auditorium. Dave Campbell spoke clearly, lovingly, kindly, openly and invited others to come up to the stage and share their memories.

Dave planned the evening wisely. There were enough people, friends, relatives and strangers to me, who spoke in remembrance of Ben, that an intermission was called. But just before the break, in as touching a moment as I had ever listened to, friends of

Ben's reprised a moment that had taken place at their high school graduation in 1998. At that ceremony, a trio sang, "With a Little Help From My Friends." On this evening of Ben's memorial, friends of Ben sang the song again, and the sweetness of their harmonies and their love for Ben and one another will resonate in my heart forever. Particularly touching, too, was Erica Brookhyser, who, playing the violin, performed a piece. I can't remember the name of it, but it was haunting, laden with melancholy. If you've ever seen Ken Bums' Civil War documentary on PBS, then you know the music. Erica simply said, "Ben didn't have a chance to hear me play, so this is for him." Later, I found out that Ben had taken Erica out in Eugene for her 21st birthday, just a couple of months before he died, and they danced all night in celebration.

During the intermission, everyone filed out into the lobby. It was jam packed and I felt claustrophobic. We had brought from home a brass ship's bell. Bob took my hand, ascended the steps to the balcony, and rang the bell. He raised a glass of Martinelli's. "To Ben," he said simply. "He was a light." And everyone drank. We then returned to our seats and more people spoke; funny, sad, adventurous, loving stories of our boy, who we would never see or touch or hear from again.

At the close of the evening, we packed up, then trudged to the car in the rain, and invited those who were still around to come over to our house. In a manner fitting to Ben's magnificent seafood parties, I had called Bornstein's fish plant earlier in the day, and Rick, the dock manager, put aside a case of cooked crab for me.

I don't remember much more of the evening. Roger Fry, Ben's adored mentor, came to the house. The people who loved Ben the most were the most comforting, but at the same time, the most disturbing and painful to see.

The last couple of days since Ben's Celebration have been a blur. My mom had left a day or two earlier. I realized the strain on her was simply too much. She has been ill in the past year, but she stood so strongly beside us, and her quiet, steadfast presence comforted me. Edie and Harvey left after Ben's Celebration as did most others. Alan and Lorna and the nephews were scheduled to spend Christmas with Lorna's parents in Washington. They left by car for Olympia, but have promised to return by New Year's.

There is no Christmas tree, no stockings hung, no presents wrapped, no decorations. As was my tradition since Ben left for college, I had put up the outdoor Christmas lights on the Saturday just before he was due, so he would arrive to a cheerfully decorated home. After Ben died, Bob gruffly ripped the Christmas lights off the house. Their twinkling cheerfulness were an incongruity.

Yesterday, Christmas Eve, we went to the video store and rented all *The Sopranos* DVD's. I've always felt sorry for people in the video store on family holidays, wondering why they were there instead of sitting around some idyllic dining table or before a crackling fireplace. Well, now I understand. We shut the blinds, turned off the phone, and watched *The Sopranos* non-stop from late yesterday afternoon until after 2 this morning, when finally we all went to bed.

Dylan, Bob and I are now alone. It is terrifying. We have been so bathed in love and warmth for these two weeks after Ben's death that I have ignored the reality that the three of us are going to have to learn to cope together as a family. How will we ever be whole again? I don't know if we can. We will have to learn to become a trio, instead of a quartet, with its violin missing.

January 2002

Friday
January 4, 2002

Pete Fones agreed to meet me at Ben's apartment in Eugene, to sort Ben's things and pack them up. The apartment owners have been very kind, telling me to take as much time as I needed to get this done. But it has been almost three weeks since the accident, and I know I have to get started.

Ben lived at the Ridgewood Apartments on East 18th Street, just across from the School of Music on the University of Oregon campus. It is a non-descript, two-story, eight-apartment building, four apartments up and four down. Ben had a studio apartment: one room that served as his bedroom and living area. It had a little alcove for a kitchen, and a bath. Ben made the place homey. He placed a table and low-seated lawn chairs outside in front of his apartment, with some plants, and a rug outside his door.

Once I walked inside and looked around, I realized how much I cherished, and wanted to save, the "essence of Ben." The walls were covered with his favorite maps: a Raven map of the state of Oregon I gave him for Christmas one year; maps of the West Indies, of Russia; maps from his travels in South America. On the walls of his tiny kitchen, he had tacked up cereal boxes, his favorite kinds, because, I suppose, he didn't have enough cupboard space. It just tickled me he had done this and even in my sorrow, I laughed. I wouldn't have thought of it myself. Since he was a little boy, Ben's appetite for dry cereal had been gargantuan.

For a young man, Ben was financially well organized. I like to think he took after me in this regard. He had expando files with different sections for his expenses, his income, his investment account statements, and his bills. There was a pile of issues of *The Economist.* For several years Ben had been after me to buy him an *Oxford English Dictionary*, to the tune of $1300. I had declined. Just this fall, Ben told me he'd bought the abridged version of this dictionary, and now there it was, two fat volumes that sat on the shelves of his desk.

Ben had bought a brand new L-shaped desk just two months before he died, in October, while Phoebe was visiting. They worked together assembling it. The desk took up half the living space. Ben's bed, a futon on the floor, was tightly sandwiched between the desk and the wall. His notebook computer was atop the desk, and receipts in the drawer showed he had just purchased additional RAM. His ubiquitous gel pens, in multiple colors, were scattered about. Ben often wore cargo pants and tucked those pens in the pockets on the legs. In the cubbyholes of the desk there were stacks of his 3 x 5 note cards: phone numbers, quotes, ideas, to-do lists. On the floor, next to his bed, was the last issue of *The New York Times*. He subscribed to it. There it was, December 8, 2001, Saturday. Ben had driven home to Newport late that evening. Also on the floor, next to his futon, was a book, *1001 Things Everyone Should Know About Science*. He'd marked his place with a business card of Bob's that read "*F/V Nesika*."

What struck me the most was that Ben's desk surface was perfectly clean, except for one thing. There lay a book of Bob's poems published while Bob was in college, entitled *Burning the Slash.*

As Pete and I looked around Ben's apartment, I decided not to pack his belongings. I wanted Bob and Dylan to see what I had seen, to feel what I felt as I sat at Ben's desk, as I peered carefully into cupboards, opened bins of things important to him. I found boxes of fireworks, the knapsack that had traveled with him to South America, his favorite books, his clothes and his extensive liquor collection. I stood and looked, dumbfounded, at shoes that Ben had since he was 15. I remember the day we bought them. And a sports jacket. The jacket and shoes were for a trip to Los Angeles, for his cousin Michael's bar mitzvah.

I wanted Bob and Dylan to have the opportunity to be in Ben's spirit and space, for I knew this would be the last time we would be part of the physical life Ben had created for himself.

Sunday
January 6, 2002

Today Bob announced, "Let's go to Eugene. Let's go to Ben's apartment." It was 3 in the afternoon.

We drove to Eugene, Dylan and Bob in the truck, me in the Subaru. By the time we arrived, shortly after 5 p.m., it was dark out.

They both cried. Bob was speechless when he saw the book of his poems, sitting out on Ben's desk, surrounded by nothing else. I don't believe in much, spiritually, but felt if there ever was one, this was a cosmic connection between Ben and Bob.

Bob and Dylan found some photos in Ben's desk of the beginning of Ben's trip to South America, where he met up with Peter, and when they visited Ethan on the sailboat in Costa Rica. The pictures were just stunning. Bob's favorite, the one he took to keep on the boat, was of Ben standing on a sailboat, the night sky the background. Ben wore a black cap my father had given him. He is broad shouldered, bare-chested, brown-skinned, with loose gray pants billowing down from his hips. He was playing a harmonica.

"This just so embodies his spirit; this is Ben, Bob said. "And he didn't even know how to play a harmonica."

We laughed.

We spent several hours at the apartment loading and packing and crying. Bob and Dylan were both so glad they had come and I was glad we could do it together as a family. We read letters and we held things up and we looked and we laughed and we cried. Once, I asked Dylan what he wanted to keep of Ben's things. Dylan looked at me and said, "Whatever Ben had that I wanted, he took with him."

From:	**Dylan**
To:	**Mom**
Date:	**Wednesday, January 9, 2002**
Re:	**Made it!**

Hey, I'm just writing to tell you that I am here in Whitman…finally. I just got in around 5 a.m. because the car kept overheating, so I went like a slug until Pendleton and then got an AAA tow the rest of the way. It's really weird to be back. I don't think I like the feeling. My room's so tiny and full of crap. Also there aren't really any people here. Take care and give Dad my love, too.
Love,
Dylan

I got off the computer and called Whitman College as soon as I received this email from Dylan. I talked to the person in charge of counseling students, and asked them to call Dylan and check in with him. I explained what happened; that Dylan's brother had died. The counselor knew about it. He said to me: "Well, I'll have to tell Dylan when I call him that it's at your request. And whatever he says to me will be confidential."

"Fine," I said.

This guy seemed more concerned with the technical niceties than the fact that I thought Dylan needed help. I really didn't give a shit whether Dylan knew I called this counselor or not. Christ, I was Dylan's mom—not somebody looking to win a popularity contest. I just wanted him safe.

From: **Mom**
To: **Dylan**
Date: **Wednesday, January 9, 2002**
Re: **Will come and see you**

Hey Honey –

If you like, I'll get in the car and come hang out in Walla Walla for a few days. Keep you company for meals and a movie or something, in between your doing what you need to do. Just say the word -- I'd love to do it.

Love,
Mom

From: **Dylan**
To: **Mom**
Date: **Wednesday, January 9, 2002**
Re: **Will come and see you**

Thanks for the offer Mom, but I will be fine. People will be showing up tomorrow and I already met my R.A. and stuff. I am taking my religion final tomorrow and my core final on Friday. That counselor called me. Everything is fine. Take care.

Love, Dylan

Thursday
January 10, 2002

I can't decide which is worse: bagging up Ben's toothbrush or writing his obituary.

Yesterday, I got a call from Swede Pearson, a sergeant with the Oregon State Police. Some human remains washed ashore just north of Depoe Bay at the Surfrider Motel. Swede wanted to let me know before I heard it on the news. Bateman's, the funeral home, was en route to retrieve the remains. I started to cry on the phone. My reaction surprised me. I had often, in the last month, talked about how finding Ben's body didn't mean anything to me. But when I heard Swede say that pieces of torso washed up, all I could see was Ben's chest and stomach with no legs and no arms and no head, lying on the beach.

I pictured his appendicitis scar from the spring of his senior year of high school. Ben had fallen to the floor in his bedroom in pain. I remembered the drive to the hospital, Ben's incredible pain in the emergency room, injections of morphine which made him vomit, exacerbating his misery.

Afterwards Ben said to me, "You called it, Mom, I was on the floor and you said, 'Appendicitis, let's go.' How did you know?" he asked.

I smiled and shrugged and said, "I just did."

And then there was the other scar on his torso, opposite his appendix, the one he'd gotten when he'd ripped open his side on a bike ride down Mt. Ashland. That happened on a camping trip Ben and Bob and Dylan had taken to Yosemite in our infamous blue Volvo station wagon. Bob had left them at the top of the hill with their mountain bikes, and as they rode their way down, Ben crashed. It was a big scar; Ben really ripped himself open.

Today Ginny called me at my office. The remains found on the beach were to go to the medical examiner's office for identification. Ginny said the police wanted a toothbrush to extract DNA, so I called Swede.

"Yeah, just bring it by in the next couple days," he said. "There were pretty small pieces of a body that were found. Don't know if we can identify it."

I hung up the phone, went into the bathroom and vomited.

Was it worse to have written Ben's obituary? He died on December 11 and the memorial service for all four fishermen was held on December 15. I had risen early one morning around 5:30, while everyone else slept. It was still dark out. I made a pot of coffee and I sat at the table in the kitchen and began to write on a yellow legal pad. "Benjamin Alan Eder was born on March 22, 1980 in Coos Bay, Oregon."

Saturday
January 12, 2002

My lower back is killing me. Yesterday I spent the day in Eugene with Peter Fones again, and finished packing up Ben's belongings. Peter took apart Ben's desk; we both lugged it down the stairs in pieces and loaded it in the truck, Peter lamenting that this was a job that our sons, Isaac and Dylan, should be doing. I laughed, and agreed.

We packed the kitchen dishes, took apart Ben's pressboard bookcase, stuffed miscellaneous desk supplies into plastic bags, and carefully wrapped Ben's martini glasses in his bathrobe. We rolled up his futon and, while I sat on it, Peter wrapped it with bungee cords.

One last time, I stuck my head in the cupboards where Ben's clothes had been, and breathed deeply, smelling his essence. I laid my head on a shelf and cried.

Arriving home, Pete Gintner and his little son, Zack, met me at our storage shed in South Beach and we unloaded the truck. A few weeks before Ben's death, I had given Zack some crystals, known as Herkimer Diamonds. My mother had given them to me when I was a child. Pete Gintner mentioned that Zack was enthralled by crystals, so I had tucked a few of them in a little velvet jeweler's bag, certain that these would enchant him.

Pete told me that when he gave them to Zack, he told his son that not only were these crystals, but that they carried good luck. Yesterday, while unloading the truck, Pete said that after the accident, Zack looked at his little bag of crystals and said, "Maybe Auntie Michele shouldn't have given me these crystals. She needed the luck more than I did."

From: **Michele**
To: **Steve Ganz**
Date: **Saturday, January 12, 2002**
Re: **Hello there**

Hi Steve –

Hope all is ok with you and family. I'm sorry for not calling or writing back sooner, but I think you understand.

Dylan is back at school. The last three days he was at home we were quite close, but after his return to school, I managed to piss him off like a good parent should. I called the counseling office at the college to let them know he was back early, and asked them to touch base with him.

Dylan went out fishing on the *Michele Ann* on Christmas night. Bill Retherford was running the boat for Bob. Going out on a trip for four days was healing for Dylan, I think. In any event, I knew Dylan wanted to get away from the house, and the ocean was as good a place to go as any. It was tough to let him go; had I thrown a fit, he would have stayed home, but I was not at all inclined to tell him what to do. From our back deck we watched as Dylan and the crew on the *Michele Ann* laid a wreath at sea for Ben and the other men. Dylan wrote Ben a letter of goodbye and placed it with the wreath.

You would have enjoyed New Year's Eve here at the house. We watched Ben's favorite movie, *The Big Lebowski.* True to the spirit of the movie, Alan and Bob were drinking White Russians. They sobered up enough for us all to walk on the beach at midnight -- Alan, Lorna, Harvey, Edie, the nephews, Dylan, Bob and I. Then we came back and watched *Blazing Saddles.* I had never seen the movie before and thought I'd fall off the couch laughing. I am shocked that in my sadness I could laugh so.

Bob went out fishing a few days ago. He is getting ready to go out again tomorrow. He wants to stay close to me and to home, but I am grateful he is able to get back on the boat, if that is what he wants to do.

I am overwhelmed by paperwork requests from the lawyers representing the families of the *Nesika* crew members, as well as demands from the lawyer for "our" insurance company. I also have to do crew payroll for the *Michele Ann*, and get the 1099 information for our crew to the accountant.

Little things devastate me. Today I was at Safeway in the grocery line. Charlene was there, who has checked me through my huge grocery orders ever since Ben and Dylan were small. They would push the carts and carry the coupons. Charlene has always asked about the boys since they've been grown. As I pulled out my checkbook to pay, Charlene grabbed my hands tightly, and I just broke down.

Thank you so much again for your friendship. You have been a wonderfully non-judgmental rock.

Love,
Michele

From: **Dylan**
To: **Mom**
Date: **Tuesday, January 15, 2002**

Hey Mom –

Things are going okay here.

I have still only made up two of my exams, but this weekend is a three day weekend, so I hope to use it to study and maybe take my other tests next week. I am really happy with my classes so far. They all look really interesting and the reading material is great. I had bio lab yesterday and we went to a wildlife refuge. Everybody is back and it's nice to see my friends again. There are a bunch of new people in our dorms -- a couple of cute girls, too. One of them is even Jewish.

Anyway, as you can see, I am very well distracted here. Or maybe I am just healing somehow, because I haven't broken down in like a week. Anyway, I hope things go better for you.

Take care.
Love, Dylan

January 15, 2002

RADM Erroll Brown
Commander, 13th Coast Guard District
915 Second Avenue
Room 3590
Seattle, WA 98174-1067

Dear Admiral Brown:

On behalf of our families and friends, we would like to commend the personnel of the U.S. Coast Guard that assisted in the search and rescue mission for the crew of the *F/V Nesika*, on December 11, 2001.

Captain John C. Miko of the North Bend station, whom we understand was in command of the rescue efforts, committed every possible asset, and communicated openly and honestly with our families at each step of the mission.

CWO John Dodd of the Yaquina Bay station -- we will forever hold him in our hearts. He led the men and women stationed in Newport and Depoe Bay, at the same time making sure that the needs of the families were met throughout the day and the evening as the search wore on.

During the day, my husband was at sea, on the *F/V Michele Ann*, and participating in the search, while I was at the Coast Guard station, receiving updates on the rescue efforts and calling the family members of the men who had been lost, including our own, as our son, Ben Eder, had also been aboard. I was extended every possible courtesy and accommodation.

We would also speak with the highest regard of Ken Lawrenson, Tony Keller and Bob Beck of the Marine

Safety Office. The respect with which they treated our family in our time of grief will not be forgotten.

The professionalism, care and deep and profound sense of mission exhibited by all the men and women of the United States Coast Guard on December 11, 2001, was exemplary. We are honored by your service, and will be forever grateful.

Sincerely,
Michele and Bob Eder

Newport News Times
Wednesday, January 23, 2002

Newport Fishermen's Wives
A Remembrance
by Michele Longo Eder
Special to the *Newport News Times*

No one loved eating seafood more than our son, Ben Eder. Even more than he loved fishing, there was nothing that pleased him so much as to boil a pot full of Dungeness crabs, or quarter, marinate and grill loins of tuna he had caught, or fillet fresh rockfish, and eat all of it that he could in a sitting.

At our kitchen table, as a young boy, he would painstakingly pick the crab from the shell, as his father had taught him, taking particular delight in using the point of the crab leg to dig meat out from the hard-to-get-to spots. At that age, the hunt was as much fun as the eating, drawing the meat through the melted butter, savoring the taste. It was hard work, that eatin' crab, and hard work was something that Ben enjoyed his entire life.

Ben first acquired a taste for tuna courtesy of Tom Shafer, a long-time Newport fisherman who used to own the *F/V Donna.* In 1990, when Ben was 10, we were at a party at the Shafers' and Tom was barbecuing his famous tuna. He handed chunks of it off the grill to Ben and Ben hung out with Tom all evening. On the way home, Ben did nothing but rave about the taste, and wanted to know when I would make it for him. I'd never cooked tuna before, but I soon learned.

Later, as Ben began to fish regularly, he caught his own albacore, learned to quarter it, and developed his own secret marinade. I begged for the recipe, which he wouldn't divulge, but as I surreptitiously watched him, I discovered it had a lot to do with bottles of Yoshida sauce and a lot of garlic. There were half a dozen bottles in his cupboard in his Eugene apartment, where he last lived.

Ben shared in the bounty of the sea. His fellow students at Reed and many other friends were the beneficiaries of his largesse. Often, he'd stash a couple of albacore in the freezer in the garage, then swing by and pick one up on his way to school. "I'm takin' some tuna, Mom!" I'd hear him yell. I heard stories that he'd defrost them in the bathtub. I believed it.

On the Fourth of July, I'd make a big pasta salad tossed with pounds of pink shrimp for our traditional picnic with Aunt Mary and family friends. Ben would devour plates of it. This year, the *F/V Michele Ann* had come in with a load of crab just in time to have some fresh-cooked for the party. Ben stood with me on our back deck, showed me how to grab the still-alive crab by their legs, close in to their bodies, so as not to get pinched, and slam them on the rail, so their backs would pop off and I could shake the guts out and then boil them. I had always cooked them whole, then cleaned them, but Ben taught me the "real way" to clean crabs.

And how he loved sushi. Some parents groan over their kids' bar tabs; Bob and I would sometimes roll our eyes at Ben's expensive appetites. We knew he had a table at Sada's on the bayfront, where he and his dear Phoebe, best friend Peter, brother Dylan, and other friends ate regularly. Ben savored the freshness, the beauty and the delicacy of the presentation of each morsel. His T-shirt from Sada's was a favorite part of his wardrobe. Last summer he was thrilled to bring Sada live side-stripe prawns which he had caught in traps in an experimental fishery, for Sada to prepare and serve. At home, he sat and painstakingly peeled these prawns by hand for he and his father and Dylan to cook together and enjoy.

Off to school this fall at the U of O, Ben did what he could to maintain a seafood diet. Though he lived in a studio apartment, he'd bought himself a half-chest freezer for his tiny kitchen to store the rockfish, salmon, tuna and halibut he'd caught in the past summer. He had invested in a commercial vacuum sealer to preserve the freshness as best he could. Opening his freezer last week, I found some of his favorite specimens from the sea, as well—a couple of deep-water tanner crabs, and a couple of box crabs were sandwiched in with ice cream and rockfish fillets. Ben's latest purchase was a Little Chief smoker, which he envisioned setting out and firing up on the narrow deck of his Eugene apartment house.

Ben understood and enjoyed not only the health benefits of eating seafood, but relished every moment the experience of catching and providing food for others. "We feed people, Mom. That's what we do."

January 26, 2002

Commander
13th Coast Guard District
Federal Bldg.
915 Second Avenue
Room 3590
Seattle, WA 98174

Dear Bob, Michele and Dylan,

Your letter deeply touches the men and women of the Coast Guard who daily stand ready to risk their lives to save others. I can tell you when they are not able to make a rescue they share personally in the pain of any loss of life. While they too are deeply saddened for your loss, your letter touches their hearts and strengthens their resolve. Your family's love for Ben is abundantly evident. Thank you for openly sharing your deepest emotions for those you loved the most.

Respectfully,
Erroll Brown

February 2002

February 25, 2002

Joy Bailey
State Medical Examiner Office
301 NE Knott Street
Portland, OR 97212-3092

RE: Benjamin Alan Eder
December 11, 2001

Dear Ms. Bailey:

Enclosed is a partially completed death certificate. We are requesting that a completed presumptive death certificate be signed by the Medical Examiner.

The *F/V Nesika* went to sea on December 11, 2001 and capsized. Our son was one of the four men aboard. To date, no bodies have been recovered.

We've enclosed reports/news releases from the Coast Guard.

A certificate is being requested at this time because a certificate is required to access information pertaining to our son's assets. My husband has been appointed personal representative of Ben's estate and needs to complete the inventory of his assets and file it with the probate court. A copy of the letters testamentary is enclosed.

Thank you for your assistance in this matter.

Very truly yours,
Michele Longo Eder

Tuesday
February 26, 2002

This morning I picked the first flowers of spring from my garden—a cluster of purple spikes, yellow daffodils and hot pink azaleas -- and took them to the Fishermen's Memorial. I left the flowers with a note. "For Ben -- the first flowers from my garden. Love, Mom." The podium was strewn with flowers, notes, cards of all sorts. There were crayon drawings from children, remembering Steve Langlot. There were handwritten notes from Kelly, Jared's girlfriend. Letters from strangers, people from all around the Western states and Canada, who left messages that all our men were in their prayers.

It is a clear, cool, false spring day, but maybe spring will come early this year and relieve us of some of the pain. I will never forget the drenching rains that pounded us mercilessly this winter; they served to emphasize our loss. Instead, today the air is clear and makes you want to breathe so deeply. I think of Ben, on a day like this, the air so clear and clean and cold, and how he drank so deeply of life; and then I think of him gasping for air as he struggled so hard and fought and fought to live, but drowned.

Wednesday
February 27, 2002

I'm dreading today. Bob and I have to go and talk to one of the lawyers and the investigator for "our" insurance company. Actually, Bob has to talk to them; I'm just along for moral support. The asshole lawyers are insisting they want to interview Dylan, since he is the surviving owner of the boat. I told Doug Fryer, our lawyer, "Over my dead body will they talk to Dylan." Big talk from me, but if our insurance company refuses to pay the families, their lawyers will be hounding Dylan. I can't bear the thought that, on top of everything else, Dylan would have to go through the litigation, too.

What's absolutely rotten about today is that our own insurance company is trying to deny paying what's known as the "hull coverage." If our own insurance company can show Bob was negligent in some way, or that the manner in which the boat was loaded with crab pots made the vessel unseaworthy, then our insurer can refuse to pay out the million dollars in insurance coverage to the surviving families.

The situation is so bad that we hired our own lawyer, Doug Fryer, to threaten our insurance company. We will sue them if they fail to pay the entire policy limit to the families. The lawsuits, and the ensuing nightmares, could go on for years. What it will come down to, however, are the results of a stability study being done by Dave Green, a marine architect. He has been "hired" by our insurance company to independently investigate what happened. If he confirms the boat was loaded correctly for the way it was built, our insurance company has no choice but to provide the families with coverage and pay their claims. Still, that won't make today any easier.

Dave Green. Now, that was a day I'd rather never repeat. I can't, right now, even place exactly what day it was. I knew he had to be a hell of a marine architect, because our insurance company had its hopes pinned on him saying the vessel was unseaworthy. Our lawyer, Doug Fryer, told us Dave Green would be honest and fair. I had to meet with Mr. Green and assist him in seeing the gear and the *Nesika.*

He arrived at my office, with an assistant who was to help in the tests and measurements of the vessel. Mr. Green is retired from the Coast Guard and he is modest and quiet-spoken. In the lobby of our law office, numerous pictures of vessels we represent hang on the walls. A photo of the *Nesika*, fully loaded with crab pots, is still up, and I gave him a copy of it.

We left the office and Mr. Green followed me first to Port Dock 7, where the *Nesika* crab pots are stored. A couple of weeks after the accident, Bob, Joe Rock, and Doug Rose on the *F/V Grumpy J*, retrieved these pots from the bottom of the ocean. I remembered again how relieved we were when they pulled up the gear; no human carcass had been entangled in the pots that rolled off the deck when the *Nesika* capsized. As Bob, Joe, and Doug on the *Grumpy J* pulled up those pots, I stood outside our house, with binoculars, watching them work. When the pots were all on board, Bob called me immediately with the news. I had asked Ginny Goblirsch to "stand by" while this gear was retrieved. In the event a body was recovered, Ginny agreed to notify the family for me, if it was someone other than Ben.

Now, today, at Port Dock 7, Dave Green took photos of these same pots recovered from the bottom of the ocean. I also showed him the line and buoys and bait jars and how the pots were rigged when loaded on the *Nesika.*

We then drove out the Bay Road to our shop. I hadn't been to the shop since the accident, and I struggled very hard not to cry. I have so many good memories here of the boys playing in the meadow when they were smaller and then working here as they got older. Instead of the gray cold day that it was, I envisioned the sun shining, the green meadow encircled with turquoise line and hundreds of bright orange and yellow buoys, freshly painted, hanging to dry. It was a scene repeated each year, as we got ready for crab season.

I had to show Dave Green the outriggers. These are long aluminum poles used on board, extending out from each side of the vessel, to help with the stability on the ocean. Bob had told me where they were located on the hill above the shop and Dave measured and examined them. At one point I had to walk away; images of Ben and Dylan in happier times kept flashing and I again teared up.

Done at the gear shed, we then drove further out the Bay Road to a boatyard where the *Nesika* had been hauled after the accident. It was the first I'd seen the boat since it washed ashore at Beverly Beach in the early morning hours of December 12.

As inappropriate as it might be to say that an inanimate object was heartbreaking, the sight of the once-proud *Nesika* up on blocks, the bow smashed, its mast broken—I was sickened.

Ladders were placed up against the side of the boat, and I climbed aboard while Dave and his assistant shot photographs and took measurements from below.

I hadn't really thought about standing again on the deck of the boat where my son and three men stood before they died. When the *Nesika* beached, a few personal items washed ashore and been returned to the families. Ben's knapsack had been found and given to us. But I had not been prepared to see the boat still loaded with diesel-soaked clothes, and, most difficult of all, items belonging to Ben.

On the deck was Ben's windbreaker, one my parents had given him. I picked it up and cried. I went into the cabin and into the foc'sle below, where there were broken bunks and clothes tossed about. Despite the stench, I crawled in and pulled out a half-dozen of Ben's t-shirts. Somehow, I had imagined the interior of the foc'sle, indeed, the boat, as completely empty. It wasn't. I climbed out of the foc'sle, and stood in the cabin, and ran my hands on what I incorrectly referred to as "the wheel," but what I knew was the helm. Bob had told me the only thing he wanted from the *Nesika* was the helm. I tried to figure out how to unscrew it, but didn't have any luck.

I took one last look before I left the cabin. Still attached to the dashboard on a Tyco label, as it had been since the day the boat was launched in 1979, were imprinted the words: "May the life of this boat be bountiful and safe."

Interview of Bob Eder

Tape Recording made February 27, 2002 by David Willoughby

Present on tape recording are:
DW: Dave Willoughby, investigator for hull underwriters
NM: Nick McDermott, attorney for hull underwriters
DF: Doug Fryer, attorney for Bob & Michele Eder
BE: Bob Eder

DW: It's the 27th of February, 2002. I'm conducting an interview at the La Quinta Inn in Newport, Oregon. Present in the room is Nick McDermott, attorney for hull underwriters. On the telephone is attorney Doug Fryer, representing the Eders. Bob and Michele Eder are here, and also Jon McKnight. I'm tape recording this with everybody's knowledge and permission is that correct, Mr. Fryer?

DF: That is correct. And as I understand it, you're the lead investigator for hull underwriters and you're doing this as part of hull underwriters' investigation of the loss of the *Nesika* and the purpose of the interview, as I understand it, is to ascertain the facts concerning the circumstances of the loss as best you can from Bob Eder.

DW: That's correct. Also some background on the vessel itself. I have not had a chance to meet with the Eders since the loss of the vessel.

DF: Okay.

BE: The vessel was constructed and launched in June 1979.

DW: And did you buy the vessel before, during or after the construction?

BE: The vessel was constructed for me. It's a one-owner vessel.

DW: And my understanding was the vessel was built or at least designed by Lucander, is that correct?

BE: Nils Lucander.

DW: And so did you have any specific design differences that you wanted to see in the boat when you ordered it, or just basically went with that plan

BE: I was having a Port Orford crab boat built. A boat that would be suitable for the sablefish trap fishery also. We were taking what had become an established and proven design for fishing crab out of Port Orford, untanked vessels for day fishing, light enough to fit the constraints of the hoist, 25,000 pounds of weight, and less than 42 feet. Aluminum seemed an even better material than plywood because of the pounding on the docks, aluminum being the toughest, lightest material. I chose to go with the conventional engine forward, single screw design, more like the plywood Lucander boats.

DW: Okay. Besides crabbing, were there other fisheries that you wanted to have built into this vessel also?

BE: Yes. Although I don't think it affected work that Lucander did. But I intended on going sablefish trap fishing and salmon trolling, also.

DW: Since taking possession of the vessel, have you made any changes from the original design?

BE: Changes of what nature, Dave?

DW: Engine size or compartment size or lengthened it or widened it, or...

BE: I've made no major changes as far as engine size or compartment size or length and width. The biggest alteration made to the boat was upon moving from Port Orford, which was a "dry crab" port, to Newport. It was requested by the buyers here that I deliver a wet, live-tanked crab. And there are two alternatives for doing that. One is an insert tank and the other is flooding the hold. And I had contact with Lucander and flooded part of the hold. So we did not change the hold's size, but rather we inserted foam into the aft 35 percent of the fish hold, so that we could flood the hold and still carry a full load of pots. That's probably the biggest change. I made many minor changes. Many, many. I owned the boat for 23 years, 22 years. But nothing substantial except for that.

DW: How many crab pots would you carry on a normal load? Assuming you were setting pots out, how many pots would you carry on a normal voyage?

BE: That would depend sometimes on the weather or the distance I planned to travel. As I recall, we typically took out a load of about 135 to 138 pots at the beginning of the season. To illuminate a little bit more, I'm a little bit conservative in the loads I hauled. Dick Burkett, owner of the *Dawn Treader*, typically put 145 to 150 on his Lucander plywood vessel, just for perspective.

DW: Have you had any discussions with Lucander besides changing the wet tank, on the hull side? Are there any problems that might have come up afterwards, after you took delivery of it besides the changing to the wet tank? Were there any conversations about any problems with the design of the vessel?

BE: No, not about design problems. We've had a few conversations about possible improvements, exploring things like that. We were very happy with the vessel. Until this accident, it'd been a remarkably successful 40-foot vessel.

DW: When you took delivery, did you run the boat yourself, when you took delivery of the vessel?

BE: I was the primary operator, that is over 90 percent of the time from 1979 to 1989 and I've operated the boat at least a little bit, or been on the boat every year since, even after I became the primary operator of our larger vessel.

DW: Were there operating instructions for the vessel, either written or verbal?

BE: There were no written operating instructions. I recall specific maintenance instructions when I leased the boat a time or two, which we could provide if we still have them. There's no stability book, as far as loading, like I have with our other vessel.

DW: Okay. Are there any specific instructions on the amount of fuel that needs to be on board the vessel at any given time?

BE: No.

DW: Okay. You ran the vessel for several years. When you got away from the dock, were there recommendations to a new captain or a different captain that you should go out there at least half full or three-quarters full or, was it 900 gallons of fuel on the boat, or were there any instructions that you had to have that much fuel on board before you got away? Or was that up to each individual captain? Each individual operator?

BE: I assisted subsequent operators with recommendations on fuel, yes. Such as when salmon trolling, fill the stern tank, bring the stern down, it's easier to land fish, it's a nicer ride. When sablefish fishing and loading the boat with fish and ice, burn off the stern first, then return to the stern because the tanks are integral and returning fuel is warm, and it would melt the ice. When hauling crab gear, empty the stern tank so the boat does not squat with the heaviest loads.

DW: Okay. At some point the ownership of the vessel changed. Can you explain to me what happened or how it happened or why it happened?

BE: In the summer of 2001, the ownership was transferred to our sons, Ben and Dylan, so that we could utilize a couple of sablefish permits, which we wouldn't be able to use if the boat had been still in our ownership. We found this out two weeks before the season commenced. It had not been clarified. We thought everything was okay. And that was done in response to a confused policy through the National Marine Fisheries Service, that kind of jumped us at the last minute. And that was the status officially of the vessel on December 11 of 2001.

DW: Along the same lines, do you still hold the management part of the vessel yourself, so if a captain had a question, would he go to you or would he go your sons?

BE: I think it's fair to say I was still the manager.

DW: Okay. And you retained that up until the time that the boat was lost?

BE: Yes.

DW: Captain Thompson, he came to work for you in 2001 as the captain? Is that correct?

BE: As the captain, the second time I employed Rob, was 2001, correct.

DW: And the first?

BE: The first time I employed Rob was 1988.

DW: And was he employed as captain that time?

BE: No.

DW: As a deck hand?

BE: Yes, crabbing.

DW: When he was employed in 2001, was there any specific guidelines given to him about the crabbing or the crab gear on the vessel? First of all, how many pots would be there?

BE: I gave him guidelines as to the specifics as to how I loaded the boat. We discussed that. Yes.

DW: And when the crab pots would be set, was that something that the owner of the vessel tells the captain where to set the pots, or does the captain have his own specific places he likes to set pots?

BE: Are you talking about my operation, Rob's operation, or the fleet in general?

DW: Rob's operation, but on your vessel.

DF: Let's make clear, the only thing we want to talk about is the *Nesika* operation.

DW: Yes, exactly.

DF: In December of 2001.

DW: When the vessel departed, and I'm not familiar with your operation. Is there a certain line that you like to have crab pots set or does the captain pick out where the crab pots are set, from past experience?

BE: The initial load, the only load on December 11, the whole load of pots was rigged identically as far as the length of line and the buoy configuration, and we had a plan, and it was recommended by me.

DW: And can you tell me where that plan was to put the pots out?

BE: The strategy was to put the pots in the early or mid-20, 20s; 24 or 25 fathoms from off of Newport across the mouth of the Yaquina River and down to approximately the Seal Rock area. The strategy was to lay that gear close to town and be able to come in to get more gear.

DW: The date of the incident, do you know what time the *Nesika* got underway that morning?

BE: Approximately, yes. I know the Coast Guard has information spotting the *Nesika* driving by, and you probably already have that information. I think it was 7:49.

DW: Were you underway on the *Michele Ann*, I guess it was the same day, is that correct?

BE: Yes.

DW: Were you already out there on the ocean when the *Nesika* got underway?

BE: Yes.

DW: Did you have any conversation with the *Nesika* that morning prior to getting underway?

BE: Yes.

DW: Can you tell me what that those conversations entailed?

BE: With the *Nesika*, the vessel?

DW: Yes, the vessel. Or anybody on the vessel.

BE: I phoned Rob Thompson at home, probably soon after 5 in the morning to give him a "heads up," that the weather conditions had improved and we were mobilizing to look at going to set gear. I made a call to his home then. I talked back and forth with the boat. I know I spoke with the boat at approximately 6:30 a.m. also, and I think the boat was moving around the harbor, beginning to load bait at that time. And I was underway, either going down the river to the bar or, I'm not certain of the times, but I know I spoke with the boat after I crossed the bar, and gave a weather report.

DW: Was the weather consistent with times that the vessel could go out in that type of weather? Was the weather too rough, not too rough, so the vessel could go out? It's a small vessel, so, I mean, did it look like the weather was breaking enough so it could set gear?

BE: The weather had improved dramatically from the afternoon and evening before and was definitely usable weather in the early hours of that morning. When we mobilized at 5 to 6 a.m., the seas had come down from 20-plus feet to 10 to 12 feet. The winds had come down from westerly northwest, to light south or southeast winds, very light to where at 3, 4, 5 in the morning there was very little wind. And the conditions were good to go, yes.

DW: After the vessel got underway and crossed the bar, did you have any more conversations with the vessel?

BE: No. I called the vessel after we'd set 150 pots and were transiting, just to make sure everything was okay. I got company recordings on Rob's phone and on the phone that we'd installed on the boat. And I, I know I called Ben's phone and left a message but this was approximately 10. I just wanted to make sure he was okay.

DW: I'm sorry, sorry for your loss, by the way. Do you want to take a break?

BE: No. The pain doesn't stop.

DW: Do you know if anybody had any conversation with the boat after it crossed the bar?

BE: No. Not that I know of. We were not close by. We went in a different direction. We were in a VHF communication. I wouldn't hear.

DW: Do you know how many pots were on board the vessel when it got underway that day? Crab pots total?

BE: Not for certain, no.

DW: Before the vessel got underway that day or the day before, I understand it was fully loaded or at least, the pots were on board and ready for the vessel to get underway. Do you know how many pots were on the vessel at that point? Before it got underway?

BE: I understand through this investigation that Rob Thompson reported he had 149 pots on the boat to the Coast Guard when they made the inspection. There was some confusion, but that was the number he reported to the Coast Guard.

DW: And these were 90-pound pots?

BE: Negative.

DW: How much did the pots weigh then?

BE: The pots that I weighed, three of the load of 98 pots we recovered from the ocean seventeen days after the accident, averaged 72 pounds. These were pots that had been 90 pounds when they were new, but the pots' age was from 1979. The newest one would have been 1988, and the weight bars are eaten up in the electrolytic process of the pots aging, so these pots had gotten substantially lighter, 15 to 20 pounds lighter. So for example, if a person had 149 pots that weighed 72 pounds each on the boat, he has a lighter load than 135 pots that each weighed 90 pounds.

NM: The decision to fish that day, was that your decision or was that the captain's decision?

BE: The decision was the captain's decision.

NM: The total amount of pots that were on board that day, was that your decision or the captain's decision?

BE: The captain's.

NM: The area where the vessel would have fished that day, was that the decision of the captain or your decision?

BE: Where it was going to set gear or where it set gear?

NM: Where it was going to set gear first.

BE: My recommendation.

NM: Where the vessel set gear that day, was that a recommendation made by you or was that the captain's decision?

BE: The captain's decision.

DW: I'm not sure how far away your vessel was to the *Nesika* in miles when the incident occurred.

BE: With my notes and my plotters I could accurately answer that. I guess, hang on just a second, I guess about 20 miles.

DW: What was the sea condition where you were at the time, on the *Michele Ann*? I understand you were on the *Michele Ann*?

BE: Correct.

DW: What were the seas like where you were at that morning at the time of the incident?

BE: Difficult question to answer because the sea conditions changed significantly that day.

DW: What were there, confused seas?

BE: Yes.

DW: And wind status?

BE: Well, for instance, there had been a large swell, west northwest swell, and the wind the day and evening before, such that the bar I would not have considered safe to pass. It came down, as I said before, significantly and dramatically during the night, such that 36 boats went out hauling crab gear. Vessels smaller than the *Nesika* went out and vessels larger than the *Michele Ann.* The wind was less than 10 knots in the wee hours of the morning. When I spoke with Rob after I had crossed the bar, the wind was approximately 15 knots out of the south, and it rose. About the time that we understand that Rob went by the Coast Guard station, it was coming up and it rose at 8 and 9 and 10; it was up to about perhaps 30 west southwest against remaining west northwest swells. You say 10 to 12-foot seas; a lot of them were only 8, some of them might have been 18. By the time I joined the search in the afternoon the wind was already dying.

DW: What time did you get on scene that afternoon?

BE: That information is on my plotter and in my logbook. I think a few minutes before 2 p.m., 1 p.m. As fast as I could.

DW: Do you know if there were any other conversations with the *Nesika*, with any other vessels that morning after it crossed the bar? Do you want to take a break?

BE: No! It doesn't stop!

DW: I'm sorry.

BE: Repeat your question, please.

DW: Do you know if there were any other conversations from the *Nesika* to a different vessel that morning besides to your vessel?

BE: You already asked me that question, sir...

DW: I'm sorry.

BE: ...and to my knowledge, no.

DW: Okay.

BE: I haven't talked to anybody who spoke to them. Have you?

DW: No, not that I know of. The vessel got underway that morning, I understand, without the outriggers on it.

BE: Correct.

DW: Was that a decision that was made by the captain or a decision that was made by you?

BE: Decision made by the captain.

DW: Do you know why they weren't on there that morning?

BE: They weren't on there because he'd removed them and he had no intention of putting them back on, that I knew of, while crabbing.

DW: Okay, Captain Thompson had removed the outriggers then.

BE: Yes.

DW: Did the captain discuss why he took the outriggers off with you?

BE: It was clear to Rob that it was optional whether he had the outriggers on or off. And it was clear to me by his decision that that was his preference. I told him either way is fine.

DW: Okay. Did the captain discuss with you how many pots he intended to take that day on board the *Nesika*?

BE: No. We've been told that he had 149 pots on the vessel. We had an understanding that he could always take some off if the weather was real poor. During one of my conversations with Rob, either when I alerted him to the possibility of going shortly after 5 a.m., or when he was putting bait on the boat, one of those two times, he asked about taking the full load or taking a few off. And my response was, "It's your call."

DW: Can you elaborate what the "full load" meant?

BE: I assumed it meant the load that had been sitting on the boat for two weeks as we were tied up in a price dispute. The load that Tom Curry inspected, during his survey of the boat, while it was sitting there loaded at the dock. That load.

DW: You operated the vessel for a lot of years. You own the vessel. Can you describe the seaworthiness of the vessel?

BE: I am absolutely shocked at this accident. I probably drove the boat two thousand days. If you go to sea that many times, you can have some experiences. I had a very high degree of confidence in the boat. It was an extremely tough boat. Very seaworthy. I've been stuck in seas in excess of 30 feet, no problem. I remember coming around Cape Blanco, into 96 knots of wind, no problem. I have hauled large loads of pots in seas and wind far in the excess of December 11, 2001, no problem. We fished the boat, and in a like configuration, without poles. I fished crab and sablefish all those days, all those millions of pounds without poles, including sablefish trapping, pulling on sets of gear, in deep water and in gale-force winds, with nothing in the fish hold. We put on the deck and in the hold the heavy pots we used to use, and a drum on deck, nothing in the fish hold, running the boat all courses of the compass and setting gear in gale-force winds, again and again. I'm very confident in that boat. I had been to hell and back many times in that boat before December 11th. Just a damn good boat. That's all I have.

DF: I wanted to clear up a couple of things because we don't know the extent of the hull underwriter's investigation. Bob, could you tell us what Rob's experience was between the time that he fished for you back in 1988 and when he came on as captain of the *Nesika* in 2001? You've indicated that you gave a certain amount of deference to Rob Thompson in his decision to fish and in his decision to take a full load. And maybe you should state why you gave him deference to make those kind of decisions.

BE: Rob had extensive experience operating crab boats out of Newport. Nine years on the fishing vessel *Ms. Law*. The reason Rob was given the deference is from a couple of sources. I had a lot of confidence in Rob's ability. I felt damn lucky to have Rob as our skipper; he was, frankly, over qualified. He'd been bumped off the boat he was operating and I felt extremely fortunate to have him on the boat. I didn't want to micro manage his decisions. He'd fished out of Newport, plenty. He understood the bar, he understood the fishery and I felt lucky to have him as our skipper.

DF: Okay. Now the other thing I wanted you to clear up possibly is this potential issue over the outriggers. Can you tell us what would be the consideration, in your opinion, in removing those outriggers for fishing.

BE: I operated the boat as a crabber and a sablefish boat without the outriggers for years. I considered the outriggers a nuisance on a very small vessel. I was very aware of having extra shit on the boat. With the outriggers on the boat, they are a little bit of an inconvenience as far as being in the way. With the outriggers up, it probably did diminish the stability of the vessel. The fellow who ran the boat previous to Rob, Richard Wood, preferred to use the outriggers and that was okay by me, too. It's not the way I would have done it, but that seemed to work. You had to mess with them and put them up and down and we had them break a few times. If an outrigger breaks, you could take an extreme roll to the other side. It could be dangerous. Outriggers functioning, with the stabilizers in the water in an ideal situation, is one thing. Things falling apart are another thing. Maybe the underwriters are aware of the death in Bodega Bay that happened two years ago, where a boat was hauling crab pots out. They threw one stabilizer in the water, the boat rolled over and it killed a guy. These are some of the considerations. Aside from damage to the outriggers themselves and a little bit of a nuisance, it worked fine for the eight years that Richard Wood operated the boat with the outriggers on. And I know it worked fine for the 10 years that I operated the *Nesika* with the outriggers off. Is that a satisfactory answer?

DF: I think that covers it. Yeah, those are the only points I had, Nick.

NM: Okay. Then I will let Dave take over and put whatever he needs on his tape recorder to deem the matter concluded.

DW: Well, once again, that was tape recorded with everybody's knowledge and Mr. Fryer, if you could speak for yourself and your clients on my recorder?

DF: Yes, this was with our consent. And we, of course,

we request a copy of this transcript and, now that this is complete, we'd like to have copies of the transcripts of the other witnesses interviewed.

NM: Doug, the Eders obviously have expressed a desire to have those. I didn't think to bring a copy of them, but I'd be more than happy to stop by Jon's office and make a copy for them if that's of interest.

DF: I think that would be appropriate.

DW: I'm going to go ahead and stop the tape at this time.

March 2002

Friday
March 8, 2002

Today I received a copy of Dave Green's report. He's the marine architect from Jensen Maritime, who our insurance company hired to try and say our vessel was unseaworthy, so they wouldn't have to pay the families of the men who died. Green's report states that although for vessels the size of the *Nesika*, there are no formal regulatory standards, that the boat, as loaded, met or exceeded all of the recognized stability standards used in the industry for this type of vessel.

Green also concluded, "Regardless of a vessel's stability characteristics, a standard clause of any formal stability or loading document relates in some way to the exercise of good seamanship. In this case, it is my understanding that sea conditions involved at least two significant wave systems and that the incident occurred during a passing squall. The survival of a vessel under these circumstances remains heavily dependent upon the exercise of seamanship, regardless of a vessel's stability characteristics."

I can't help it. I feel an overwhelming sense of relief. The boat, as loaded, was seaworthy. We knew that. Now our insurer will have to pay our crews' families the insurance money.

March 13, 2002

Mr. Eugene Gray
State Medical Examiner's Office

Re: Benjamin Alan Eder
Date of Death: December 11, 2001

Dear Mr. Gray:

By copy of this letter to the State Medical Examiner, and to other appropriate persons, please consider this a complaint about the method of operation in the office in which you work.

It is unacceptable to be told that a file will not even be looked at for five weeks after it has been received by an agency. You told me on March 13th, you had received our request for a presumptive death certificate on February 28, and that it could be three more weeks before the matter was even begun to be looked at. Five weeks after a matter had been received? To add insult to injury, you also stated that it could be up to three months before a presumptive death certificate could be issued.

Mr. Gray—in all my years of law practice and in dealing with the state government, I have never heard of such poor service to the public. Never.

On the previous day, March 12th, I spoke to the woman who answers the phone in your office. I called because I had sent in the request more than two weeks ago and had heard nothing. When she said it would take several months for the death certificate to be issued, and I asked her why, she said "Because sometimes people show up after a few months." After I explained to her that in this case, our son and other men died at sea on December 11, 2001, more than three months ago, and that none of them were coming back, she still said it would take three months for a presumptive death certificate to be issued.

After I repeatedly asked you on March 13th if there was additional information that was needed in our file so that it could be processed, you finally deigned to look at the file (in advance of the three additional weeks you said it would take to even get to it) and said that I needed an official Coast Guard report, if that was the investigating agency (it is) and also a newspaper article to prove, then corrected yourself to say "confirm," that the events had taken place. I have now enclosed a copy of the Coast Guard Log for the time period of December 10 - December 12, which details the report of the capsizing of the *F/V Nesika* on the 11th, and the subsequent search and suspension of the search.

In regard to the "confirming" newspaper article, you told me that the reports I had sent you, downloaded from the internet, were "unacceptable."

I beg your pardon, Mr. Gray. The reports that I downloaded came from the US Coast Guard Group North Bend Web Site, which consisted of three separate press releases from the Public Information Officer, and described in detail the search and the suspension of the search for my son and the three other men lost at sea. Included in the press releases were the names and phone numbers of the Public Information Officer and the Commanding Officer of the North Bend Station.

In telling me that the information I provided was "unacceptable" to confirm their (and our son's) presumptive death, "Because we don't take anything downloaded from the internet," were you suggesting that I somehow had fabricated the excruciatingly painful details of the ship's capsizing and the loss of these men?

Mr. Gray—those articles are sufficient. Consider their deaths confirmed.

I do not expect special treatment. I expect a public servant to do their job. In a manner that is timely, efficient and sensitive to the needs of the public and the facts of each case.

Very truly yours,
Michele Longo Eder

cc: Dr. Karen Gunson, State Medical Examiner
Captain John Miko, US Coast Guard
Ms. Ginny Goblirsch
Senator Ken Messerle
Representative Alan Brown

March 17, 2002

Karen Gunson, MD
State Medical Examiner

Dear Doctor Gunson,

Attached you will find a letter I received from the mother of a young man that lost his life in a commercial fishing accident at sea off the Oregon coast.

I take pride in the service State of Oregon employees provide for the citizens of Oregon.

The story Mrs. Eder relates in her letter is one of unbelievable bureaucracy and seemingly indifference. There were three other people on board that fishing vessel. Are these families experiencing the same treatment at the hands of your department? Does reason and common sense have a role in government? I cannot think of any reason for this kind of service. As employees of the State of Oregon, all we have to offer is service.

Doctor Gunson, I know you are sensitive to the needs of the people you serve. Please help the Eder family resolve this matter.

Respectfully yours,
Alan Brown
State Representative
House District 10

cc: Michele Longo Eder

March 19, 2002

Robert L. Eder
Michele Longo Eder

Dear Mr. and Mrs. Eder:

This is to inform you that a presumptive death certificate has been filed with the State of Oregon Vital Statistics on your son, Benjamin Alan Eder, who has been missing since December 11, 2001.

Please allow two to three weeks to request your copy of the presumptive death certificate from the State Health Statistics. Please contact Vital Statistics directly at (503) 731-4108 for instructions on receiving your copy of this death certificate.

If you have any further questions please do not hesitate to contact this office at the number noted above.

Sincerely,
Karen Gunson, M.D.
State Medical Examiner

To:	**Friends and family**
From:	**Michele**
Date:	**Thursday, March 21, 2002**
Re:	**Tomorrow is Ben's birthday**

Dear All –

Tomorrow is Ben's birthday. He would have been 22. I hope you will all find your own way to celebrate his great life.

With love,
Michele

April 2002

Tuesday
April 9, 2002

I keep the door to Ben's room closed. Not because, as most people think, it's too painful to go by every day and see his things and think of him, but for an entirely different reason.

I've captured his smell. I can go in his room and smell him, nice big gulps of him, from his clothes I unpacked and put on the shelves of his closet. Actually, it was best when all his things were still in soft duffels; then I would just stick my head inside one and breathe him in. But in sorting through his clothes, I took them out of his bags, and I regret that now.

How long until the smell of him dissipates? What will happen when I can no longer grab at him as I walk in there, the room that faces the ocean where he died, the smell so real I can grasp him, hold him in my hands, put my arms around him. I'd live in there if I could. But then it would begin to smell of me, and that wouldn't be good at all. No, not at all.

Sounds.

I haven't cancelled Ben's cell phone. I can't. At $37.37 a month, I know I'm wasting money, but what price is it worth to still hear him? To cancel the phone would be to cancel him in the one last way I have of holding on to his physical life. Once in a while, I call his number to hear his voice on his message. Ben has, or had, a deep voice. Even though I know that Bob, Edie and I left him messages, the only one left is Dylan's; a message of love to his brother Ben, the saddest, most plaintive cries I have ever heard in my life. Heartrending sorrow, weeping, moaning, Dylan was begging Ben to come back, that it all not be real. If there is anything worse than Ben's death, it is Dylan's pain.

This morning I did the last bit of laundry I will ever do for Ben. In one of the bins that Bob, Dylan and I had packed in Eugene, in among Ben's shoes and hiking boots, was his laundry bag. It was a gift from his Aunt Mary, and made of heavy green cotton. One of us had picked it up from the floor of his apartment in Eugene. I thought it was empty, but no. Two days worth of worn underwear and socks were inside.

His last load of laundry. What I wouldn't give to see him again, with a pile of dirty clothes in his arms, his t-shirt stained with spaghetti sauce, the pockets of his pants loaded with sand and treasures: little cars, Legos, enough to choke any washing machine to a halt. Or to see his clothes stained with paintball ink, crusted with dried mud from playing rugby, or smelling of bait from chopping mink at the fish plant. I miss all his smells.

As an adult, Ben had become particular in the care of his clothes. "Fleece doesn't go in the dryer, Mom," he'd tell me, and his eye-rolling exasperation when I'd forget.

Tuesday
April 23, 2002

Swede Pearson, the sergeant with the local state police office, called me at the office today. I was sitting at my desk, computer screen on, phone receiver caught between my shoulder and my ear, typing and chatting away, when our receptionist stuck her head in my office to let me know he was on the other line. Shit. I finished the other call, took a deep breath and took the call from Swede.

The human remains that had washed up on the beach in January belonged to Steve Langlot. Swede said he would fax me a copy of the DNA report. I hung up. Not much else to say.

Dear God. Such horrific deaths for them all. I put my head down on my desk and wept. How long were they in the water before they drowned? Did they see the rescue efforts, or were they already dead? Did they see the other fishing boats and try to call for help? I pray that they died instantaneously, but I know that's not what happened.

The lawyer representing our crewmen's families writes horrible missives, warming up to his case, imagining himself in front of a jury:

"Robert Thompson, Stephen Langlot and Jared Hamrick have suffered the ultimate damage, death. It is probable that they suffered torturously before being overcome by hypothermia and drowning."

"Given the ocean temperature, the crewmen undoubtedly suffered for 30 minutes to one hour before drowning. Tragically, all of the *Nesika* crewmen would have known they were doomed to die. Undoubtedly, Ben, Robert, Steven and Jared's last thoughts were memories of their families, which they would never see again, and the crushing reality of just how short their lives had been."

"Plunged into near freezing waters of the Oregon coast, as

minutes slowing ticked away, the life trickled from the grasp of these four men. Death, the ultimate damage, was not a possibility, but a certainty. Because this boat was overloaded, four men treaded water simply waiting to die."

"As you know, the physiological and psychological aspects of drowning has been extensively studied. Through scientific experiments, we will be able to prove that each drowning victim endures a torturous process: first, fighting for their lives in panic; then gulping salt water into their lungs causing laryngospasm; cutting off the air supply resulting in the build-up of lactic acid in the muscles causing severe burning pain; convulsions next occur; and death is the result of ventricular fibrillation."

"Because of your client's negligence, four men are dead. They were not hit by a meteorite and the *Nesika* didn't catch fire. As you and everyone else knows, the crew of the *Nesika* were in the process of setting their gear; they had, in fact, set some of their gear. All hands would have been on deck. The boat undoubtedly capsized as a result of overloading, and the four men drowned. Photographs of the vessel after the accident clearly show the hull to be entirely intact from which we can conclude that this is a capsizing due to loss of stability. I understand that the first boats on the scene saw bodies in the water, but were unable to retrieve them. There were no bodies in the hull of the vessel. Steven Langlot's headless torso has been washed up on the beach. What is your theory, that all four men suffered an instantaneous death? Does the Eder family believe Ben didn't drown? A jury is going to reject any silly argument that these four men did not suffer prior to their deaths, and if such an argument is made, you can anticipate a verdict that punishes the insurance company and invades the Eders' personal assets. Is it necessary to not only put my clients, but also your clients, who lost a son in this same accident, through the pain of a trial?

May 2002

Tuesday
May 7, 2002

Today is our 14th wedding anniversary. Bob and I got up this morning and went for a walk on the beach. To celebrate, we'd been out to dinner last night at the Blackfish Café, a restaurant in Lincoln City. Fresh fish was served, halibut and black rockfish, bought locally. "Celebrate" is not quite the right word for what we did by going out to dinner. Honor our marriage, go through the motions that will hopefully lead us back to a measure of normalcy. Normalcy isn't the right word either. I have no right words.

I still cry every day. The hole in our hearts is so deep. I can't talk with Bob, or anyone, about our wedding day, because it involves memories of Ben and Dylan. We were married as a family, not as a couple.

We were married at the "Jew Dome," as Bob called it, that beautiful Temple Beth Israel in Northwest Portland, by Rabbi Rose, the only rabbi in the state of Oregon who would perform the ceremony. As Bob was unaffiliated with any temple, and me being a shiksa to boot, it wasn't easy for us to find a rabbi, mind you. We had meetings with Rabbi Rose and he gave me books about Judaism that I read and enjoyed, and he married us. The ceremony wasn't long. In the cavernous temple we were but few, but we had the traditional hoopah that came down from the ceiling and we stomped on and broke the wine glass. Before the ceremony I almost fainted in the rabbi's office. Bob said I turned completely white. My knees literally went out from under me. Bob grabbed me before I hit the floor. I think the enormity of what I was to undertake struck me. During the ceremony, Ben and Dylan held our wedding rings in gray velvet jewelry boxes. This past weekend, while going through another bin of Ben's things, I found the gray velvet ring box from our wedding.

Thursday
May 16, 2002

I've given up on trying to think I can overcome my crying. "If only I try hard enough," I say to myself. At night, restless in my sleep, I get up and wander the house, so as not to wake Bob. Sally gets up from her bed and follows me downstairs, tentatively, her old joints aching. I go into Ben's room and touch his things: his clothes, his books. I look at his biochemistry text, and the page that he marked, where he was reading as he sat in the black leather chair in the living room with me the night before he died.

I give up. I go and see a psychiatrist in Newport. I'm so desperate, I don't even care that I will see people I know in the shrink's office. I'm not crazy, but I know I'm depressed. But depressed people are supposed to lose weight. I haven't stopped eating and have easily gained twenty pounds since Ben died. Still, I know I need help. I need some relief.

The psychiatrist gives me Wellbutrin, and Xanax, an antidepressant and anti-anxiety medication.

Sunday
May 19, 2002

Today was the "Ben Eder Memorial Coast Hills Mountain Bike Race." Dave Campbell, the high school teacher who had led Ben's Celebration of Life, was the race promoter. This is an event that has grown out of the mountain bike club when Ben was a junior.

Ben, and his friends Peter Jordan and Daimeon Shanks, had been inspired by the races, and wanted to start their own. The race began in 1996 with a 26-mile course made for expert bikers, as well as a shorter course for novices. I remember the many days that Ben and fellow club members worked on the course clearing brush and building bridges. Dylan had volunteered at the race as well while in high school, and we always donated support: money, cell phones, a truck. Now, today, the race was held again, this time in memory of Ben.

Dylan is home from college, having finished his freshman year. At the dinner table last night neither Dylan nor Bob had much enthusiasm for going to the race. It wasn't that the race isn't important to them; it was the act of appearing in public, as if it is somehow normal to put yourself out in front of strangers at an event named to honor your dead brother, your dead son.

At the race site, a winding track up through the hills of South Beach, we helped the Honor Society students set up. While Bob and Dylan pounded stakes in order to string the multi-colored banners of the race sponsors, I split bagels and sliced oranges to feed the bike racers after the event. The young people who were volunteers avoided our eyes, and we avoided theirs. A blown-up photo of Ben was on a tall stake pounded into the ground at the start/finish line. Posters of photos from past races, including Ben and his friends, were on display. It was so painful. An hour or so into the race, Dylan announced he was leaving. He was going to a friend's house, and would see us later. I didn't blame him. It was awful. The announcer for the race, Dave O'Donnell, Dylan's wrestling coach and a wonderful man, wanted to know if we wanted to say a few words about Ben. Both Bob and I shook our heads "No." We just couldn't.

Afterwards, Dave Campbell invited us to his home for a meal with his family and the other adult volunteers, a post-race tradition. Although I'd made food to contribute, I dropped off a cake and a salad at their house and went home. It was too difficult to be with people. I could hear Ben saying to me, "Come on, Mom, you've got to go," but I had to tell him, "Honey, I just can't."

Thursday
May 23, 2002

Awards night. Newport High School.

How many times have I crossed this threshold into the high school for teacher conferences, wrestling meets, choir concerts, talent shows, to volunteer in the snack bar, to help teach Street Law classes? In the late summers when the boys were fishing, I'd even registered them for school, signing up for classes, making the adjustments to their schedules. Sometimes the boys wouldn't get off the boat until well after the first day of classes.

How many times have I been in this Multi-Purpose Room, the site of dinners, fundraisers for athletic teams, for Honor Society ceremonies, both when Ben and Dylan were inducted, and when they each acted as officers to welcome new students into the society. And I'd been there for two other Awards Nights, one in 1998, when Ben had graduated from Newport High and one in 2001, when Dylan graduated, both receiving scholarships.

I'd always told the boys that their teacher conferences were as wonderful as Christmas morning to me. Each of their teachers had a "present" for me; an insight into the boys I may not have seen, or a warm comment about their intellectual curiosity, their motivation, their responsibility, their kindness to others. And how I remember Ben's Awards Night. His name was called so many times: for Honor Society and Mountain Bike Club Scholarships, as a scholar athlete, to receive the Optimist Scholarship, the Lincoln County Medical Staff Scholarship, a Joanne Hamilton Scholarship. Ben grumbled about not being eligible for any need-based aid, but was happy with the total scholarship money he racked up that evening.

I remember all the shining faces, the seniors, some of them on the edge of their chairs, hoping for awards, delighted when their friends received them, the love of the parents who surrounded them, and the pride of the teachers who had helped them.

This night was different, though. Tonight, Bob and I walked into the Multi-Purpose Room at the high school to give an award in Ben's name—the Ben Eder Memorial Scholarship.

About a week before Awards Night, our "committee" met—Gretchen Nelson and David Hesse, Hannah Robbins, Nancy Reid and Jerry Robbins, and Bob and I. They were the parents of Ben's friends, and good friends to Ben, too. We sat around our living room, carefully reviewing applications and eating apple pie. We added an unusual twist to Ben's scholarship. Each student had to write an essay: "You have one week, $500 and a reasonably reliable-ten-year old Volvo station wagon. Describe your ideal road trip." All of the students were highly qualified, but it was the essay that tipped the balance in favor of a young man named David Giles.

On the evening of Awards Night, we sat in Bob's truck in the parking lot at Newport High School before going in. Bob told me he wasn't going to be able to speak in public. It was too soon, and simply too hard. I'd jotted out some words about Ben, but of course, they were inadequate. Sitting in the truck, Bob cried for awhile, then gathered himself and we went inside. Bless their hearts. Nancy Reid and Jerry Robbins were there, having promised us that they would be our "second," in case neither of us could speak. Such true friends, those parents of Ben's friends, who surrounded us with such love at the time and in the months after the accident.

Al Fitzpatrick approached. Al is a government teacher at the high school, the teacher for the Street Law class, where I'd helped coach a mock trial team for the last couple of years. Al is also a member of the local Optimist Club. Ben had volunteered many hours for club activities all four years he'd been in high school. The Optimists have also named a scholarship in Ben's honor. We are so moved.

When it was our turn to present the awards, Bob and I approached the podium. It was a hard balance: with our words we wanted to remember and honor Ben, but not bring grief to these young people and their parents for whom it was an evening of great joy, a culmination of hard work and recognition by their community, their family, and their peers for their success. I spoke, and Bob stood next to me. I remember speaking very slowly, for it was the only way I could get through it without sobbing. We shook David Giles' hand. Then Al Fitzpatrick stepped up and announced the Optimist Club Scholarship made in Ben's name. We thanked the Optimists, who spoke of Ben's volunteer service to his community.

Tyler McNamara won this award. We are glad the Optimists selected him, for although we don't know Tyler, we'd had a chance to see him as a volunteer at the bike race. Quiet, unassuming and needing neither direction nor attention, Tyler did the jobs that needed to be done and led others in doing them. He is an excellent choice for this scholarship.

Thursday
May 30, 2002

Swede Pearson, the sergeant with the Oregon State Police, called me again this morning. Another nightmare begins when the receptionist buzzes me to say, "Swede is on the phone." More human remains have washed up on the beach, just south of Lincoln City.

Swede says he doesn't believe the remains are Ben's. I wonder how he knows. We talk about "distinguishing marks." Swede wants to know about Ben's scars. I tell him of Ben's shoulder surgery, the pins in Ben's arm. Ben had a subluxated shoulder from playing rugby at Reed. Swede suggests I get Ben's x-rays sent to the medical examiner. The DNA analysis may take months, but the x-rays of Ben's upper body will help to quickly exclude him from the list of possibilities, if indeed, it is not Ben.

Obliquely, Swede is telling me they found an upper torso.

I write a letter to Ben's surgeon, Dr. Robert Wilson, asking for Ben's records to be sent to the state medical examiner.

Friday
May 31, 2002

Cause of *Nesika* Capsizing Not Determined
***The Oregonian*, Matt Sabo**

U.S. Coast Guard investigators are unable to pin down what caused the *Nesika* to capsize on Dec. 11 in an accident that claimed the lives of all four fishermen aboard the Newport fishing boat.

The *Nesika* overturned about a mile offshore of Newport just hours after the Oregon Dungeness crab season got under way. Crew members aboard a passing boat, the *Gary Lee*, notified the Coast Guard at 10:44 a.m. that the *Nesika* had capsized.

The boat washed ashore the following morning. The bodies of the skipper, Rob Thompson, 40, and his crewmen, Ben Eder, 21, and Jared Hamrick, 20, were never recovered. Partial remains of another crewman, Stephen Langlot, 34, washed ashore in January near Depoe Bay.

Skeletal remains were found on the beach Thursday morning south of Lincoln City, but it will take some time for investigators to identify them. A six-month Coast Guard investigation concluded that the 36-foot boat was not overloaded, as some Newport fishermen had speculated after the accident, said Lt. Tony Sellers of the Coast Guard's Marine Safety Office. The report is under review at Coast Guard headquarters in Washington, D.C. Sellers said there was not a "direct cause (of capsizing) that was actually found. Just like any situation where there were no survivors, it was pretty hard to piece this together," Sellers said.

Nesika crewmen did not call for emergency assistance, and an emergency beacon signal did not trip until nine minutes after the crewmen aboard the *Gary Lee* called the

Coast Guard.

Sellers said *Nesika* crew members had dropped about two dozen crab pots into the ocean and were dropping more when something catastrophic caused the vessel to overturn.

The capsizing could have been caused by a number of factors or combination of factors, Sellers said. Those include a shifting of the load, a freak wave or a problem with dropping crab pots. "Once you start offloading equipment, stability situations change," Sellers said.

The deaths of the fisherman, among 105 Newport fishermen who have died at sea since 1900, hit the community hard, said Jeff Feldner, a fisherman. He was at sea with 150 to 200 other Newport area fishermen on the morning the *Nesika* capsized. "This one was pretty profoundly significant," Feldner said. "It affected a lot of people."

Weather on the morning of Dec. 11 was worse than predicted and had turned terrible, Feldner said. Seas were running "close," meaning a boat doesn't have time to stabilize before the next wave hits, Feldner said. "Everybody was there," Feldner said. "Everybody was almost in exactly the same situation. There were so many of us that were exactly in the same predicament that day."

Thompson's crew also was considered competent and extremely professional, compounding the shock in the Newport fishing community. "The unknown is so much more in this one," Feldner said.

Thompson is survived by his wife, Trish, and three teen-aged children. The oldest, Josh, graduates on June 8 from Newport High School. Trish Thompson said she has been unable to claim Social Security benefits because a death certificate for her husband won't be issued until the Coast Guard releases its investigative report. "It's just awful that the Social Security office more or less looks at us and says, "It's your fault that Rob died, and we're not going to help you until we get this," she said.

Thompson said she has tried not to think about the forces at sea that caused the accident. "I didn't want to get worked up about it," she said. "I'll probably want to think of a reason later, but I was more concerned about how I was going to support my family."

June 2002

Wednesday
June 5, 2002

Dear Ben,

Tai sent us his senior thesis from Reed, dedicated to you. Here at the Fishermen's Memorial, Hannah has left you her corsage from graduation at Reed, and Noah carried your picture when he "walked" to receive his diploma. Karina climbed Mount Kilimanjaro, and at the top, carried a sign "In memory of Ben Eder. Learn, learn, learn!" Sugar maple trees, in your honor, were planted by Peter and Sunny behind Bragdon Hall at Reed. You are so loved by all.

Mom

July 2002

Tuesday
July 25, 2002

I read in the paper this past week that Barbara Roberts, the former governor of Oregon, would be speaking at the Nye Beach Writers' Series at the Newport Performing Arts Center on Saturday, July 20, at 7 p.m.

Barbara Roberts, her husband, Frank Roberts, and other members of the extended family had long been active in Oregon politics. While Barbara served as governor, Frank served in the Oregon Senate, only to be stricken with cancer during his last years of service. I cannot imagine how she did it, but as governor, she cared for her dying husband in Mahonia Hall, the governor's mansion. He died in 1993, while she was still in office. In the years following her husband's death, Barbara wrote the book, *Death Without Denial, Grief Without Apology*. She was to speak at the Performing Arts Center of her experience with death and loss.

I've always admired Barbara Roberts. A girl from Eastern Oregon, high school educated, had risen to become the leader of our state. I thought that was pretty good stuff. Although I'd found no comfort in any of the self-help books people offered me in the months since the accident, I thought Barbara might have something to say to me.

I went alone to the Performing Arts Center that evening. Bob was fishing. I walked into the small theater just a few minutes before 7 p.m., into a room that was dark all around, with small tables and chairs set up, café style, and chairs lined up along the back of the room. One of the last to arrive, I made a beeline directly for an empty seat. I was sitting next to Taylor Bortz.

Taylor was a senior in high school and for the last few years played high school soccer with Dylan as the only girl on the varsity team. If for no other reason than her bravado in playing defense on an all-male team, I liked her very much. In the few times I'd spoken with Taylor, she seemed bright and sassy and very self-contained.

Taylor and I looked at each other, and by an almost imperceptible shake of the head, indicated how surprised we were to find ourselves sitting next to each other, both alone. I knew there was an open mike following the speaker. Taylor clutched a folder of papers.

I asked Taylor if she was going to read at the open mike. She took a deep breath and stammered, "Yes, but I'm not sure if it's appropriate." I wondered what she meant.

At the end of Barbara's reading and questions from the audience, it was time for the open mike. Taylor looked a little panicked and at first, I thought it was just normal nervousness, as any young person would feel in front of such a large and adult crowd. I admired her for coming alone—not with a gaggle of girlfriends or boyfriends, but simply by herself to read her work, her art.

Still in her chair, Taylor turned to me and blurted, "I wrote about the *Nesika*—the accident. I don't know if I should read this."

It took my breath away, but I told her, "Read, Taylor. I really want to hear what you wrote. It's really important to me."

"But I don't know if what I've said is okay. I don't want to hurt you."

"It's okay, Taylor. I really want to hear what you wrote."

Taylor read.

FOUR MEN DROWNED TODAY

Four men drowned today
how long does it take for the December water to quench his
thirst for the sea
When they are suddenly
gone
from our lives
look back and remember
the boys and the lovers
Everyone knew by dinnertime
every fisherman in town had a private mourning
they know how any weight
can disappear under
gray benign waves
and how one longs for the gusty solace
of the never ending horizon

The wives will receive stiff lilies,
pyrex casseroles, grievances
she will grow cold over the loss
of a son, a husband
we murmur things to the effect of "I'm sorry,"
and think 'why do bad things happen
to good people?'
secretly grateful it wasn't our own

Yet no answer will come
the tides will rove across the beaches, our backyards
and whisper in our dreams
"Your bones are like water
you are sons of the sea."

-- Taylor Bortz

Taylor couldn't have known that I would be there, and I couldn't have known that she would have written a poem about our loss, and neither of us could have known that we would each come together that evening, me to listen, and her to share.

August 2002

Sunday
August 11, 2002

Dear Ben—

Phoebe left for Argentina on Thursday. She'll be in Buenos Aires for at least a few months, maybe longer -- studying their economic policy. Or really, their economic collapse! You'd be so proud. She is so brave.

Love,
Mom

Thursday
August 15, 2002

The phone on my credenza buzzed. The receptionist told me it was Kerry Tymchuk, with Senator Gordon Smith's office, on the line. Hmph, I thought. I wonder what this is about. Although I made no financial contributions to his campaign, I did support the Republican Senator as a "Democrat for Smith."

"Michele!" said Kerry, in his irrepressible manner. "Guess what? President Bush is going to be in Portland next week with Senator Smith, and you're invited to meet with him—just a group of people who want to talk about issues of concern to them. Want to come?"

I almost choked with surprise. Regardless of whether I agreed with many of the President's positions, this was the President of the United States, and I am being offered a chance to meet him. I was ecstatic, quickly expressing my acceptance to Kerry.

"OK," he said. "Just a formality, but we need your social security number for a background check."

I gave it to him. Kerry told me he'd call me in a day or two with all the details as to the time and place of the meeting.

I am flabbergasted. It feels like the first sign that not every day of my life will be heavy with nothing but grief. I saw I could actually get excited about something again, and that gives me a sense of optimism I haven't felt in a very long time.

Kerry called me back with the details. The event is to be held at the Portland Hilton and our meeting with the President is at 1:30 p.m. Quickly, I made reservations at the Hilton, checked my wardrobe for a presentable suit, and looked at my shoes. Oh, brother. Run down heels wouldn't cut it. I figured I'd go up to Portland the night before, so as to not worry or be caught in traffic, and then I'd have a chance to hop over to Nordstrom's that morning for some new shoes.

Saturday
August 24, 2002

I arrived at the Hilton Wednesday evening, having reserved a room in their main tower. When I checked in at the desk I was told by the clerk there were "no rooms at the inn" so to speak, because the President, his White House staff and his security detail were arriving. The clerk offered to put me in a hotel eight blocks away.

"No," I said, "You don't understand. I have a meeting here tomorrow I need to look good for, and I can't be walking eight blocks outside to get to it. My hair will get ruined," I said.

"Sorry," said the clerk. "The President's here."

"I know that," I replied. "That's why I need the room I reserved and I need to be in this building."

The desk clerk then offered me a closet, with a pullout bed, and a shower down the hall. I declined, and after further discussions with the manager, realized the best I was going to do was to stay in the hotel annex, kitty corner to the main building. Oh, well.

The next morning I made a successful foray into Nordstrom's, emerging with both new shoes and a new handbag. The meeting was at 1:30 p.m., so just after noon I showered and dried my hair. Wrapped in a thick terrycloth robe, I began setting my hair in electric rollers. If the humidity hit me when I left the building, no matter how much I shellacked my hair, my "Texas big-hair" would collapse.

Pound, pound, pound. Loud knocks at my hotel room door. I peeked out the hole. Two guys, in cheap-looking sports jackets and slacks, one holding a badge, stood there. What the fuck? I thought. I opened the door.

"We're FBI, ma'am and we have some questions to ask you," the taller of the two said.

"Let's see some I.D.," I demanded. Oh, yeah, I was real smart—opening the door to two strange men and then asking to see I.D. I think I got it backwards.

They produced their I.D.'s. All I could think of was they looked pretty seedy to me. Where was Clint Eastwood? Tommy Lee Jones? Dark glasses, ear pieces. You know, stud muffins?

The taller one spoke first. "We understand that last night you arrived at the hotel and were demanding to stay in the main building, where President Bush was going to stay. We want to know exactly why you wanted to stay in that building, and why you wouldn't move. You were reported as a potential threat."

I almost started to laugh. I began to sputter. "Look, I made that hotel reservation, and I wanted to be there because—well, because—look at my hair," and I pointed to my head. One side was done up in giant rollers; the other side hung down, stringy straight. "See this?" I asked. "See this hair? I have a meeting with the President at 1:30 today, and if I had to go to a different hotel and walk eight blocks in this weather, my hair would have looked like hell. And that's the God's honest truth."

It was clear the agents were convinced of my sincerity and had already started to back away and retreat down the hall. "See this?" I kept pointing to my curlers. "This is why." They had heard enough, and made their escape in the elevator. So much for investigating me as a security risk.

Later, walking into the main lobby of the Hilton, I saw the FBI agents. I was all spiffed up, complete with "big hair," and when I saw the men, I tilted my head, gently patted my hair, and smiled at them. Neither of them cracked a smile in return.

Newport News Times
August 28, 2002

Michele Longo Eder Meets with President during Portland Visit

On Aug. 22, fisheries attorney Michele Longo Eder of Newport was invited by the White House and U.S. Senator Gordon Smith to participate in a bipartisan roundtable discussion with President George W. Bush, U.S. Senator Gordon Smith, R-Ore., U.S. Congressman Greg Walden, and 16 other Oregon community leaders, during Bush's visit to Portland.

"It was a great opportunity to speak directly with the President about issues of vital significance to Oregon's commercial fishing industry," Eder said. "The President spent over 90 minutes with the entire group in private, and a wide range of issues was discussed, from education, homeland security, fishing communities and ports, to the need for community health centers, funding of faith-based social programs, and forest policy."

"I spoke with the President about the need for tariffs on Canadian pink shrimp that our West Coast fishermen believe is being dumped into U.S. markets," she said. "I also asked for the President's support in moving forward a bill in regard to a change in the tax law to allow Capital Construction Funds to be rolled into an IRA, or for people leaving a commercial fishery to use that money to start a new business, to help stimulate the economy."

Eder, the wife of a commercial fisherman, continued, "The President was very receptive to these issues, and asked a lot of questions. He also expressed his understanding of the need for a vessel buyback program. President Bush was shocked to hear about the prospective West Coast groundfish cuts, and how it will affect fishermen and coastal communities. He was very taken aback by the stated goals of the Pacific Fishery

Management Council to reduce the West Coast fleet by 50 percent, without an economic plan in place by the Pacific Council or NMFS to address the likely collapse of family-owned businesses as a result of the cuts."

Eder described the discussion as "free-wheeling" at times, with the President speaking very frankly about his views. "I was delighted to see that not only did the President clearly grasp complex matters of importance to Oregonians, but he spoke his mind about them and he spoke from the heart," she said. "I left the meeting having no doubt about his commitment to his values, and his genuine compassion regarding the future of our fleet."

September 2002

Saturday
September 7, 2002

Yesterday I stopped at the Fishermen's Memorial after work, flowers in hand.

I saw a fellow sufferer. It was Jared's mother, Elizabeth, although I didn't immediately realize it. I stuck out my hand.

"Michele Eder," I said.

Elizabeth said, "It's me, Michele, Jared's mom."

At first I was embarrassed I had not recognized her. What I have discovered is that nothing much embarrasses me anymore; there is no gaffe that can't be forgiven, even my own. Since the accident, I'm much less hard on people now, including myself.

I have already cried three times today, in varying venues, in the company of others, and this was no exception. Elizabeth and I hugged, and I put my head on her shoulder and sobbed. Unabashedly. I made noise, the snot ran, until I was able to lift my head and wipe my face with my sleeve. She, too, cried, deeply; another woman who had lost her son.

I knew Elizabeth had long been alienated from her son Jared. Jared had a tough life and, as an adult, Jared had little, if any, relationship with his mother. Elizabeth verified that for me, not that she ever tried to hide it. Today, she asked me of her son: "Had he ever fished before? Had he been on a boat?"

Oh God, to know so little of your son's life! I told Elizabeth what I knew of her son; what Jared had told me himself. He'd said he'd been out on the *F/V Olympic*, a trawl vessel owned by Terry Thompson, on a couple of trips. So, yes, I told her he'd been on the ocean fishing before, but not on a crabber. Knowing how much it would mean, I told her how glad Bob was to know Jared, that Bob had come home last fall, enthusiastic about Jared's attitude and work ethic. Bob said, "I think Jared could be a real fisherman." I told Elizabeth what Bill Lang, the manager at Catton's dock at South Beach, had told me when I called Bill for a reference: that Jared was a hard worker, could take instruction, and he wanted to learn. I hope my words warmed her. I told her of our Crew Thanksgiving, how Jared brought his girlfriend, Kelly, to our home. How he and Tom Ramsay and their dates had joked, filled their plates with food and enjoyed themselves.

Elizabeth told me her son's birthday would be September 9, in just a few days. She wanted to know who was bringing all the beautiful flowers to the memorial and I confessed, pleased that she enjoyed them.

"You must have a green thumb," Elizabeth said.

But I explained that the secret was to plant stuff you couldn't kill off, even if you tried. Lilies, gladioli, and roses. She laughed. We left, together, and I am glad to have seen her.

Saturday
September 21, 2002

Bob has been home for two days now, and I can't think of a time when we've both been as sad or felt it as deeply. He came in from fishing on Thursday and I came home from work, to a very quiet house. I walked through the laundry room from the back door entrance into our kitchen. Sally greeted me, tail wagging. Entering the living room I saw Bob seated in "his" black-leather chair, his face contorted, sobbing. Body-wracking, shoulder-shaking sobs. I held him for a while, then he began to talk.

"You know Dale and Jerry and Doug out at the Yaquina Boat Equipment?" Bob said.

"Yeah, honey, I do," I said.

"They called me today," he said. "The fountain is ready."

Earlier this summer, Bob and I had been playing tennis at the courts behind the old middle school. A cool, stainless steel water fountain was located there. The bowl of the fountain was a sheave, which is used as part of a hauling mechanism on a fishing boat. Yaquina Boat Equipment made this one. Inscribed on the front of the cylinder of the water fountain were words to honor the late Joyce Hall, the wife of Wilburn Hall, a local fisherman. The inscription recognized her many contributions to the community.

Bob, on seeing the fountain that day, said, "I want this for Ben. Down on the bayfront. Instead of the tiles that mark the dead." Bob shook his head. "Those tiles on the sidewalk bother me. This fountain is something beautiful. This would be right."

So he'd spoken to Yaquina Boat Equipment, and Steve Dickinson with the City of Newport, and David Hesse with the Port of Newport. Yaquina Boat Equipment would make the fountain, and the City and the Port would work together to place it at the entrance to Dock 5 on the boardwalk, where the fishermen and the tourists and the locals would see it every day and be able to use it. For Ben, being a welder himself, it would be a particularly fitting memorial.

"Well, what did the guys at Yaquina Boat Equipment say when they called?" I asked Bob.

"They said they were giving the fountain to us. The men are donating not just the materials, but also all their time." Bob choked the words out as his chest heaved.

My eyes filled with tears, dumbstruck by the continuing generosity of our community who wanted to support us in every way.

"They told me they wanted to do something at the time of the accident, but they didn't know what was right." Tears continued to run down Bob's cheeks. "Dale said one of the guys suggested it, and it didn't take 10 seconds for all of them to decide to do it."

I couldn't believe it. The hand-crafted fountain was expensive and time-consuming to make. It would be such a wonderful memorial to the men of the *Nesika.* It would beautify the Port and the docks and was something functional that would be seen, and used. Bob and I talked about what we wanted to write, what words we wanted inscribed on the fountain and decided on something that had very special meaning to both of us:

May the life of this boat be bountiful and safe.

Those were the words that Bob christened the *Nesika* with in 1979, when it was first launched. Those were the words imprinted on the Tyco label fastened to the dashboard in the *Nesika.* Those words had stayed in place for more than 20 years, and they were still there on the dash after the vessel sunk, rolled in the surf, came ashore and had been salvaged and stored on blocks at the boatyard up the Yaquina River.

"May the life of this boat be bountiful and safe." Those were the same words with which I had christened the *F/V Michele Ann* in August of 1996.

Now, six years later, we would use those same words once again to commemorate the lives of our son, our crewmen, and the vessel. We decided to inscribe on the fountain, "May the life of this *fleet* be bountiful and safe." And then below it, *F/V Nesika* and list the names: Ben Eder, Jared Hamrick, Steve Langlot, Rob Thompson. No date on it. The people who knew of the incident would recognize that it was a memorial, and those who didn't, well, that was okay. There were plenty enough dates and memories of death. We wanted this to be a blessing.

***F/V Nesika* Memorial at Dock 5, Newport Bayfront**

The next morning, Friday, I went with Bob to Yaquina Boat Equipment to pick up the fountain. I wanted to personally thank the men and also take them a picture of Ben and a couple of the articles, so that everyone could read about Ben and learn more about who he was. Bob then dropped me at the office, while he went off to the Port to see David Hesse, who would coordinate the placement of the fountain.

Saturday morning we got up and went for a walk on the beach with Sally. It was a sunny, gorgeous, perfect September day. The next day would be fall, but today felt like the best of summer.

Sitting at the kitchen table after a breakfast of waffles and cappuccino I made for him, Bob sighed deeply and said, "I just don't think I've got it any more, Michele. I just don't think I can do this."

I realized getting off the ocean had nothing to do with money. Bob knew we had enough assets to sell off, so that he wouldn't have to work. Bob said his commitment to fishing cost us our son, but he couldn't stop fishing because his relationship with the ocean had brought him such joy and a sense of rightness with the world. Going fishing gave him strength again. Bob described commercial fishing as "Beauty. Beauty with a purpose. A lot of fishermen don't articulate it, but when they are on the ocean, they feel it."

We talked about Bob returning to his writing. The Nye Beach Writers' Series periodically has writers come to the Newport Performing Arts Center, do a reading or presentation of their work, and then afterwards there's an open mike for people to read their poetry or prose. Tonight two women authors would be speaking, and their work involves whales, the environment, and feminism. I pointed out the event to Bob and suggested we go, and that he read one of his poems. His eyes sparkled at the idea; he knew exactly what he wanted to read.

"You think I should do this?" he asked.

"Absolutely. It's more than time." I said.

I want to encourage him to begin to write again, and part of that process is to be around writers and to be ready to share his work. It was healing, I thought, for him to want to see people, to be out in public, and to share with others the thoughts closest to him.

Bob reading at the Nye Beach Writers' Series, Newport
September 21, 2002

THE WHALES RETURNING

We sighed and watched
For your coming extinction,
Built coliseums of grief
And waited. Beneath my forehead
I wear your tattoo:
I would love to hunt you.

You are a chosen creature, obvious
And mysterious; we accelerate
Towards our breach
And you have dived.

An epilogue, you are the mammal
Who came back, who
Sacrificed his legs for his lungs,
Who feeds and moves by echo,
Who has been there and knows.

This time
You made us hear your song,
Wet and familiar; like mercy
It holds us, a fear
So close it leaves us helpless.
To whom do we sing?

--Bob Eder

October 2002

Wednesday
October 2, 2002

This morning I took two apple pies out the Bay Road to Toledo for Dale, Jerry and Doug, owners of Yaquina Boat Equipment. Their crew has crafted and welded the water fountain that will be inscribed "May the life of this fleet be bountiful and safe," "*F/V Nesika*" and the names of our men who died. I spoke with the men at Yaquina Boat Equipment briefly. As I looked into their kind eyes, I could barely get the words out. I enjoyed bringing them the pies. It was but a small thank you for their enormous generosity.

In the grocery store in the last few days I've seen husbands and wives, mothers and fathers of other fishing families with their sons who fish, and I realize I envy them. I smile warmly and outwardly engage in conversation, but privately I wonder: Why was it my child and not theirs that was lost? I don't wish that bad things happened to other people instead of us, but I do wonder how it is in this random world that Ben and the other men were taken. I would never wish anyone the pain we have suffered, but I can't help but think: Why us and not you? Why Ben, and not your son?

Ben was such a fighter. His spirit was indomitable. He never found anything that with his sheer willpower, hard work, and determination he couldn't conquer.

What must Ben's last hour on this earth have been like? Whatever happened, I hope he was immediately knocked out. I pray he had no conscious realization that he was going to die, and I pray that he did not suffer in the ways I fear he did.

Was Ben alone in the water for a long time, and did he freeze to death? Bill Wechter, the fisherman aboard the *F/V Gary Lee*, who found the *Nesika*, saw two men floating face down near the boat. One of the men floating was believed to be Steve Langlot, identified by his long hair in a pony tail. From Bill's description, I am almost certain the other man was Ben, because Bill said that the hair was kind of reddish, and Ben had auburn hair.

I can't stop thinking about Ben. How long was he in the water before he drowned? For how long did he suffer? Did he comfort, or was he comforted by the other men who died with him? For how long did they scream for help before their life's breath was taken? Did he see other boats in the area? Could he see our home? Why did he have to die in such a terrifying manner? Why couldn't he leave this earth surrounded by those who loved him? Ben was utterly alone in his death, in his excruciatingly painful death, and I think about that all the time.

As I'm sitting here, writing this, I just received an email from Phoebe, who is in Argentina.

From: **Phoebe**
To: **Michele**
Date: **Wednesday, October 2, 2002**
Subject: **I miss my Jewish mother**

Dear Michele,

How are things going? How are Bob and Dylan? I am now completely settled into my house and I feel very fortunate to have my Israeli/Argentine housemate. We are both involved in many of the same organizations here in Buenos Aires. I am active in two independent media organizations, Indymedia Argentina and Argentina Arde.

Michele, Argentina is fascinating. They are a culture of mobilization, and the organizing I have seen so far has been inspiring. On a normal day I attend meetings in different parts of the city. I meet with the photo and press commission for Argentina Arde every Monday night at the Universidad Popular. I like to go to the community assemblies that have been organized since the government was thrown out of office. I take modern dance class three days a week, which is a nice break from speaking Spanish. Depending on the week, there are different protests and marches, all of which I attend as a member of the press. Also, I am trying to keep up on my readings about the International Monetary Fund and send papers to my professor at Antioch. I am also reading books on the history of Argentina, and lots of contemporary analysis of the current situation by authors such as James Petras and Eduardo Galeano.

I hope that explains what I am doing here. A lot of the time I feel more stressed than exhilarated. The situation here is very heavy and depressing. I have made connections with people in the Unemployed Workers Movement, the group that has come to be known as the *piqueteros* (picketers). I visited one of the communities two days ago and was hit hard by the poverty and misery so many

Argentines are experiencing. Before I came to Argentina I knew the government was a piece of shit and I knew the IMF structural adjustment programs are impoverishing millions of people around the world. It is quite another thing altogether to be here and to witness the oppressive conditions. My political consciousness is growing and I know that I will be even more active when I return to Antioch. I hope everything is o.k. in Oregon. Please write me soon.

Love, Phoebe

Thursday
October 3, 2002

Dearest Ben –

I got a lovely letter from Phoebe yesterday. She is so busy in Buenos Aires, reporting on IMF issues. Very exciting!

We are off today to L.A. to Moses' bar mitzvah! It will truly be an event. Your father is going to speak. You would be so proud of him. He has such courage. You will be with him as he speaks to all our family. And I feel your presence with me, always.

I love you, Ben.
Mom

NOVEMBER 2002

Tuesday
November 5, 2002

Dear Alan and Lorna,

This is a very hard time right now. I know you can't fix it, but I appreciate just being able to write to you about it.

The memories of last Thanksgiving are a nightmare. We had our Crew Thanksgiving, with 23 people. That evening I sat and talked with Rob and Trish Thompson and their children at dinner; Bob was down at the other end of the table, engaged with Bill and Sandy Retherford and their family. Of all the crew who were there that night, three men are dead, three men have left us, and only Javier remains. One man left fishing entirely after the accident. Another man was Jared's best friend and was on the *Michele Ann* with Bob that day, looking for all of them in the water.

If I surround myself with activity and noise, I can hide in the midst of roasting pans and pie plates and mashed potatoes, but the thought of being alone on the holiday with just Dylan, Bob and Edie makes Ben's absence so palpable that I dread it. It isn't as if I don't feel it every day, I do. I set the table for four every night and I always will. I just keep expecting Ben to bound through the door and I can't accept the fact that he never will.

The doctor's drugs don't appear to be working anymore. I've stopped sleeping again and my mouth is just beginning to heal from a massive outbreak of blisters. I see the shrink again next week, but since she can't bring back Ben, it isn't much help. I can go through the motions of trying to get better and I'm sure

I will someday, but it isn't now.

I mainly spend my time, or as much as I can, memorializing Ben. All the news articles are in scrapbooks for the bike race and the scholarships. I have made one for his writings from 1997 to 1998.

Please go through your pictures and send me as many as you can of Ben by himself and with others. I will have copies made and will take good care of them, I promise.

I know your lives are full with your own and your children's needs. Sorry it's been so much of a one way street this last year, but I so appreciate your support.

Love,
Michele

Wednesday
November 6, 2002

Bob isn't home yet. He has an annual meeting of the membership for the Newport Crab Marketing Association, and then a meeting of the Board of Directors. I spent yesterday helping him get ready and drafting agendas for the annual membership meetings. The men will begin price discussions during a conference call with Associations up and down the coast from Westport, Washington, to Half Moon Bay, California. As usual, the crab politics are a mess. I have no stomach for it this year, none whatsoever, and to some extent, I am surprised Bob does.

After eating dinner and watching TV, Bob and I turned on the VCR. Ben's scuba instructor at Reed College, Kim Johns, sent us a video he used to advertise his business, Adventure Travels. A portion of the video involves Ben in the ocean, scuba diving in full dive suit and tanks. There is a great shot of Ben coming out of the water. He is looking directly into the camera and his eyes sparkle. Ben's body is strong in the wet suit, and his shoulders and arms ripple as he pulls himself up the side of the boat and climbs in. The footage so embodied what Ben was about; the twinkle, the smile, the warmth and his strength.

Wednesday
November 20, 2002

Dear Mr. Williams:

If you are the gentleman who sits on the Board of Directors of Jenkins Insurance Company, then you met my husband, Bob Eder, and our two sons, the oldest, Ben, and the younger, Dylan, on a raft trip in Puerto Mont, Chile, in the spring of 2001. What a good time they had! My husband and sons told me about their adventure, and of meeting you and your son. Bob says he also mentioned to you that Jenkins' was the underwriter for our boats. We have been insured with your company for 15 years, maybe longer.

Some unspeakably sad news: our son, Ben, and three other men were lost at sea last December 11, when the *F/V Nesika* capsized. I've attached a photo of Ben and of our family taken last Thanksgiving, just three weeks before he died.

Also attached is Ben's obituary, and I've included an article about him that I wrote for the local paper. Neither of these can begin to describe the great light Ben was in our lives, and in the lives of his family and friends and our community, but I hope it tells you a little bit more about him. Having met Ben, even briefly, you are sure to remember his warmth. Bob told me that Ben had made a special effort to engage and talk to your son that day.

I'm writing to you not only to tell you of Ben's death, but as an insured of your company, I want to tell you how we were treated at the time of a loss so profound that we could barely function.

While our local agent and the local marine surveyor, Jon McKnight and Tom Curry, respectively, treated us with great kindness, and while we have respect for David Green, the stability engineer, and Kurt Gremmert, the investigator, that is not the case in regard to all the personnel associated with, or hired by Jenkins Insurance Company.

Although I recognize that Jenkins has a duty to its shareholders, the way we were treated by your company, a company to which we'd paid insurance premiums to for so many years, was worse than shameful.

On the hull side, Jenkins hired an investigator and an attorney to investigate and make recommendations as to whether to deny us our claim.

Even before we could hold our son's memorial service, your company's lawyer, Nick McDermott was faxing pages and pages of detailed demands for information regarding the vessel, our business and crew. While we should have been fully engaged in grieving for and honoring our son and the men of the *Nesika*, we were frantically gathering information and had to hire an attorney to protect ourselves. Instead of having some peace of mind that we were in good hands with your company, a company that had assured us it would take care of us in the event of a catastrophe, we were pushed to the edge.

Our former skippers, men who had known Ben since he was a small child and who had fished with him and taught him, were invaded by phone calls from your investigator at their time of grief, trying to "dig up dirt" about us to somehow justify the denial of the hull claim.

As late as February 27, 2002, Nick McDermott, the lawyer for your company, in a face-to-face interview he demanded with my husband, told us the purpose of the interview was still to determine whether the hull claim would be allowed.

This torment went on for over three months after the accident. It wasn't until mid-March that Jenkins Insurance acknowledged there was no basis whatsoever to deny us coverage.

One of the saddest parts in dealing with Jenkins in regard to the hull claim was the absolute irony of being attacked in this manner. As anyone in the West Coast fishing community would tell you, from the greenest deckhand to the most successful vessel owner, my husband takes incredibly good care of our vessels. They are maintained impeccably. In an industry where irresponsibility is unfortunately present, the vessel *Nesika* was a jewel in your fleet, and our son and crew were precious to us.

As we contemplated your company's threats to deny us coverage, my husband looked to me in grief and shock and said, "Did they think I wanted to kill our son?" I could only shake my head in disbelief.

I realize that you are not personally responsible for the conduct of the people hired by Jenkins Insurance. I understand that in the course of business, every effort must be made to insure that no claims are paid if there is a reason not to do so. But I had to tell someone personally at Jenkins what it was like for our family to have this experience with your company. There is a very human face to those you insure and I wanted you to hear from us.

Bob joins me in the hope that your family is well and happy.

Sincerely,
Michele Longo Eder

Friday
November 29, 2002

Will we ever again wake up in the morning without our first thought being, "Ben is dead"? Will we ever again celebrate a holiday, or any family gathering without this gaping wound?

Dylan arrived home from college on Friday, with his friend Martin in tow. Martin stayed with us for a few days before leaving to join some other friends for Thanksgiving Day. I was glad Dylan brought someone home with him; the prospect of Dylan coming home alone to this house, without friends to distract him, frightens me. The evening that Dylan and Martin arrived we had a fun dinner and played an uproarious game of *Cranium*, afterwards. Bob was quite comical; he did a great Ray Charles imitation in response to one of the game's challenges.

I strong-armed Harvey, Alan, Lorna and the kids, as well as Edie, into coming for Thanksgiving. I could not stand for it to be just Bob, Dylan and me for dinner. The three of us together reflect each other's grief so intensely, the sadness is always being mirrored back.

For many years, I kept holiday notebooks that record the guests who came for Thanksgiving, and all the other holidays: the meals I served, how the house was decorated. Well, I haven't written any notes to look back on for this past year. We haven't done much celebrating.

Lorna, Alan, Harvey, Edie, and Moses and Marley arrived from Los Angeles on Wednesday night. I fed them all hamburgers and cheeseburgers; everyone was starved. The nephews brought the latest craze with them, *Dance, Dance Revolution*. It is a video game that you plug into the TV. It comes with a mat. Dance steps are displayed on the screen, with pulsating music in the background. The patterns of the dance steps become increasingly difficult as you move up the levels, as does the speed of the rhythm of the background music. Moses and Marley were obviously the stars, but almost all of us took a try at it, even Grandma Edie. It kept us all active and busy, a good tonic for my otherwise depressed state.

On Thanksgiving Day, I woke up early and made waffles for everyone. I put Moses and Marley to work chopping bread for the dressing for the turkey. We took walks on the beach, set up the tables in the living room with pretty tablecloths and napkins, crystal, china and my mother's silver. Leah Brooks joined us again for dinner, as she had last Thanksgiving.

As we were all seated and the sparkling cider poured, Moses made a move toward his glass, as if he were going to make a toast. Dylan, sitting next to Moses, elbowed him. Dylan nodded toward Bob, who was at the head of the table. "You got to be sitting up there before you get to make the toast," Dylan said to Moses, half-smiling, half-serious. I grinned. Bob picked up his glass and said how grateful he was that our family was together, but then he broke down and started to weep uncontrollably. I looked from Bob to Dylan, Moses and Marley, who were seated directly opposite me. The boys were traumatized. Moses was crying, wiping huge tears away with the back of his hand. Marley's jaw, usually engaged in chatter, was simply agape. Dylan shoved his chair back from the table and ran from the room.

While I know that Bob has a right to his grief, and that the gathering of our clan is particularly difficult, I was angry with him. I thought it unfair for him to traumatize our young nephews further, and I was extremely worried about Dylan. I left the table and went to Dylan's room where he had shut himself in and asked him to come back to the table. He wouldn't speak to me. I went back to the table and sat down, and we all made desultory conversation, just trying to get through the meal.

After dinner, Lorna went to Dylan, and he came out of his room to rejoin us. The evening was unseasonably warm, and we all trooped down to the beach and built a bonfire. It was so warm, that we decided to have our dessert on the beach. Lorna and I scrambled back up the path to our house and retrieved the pies and cans of whipped cream from the kitchen counter. We brewed coffee, pouring it into insulated pitchers. We carried this all back down to the beach and had Thanksgiving dessert, sitting on driftwood logs around the bonfire.

I am so glad to get away from our traditional dining table, where one seat will be forever empty.

December 2002

Thursday
December 12, 2002

The Oregonian

Coos Bay – Winds gusting to 40 mph whistled in the masts of commercial fishing boats loaded with crab pots but empty of fishermen in the Charleston Harbor on Wednesday.

Bad weather wasn't keeping the commercial crabbers at dock; it was the prices offered for their catch. Fishermen were moored and angry up and down the coast.

"We're on strike," said Bernie Lindley, a Brookings fisherman. "The weather is kind of incidental."

Lindley, a third-generation fisherman, said the $1.25 a pound offered by fish processors isn't worth going to sea.

"We're insulted by an offer that is that low," he said.

Crabbers want $1.75 a pound. They received between $1.60 and $1.65 last year. In past years, prices have reached $3 a pound.

Brookings fishermen, who were allowed to start crabbing Dec. 1, have yet to set a single trap. They have no price negotiations scheduled with processor Pacific Choice.

This year the crab season started 10 days late for most Oregon fishermen because of an agreement with Washington state and several coast Native American tribes that allowed the tribes more time to fish exclusively. The agreement didn't affect California and the Oregon coast south of Bandon.

Coos Bay fishermen, who could have started crabbing Tuesday, are meeting with local processor Hallmark Fisheries today to continue to negotiate prices. A spokesman for Hallmark did not return telephone calls Wednesday.

Fishermen refused to speculate on the potential

harvest this year. Last year, Oregon crabbers caught about 13 million pounds of male crabs, measuring at least 6 ¼ inches across the shell. Oregon averages 9 million pounds a year.

Although a few fishermen have other income and can wait for better prices, others will be forced to head to sea. They might not have the luxury of waiting for calm waters.

"These guys put their lives on the line for $1.25," said Chief Petty Officer John Slack of the U.S. Coast Guard in Charleston.

The Coast Guard closed most bay entrances along the Oregon coast to recreational boats Wednesday because of high swells, but the agency has no control over commercial fishermen.

"Sometimes they get into a position where they need to make a living," Slack said. "Christmas. They've got families, and they're wanting to take care of them."

If a fisherman decides to brave the heavy surf, the Coast Guard can't stop him, but it will send rescue boats to the bay entrance to stand by for assistance.

The Oregon crabbing season begins as the coast's worst weather hits. The first of a series of storms was expected to hit the coast Wednesday night with winds gusting to 65 mph.

Competition forces the crabbers to harvest early. They catch about 75 percent of the year's total during the first eight weeks of the season, which ends Aug. 15, according to the Oregon Dungeness Crab Commission.

Last year, four crab fishermen died in December when their 36-foot boat, *Nesika,* capsized four miles north of the Yaquina Bay entrance at Newport.

The 15-foot swells washing over the bar at the entrance to Coos Bay on Wednesday were navigable for larger commercial vessels, Slack said. But crab boats carry an additional burden. The 80 to 125 pound crab pots stacked four or five high on the deck make the boats top heavy.

"It's called a "bad moment" if you're overloaded

topside," Slack said. "A big swell can create a capsizing."

Most fishermen check the weather and ocean conditions before heading to sea, Slack said.

"Every one of them here (is) experienced," he said. "The problem is they get locked into making a living. Also, there is nothing Mother Nature can't tear apart if she wants to."

Saturday
December 21, 2002

Today is the one year anniversary of Ben's Celebration of Life.

Pieces of Ben. I keep looking for him. I walked on the beach today hoping to find some bit of him washed up in the surf. There have been huge tides, giant logs rolling up to the base of the cliff below our house, depositing all manner of flotsam and jetsam on the beach and in the grassy dunes that separate the beach from the cliff. In the pools of stagnant water inside the dunes, trapped by the cliff, I look for things. What I expect to find, I don't know, but I look anyway.

What interests me are signs of life from vessels: wooden pallets, frayed mooring lines five inches thick, or crab line, yellow with blue running through it. I wonder if it was a part of a shot of line from the pots that fell off the deck of the *Nesika.* Poking up from the sand is a toothbrush: Ben's? No. His Dopp kit was intact, in his knapsack, retrieved for us by the Coast Guard and State Police after the vessel washed ashore. I remember Peter, Ethan and Dylan meticulously going through Ben's knapsack, laying out items on the top of the dryer in the laundry room. His address book. The contents of his wallet. His passport. An unopened and dry package of Pepperidge Farm Goldfish crackers. One day, a couple of months after the accident, I sat alone at the kitchen table. I opened the bag of his Goldfish crackers and ate them slowly, one by one.

Under a steely purple sky, Sally trotted next to me, making desultory attempts to catch a sea gull. As a group of gulls scattered at what I thought was Sally's approach, I looked up and saw the cause of their flight was a bald eagle; its wing span tipped with jagged edges, soaring gracefully over the beach, skimming tree tops.

Ben, I thought. It was Ben. He had come to me as an eagle today, not the first time certainly, and not the last, that he would signal his presence in our souls.

Thursday
December 26, 2002

There were tangled bullwhips of kelp in the dunes. I saw what I thought was a dead seal pup on the beach, and I wondered if it was the progeny of one of the two lions I saw a few days ago, poking their heads up out of the surf. A lone gull and several crows gorged themselves on the carcass of a salmon: a veritable feast. Had pieces of Ben washed ashore on a high tide and been similarly devoured?

I was on the beach around 9 this morning, taking a half day of leisure. I'd been up at 3:30 a.m., when Bob and Dylan left to fish. Because of the difficulties in reaching a price for the crab between the processors and fishermen, and because not all the crab are ready to be harvested, the season did not start on December 1 this year. Instead, a few days ago Bob and crew left on their first trip to dump crab pots and begin retrieving them.

Bob had come in around midday on Christmas Eve, and tied up the boat at the terminals, intending to unload his crab on Christmas Day. After arriving in port, he called for me to bring him a replacement light bulb for the halide deck lights and some weather stripping to help seal the seams of the shelter deck they were about to attach to the boat. Now that all the crab pots had been taken out to sea, the massive stainless steel shelter deck would be bolted down to the port side of the vessel, protecting the men from the weather as they worked the starboard side where the crab pots would be pulled from the water and landed on deck. The shelter deck stood a story high. In happier days I remembered a couple of the Kennedy girls dancing on its roof, level with the deck of the wheelhouse, during the celebration of the Blessing of the Fleet. That was the spring of 2001, the year the *Michele Ann* won the Best Decked Vessel Award.

Off I went to the docks with the replacement bulb and weather stripping.

Water was pouring out of the fish hold, the circulating tank doing its job of keeping the crabs immersed and alive in oxygenated sea water. With the lid on the fish hold, I couldn't tell how many crabs were on board, but I knew Bob wouldn't have come in to port without a full load. The boat held about 40,000 pounds of crab, which would mean they had earned $56,000 at $1.40 a pound, and they caught it all in less than two days. Holy cow. Bob had gone out at noon Friday, set a full load of pots, then came back in to get another load, and went right back out. They didn't start pulling gear until Sunday evening, and yet, here they were, back already. Bob was smiling, and so was his crew. I delivered the needed items and wrote draw checks for the crew, an advance on their earnings.

Bob was actually home for dinner on Christmas Eve, although he was so tired he could hardly keep his head up. I made fettucine alfredo with prawns, garlic bread and a big green salad. Bob went to bed around 7 p.m., with a promise from me that I wouldn't wake him on Christmas morning until the last minute. We would have to get our gifts opened and Christmas breakfast eaten quickly, as he needed to be back at the boat at 12:30 p.m. I promised. He went off to bed. Dylan and I watched *Men in Black II*, which I found to be much funnier than I expected.

Our Christmas Eve tradition for years has been to fill the boys' stockings and hang them on their bedroom doors. After watching the movie, Dylan, walked down the hallway to his room, turned to me and said, "Put my stocking in the living room, please Mom, I'll get to it in the morning. It's too lonely down here without him." Dylan misses Ben so much. I understand. I'd held back tears all day, until I'd gone to the Fishermen's Memorial, where I cried and cried.

I had left a candle burning, with a picture of Ben taped to the glass candle holder. I wrote Ben a note telling him that his dad was in from fishing, that Dylan was going out on the next trip, and that I'd seen a bald eagle soaring, and I knew it was him.

On Christmas morning. I was awake at 5 a.m. and got up at 6.

Bob stirred as if to get up, but I knew what he wanted, and it wasn't to make love.

"Do you want me to go down to the boat, honey?" I asked.

"Yeah," came his smothered reply, his head still buried in his pillow. "Know what to look for?" Bob asked me. "Deck lights gotta be on, mooring lines ok, water circulating in the fish hold, and the doors to cabin and wheelhouse locked," he said.

"You got it," I reassured him.

With Bob and Dylan sleeping, I drove to the terminal where the boat was docked. I saw that the deck lights were on and the mooring lines secure. The water was still pumping on the crab, keeping them alive, and the doors were locked. All was okay.

I "visited" Ben once again, walking down the bayfront, stopping along the memorial sidewalk where his name is etched in concrete with the name of the *Nesika* and the three other men who died with him. I stopped at Dock 5, and drank from the water fountain, running my hands over the bronze lettering, feeling Ben's name. I drove again to the Fisherman's Memorial, happy to see the candle I lit yesterday was still burning. Across the road from the Fisherman's Memorial, someone had decorated a shore pine tree with ornaments and a string of gold beads.

I returned home. Bob and Dylan were still sleeping. I baked a quiche and cinnamon rolls. Woke the guys up to open gifts and eat breakfast. I played my favorite tape of Christmas carols but it left me feeling joyless. Bob and Dylan then went to the fish plant to unload and sell their crab. Home for dinner, I made a salad, bread, and steamed crabs for us all to eat. Exhausted, we all went to bed early.

Bob and Dylan left this morning at 4 a.m. After helping to load their groceries and gear in the truck, I went back to bed. The phone rang. It was fellow fisherman Dave "Big Wave" Smith, so nicknamed after one particularly bad bar crossing many years ago. Dave wanted to let me know that two other boats had gone safely across the bar. "Thanks, Dave," I said. "Bob's already gone, but it makes me feel better knowing he's not the only one out there on the ocean."

I am terrified by the weather forecast. Today the weather is supposed to be okay, but the winds are expected to be gale force this evening, and the seas very big. If the boat doesn't come in late this afternoon, they likely will stay on the ocean and ride out the storm, working when the seas lay down enough to find the crab buoys. The bar itself will likely be unpassable, so they will drift. Or, if the seas are too big, Bob will point the bow into the swells and ride out the storm.

My fear sickens me. Bob called this morning before I left for my beach walk. I heard shouting in the background. "Hear that honey?" asked Bob. "That's Dylan, shouting the number of crabs in the pot."

"Twenty!" I heard; a happy cry.

"Dylan's real happy to be here, Michele. He's never seen fishing as good as this. He's doing great. Look, honey, because of the weather, we may just stay out for a few days and ride it out," Bob said.

"I know," I said. "And whatever you decide is okay by me. I'm fine with it," I reassured him.

What else could I say? It was December, and it was crab season.

EPILOGUE

Five years have passed since I wrote my last monthly journal entry. I have alternately written with great bursts of energy, and also walked away from this project for months at a time. The desire to finish this book has fought continuously with the sadness I feel each time I try to complete this story. What I have learned is that while my writing may come to an end, the grief will continue.

As a family we remain intact, in large part due to the love and strength of our friends, family and community, who have continued to support us in the years since the accident. I cannot name you all, but there are hundreds of you. We remain deeply grateful.

Dylan graduated from Whitman College in May of 2005. Even after the accident, he continued to fish with Bob on the *Michele Ann* each summer and winter. Dylan has also worked as a landscaper in Portland, traveled up and down the East and West coasts, and driven his 1984 Volkswagon van on the Al-Can highway to Alaska, where he adopted his beloved "pound dog," Beuford. A talented musician, he has written and recorded several CDs of guitar music and lyrics.

Although I worry about Dylan daily, I know he is on his own journey. I hope, as we all do for our children, that he will find love and contentment.

Bob continues to fish. The death of our son did not destroy the peace he finds while at sea. It is where he felt closest to Ben; they understood one another and spent days, weeks, and months together on the water. I think when Bob is on the ocean he feels less pain, not more. The crab seasons of 2005 and 2006 were banner years for both the resource and our business. Bob continues to land the most crab on the Oregon, Washington and California coasts. But his success is cold solace. As we sat at the kitchen table one morning, talking about Ben, Bob wept. "I have lost both my heroes," he said. "My father and my son."

In honor of Ben, Bob and I made a commitment to take time to leave work, get out of our comfort zones, and to travel to those places Ben would have gone had he the chance. In the past few years we have visited the south island of New Zealand, lived in Rome for several weeks, eaten reindeer in Lapland above the Arctic Circle, traveled on an ice breaker in the Gulf of Bothnia, and visited Ny Alesund on Svalbard, 650 miles from the North Pole. We released a picture of Ben into the sea. We take him with us everywhere we go.

I continue to be immersed in the culture of loss and grief. In the eighteen months between 2004 and 2006, my mother died, "Aunt" Mary Ridings died, and my father died. Even our sweet dog, Sally, died. Had there remained in my soul any remnants of the Catholic faith that would comfort me, it has long vanished. Instead, I have the rituals of death down pat: writing obituaries and eulogies, arranging memorial services, selling homes, administering estates. But I will never understand why any of us must suffer so. I can only remember my friend Gerry Spence's words to me: "Tragedy can be a gift. I have grown only through pain."

My work life, ironically, has flourished. As a result of my meeting with President Bush in 2002, I was appointed in 2004 as an industry representative to the U.S. Arctic Research Commission. The Commission meets several times a year at universities in the United States, in Alaska, and in Arctic nations. I can only think of Ben, his love of biological, physical and chemical sciences, and that this is my opportunity to continue to "Learn, learn, learn!

In my law practice I have also had the opportunity to do rewarding work. With nationally acclaimed attorney Gerry Spence, and Portland, Oregon, civil rights lawyer Elden Rosenthal, I have served since 2004 as co-counsel representing Brandon Mayfield. He was the Muslim Oregon lawyer wrongfully accused and arrested by the FBI, held in custody on a material witness warrant in connection with the Madrid train bombings in

2004. While we can never restore to Mr. Mayfield and his family their dignity and privacy, we obtained a measure of damages for them. In addition, based on the Mayfields' courageous pursuit of the matter, in 2007, a judge of the U.S. District Court ruled that portions of the Patriot Act violated the Fourth Amendment and were unconstitutional.

In our fishing business, however, we continue to experience what I refer to as regulatory death. In 2006, the Oregon Fish and Wildlife Commission implemented a crab pot limit program which allocated the right to fish crab pots away from the most efficient and productive fishermen, like my husband, and redistributed those pots to a majority of the fleet who are neither as talented nor as hard working. There is no ecological or biological justification for this action. It is simply social engineering of the worst degree: government intervention on behalf of the less competent and vocal majority of the fleet. These fishermen, rather than compete and succeed on their own merits, prefer to hamstring others.

It is unfortunate that being a success, purely from the dint of your own hard work, makes you a target. Bob now looks at me, puzzled, pained. He says, "My father taught me to every day to go out and try and do my best. That's all I have ever done. What is it about government, or other people, who don't understand that?"

Most likely, we have come to an end of an era. With the continued government intervention in fisheries management for social, not biological good, we will see the demise of our last hunter-gatherers, the commercial fisherman. I can only be glad this is happening towards the end of Bob's career.

In the spring of 2007, Bob and I sold the *F/V Michele Ann* and its crab permits. We retain the ownership of the sablefish permits, leasing them to the new owner. Bob will continue to fish the boat for a portion of the summer. He is undecided as to what he will do next. I expect it will take a couple of years for him to decide on his next venture.

A final note. After experiencing the bureaucratic nightmare in attempting to get a death certificate for Ben, thanks to our former State Representative Alan Brown, a bill was passed in the Oregon legislature and signed by the Governor. The law requires the State Medical Examiner to issue a death certificate within 45 days after the loss of life at sea. A small victory, perhaps, but hopefully one that will help the next family who experiences such a sudden and tragic loss.

As of December 2007, only pieces of the torso of Steve Langlot have been recovered. The bodies of the rest of our men, Ben Eder, Rob Thompson, and Jared Hamrick, are still missing.

REMEMBERING BEN

In Ben's honor, scholarships have been established in his name for students who have achieved academic excellence and volunteered in their community. Contributions in his memory may be made to:

Ben Eder Memorial Scholarship
c/o Lincoln County Foundation
8423 Yaquina Bay Road
Newport, OR 97365

or

Ben Eder Scholarship
Yaquina Bay Optimist Club
P.O. Box 1912
Newport, OR 97365

In addition, a web site with photos of Ben, some of his writings, and memories of his friends and family is located at:
www.beneder.org

May you carry Ben's spirit with you forever.